COMPUTER SIMULATION
IN OPERATIONS MANAGEMENT

COMPUTER SIMULATION
IN OPERATIONS MANAGEMENT

Keith Klafehn,
Jay Weinroth, and
Jess Boronico

Q
Quorum Books
WESTPORT, CONNECTICUT • LONDON

Library of Congress Cataloging-in-Publication Data

Klafehn, Keith.
  Computer simulation in operations management / Keith Klafehn, Jay
Weinroth, Jess Boronico.
    p.   cm.
  ISBN 0–89930–732–9 (alk. paper)
  1. Production management—Computer simulation. I. Weinroth, Jay.
II. Boronico, Jess. III. Title.
  [DNLM: WY 105 M685q 1997]
  TS155.K638   1996
  658.5′01′13—dc20   96–4849

British Library Cataloguing in Publication Data is available.

Library of Congress Catalog Card Number: 96–4849
ISBN: 0–89930–732–9

First published in 1996

Quorum Books, 88 Post Road West, Westport, CT 06881
An imprint of Greenwood Publishing Group, Inc.

Printed in the United States of America

The paper used in this book complies with the
Permanent Paper Standard issued by the National
Information Standards Organization (Z39.48–1984).

10 9 8 7 6 5 4 3 2 1

Contents

Tables, Figures, and Appendices

TABLES

FIGURES

APPENDICES

1

Simulation:
Defining the Concept

sim·u·la·tion, n. false resemblance, as through imitation.
                            —*Webster's Universal Unabridged Dictionary*

The preceding definition captures distinctly the flavor of the concept of simulation. In essence, when one simulates, it involves the creation of an artificial world which replicates as closely as possible the real-world universe from which it is drawn. Over the years, simulation has moved into high-tech areas and computer sciences, while becoming a methodology unto itself.

Basically, one can recast the formal definition provided above in one simple sentence: Simulation is a methodology whereby a user attempts to understand a real-world process. In understanding this process, the user ordinarily has an objective in mind and a problem to solve. As opposed to other methodologies in which optimal, or best, solutions are generated, simulation attempts to model a system and observe how changes in some of the system's parameters (inputs) affect the behavior of the system (measured by outputs) over time. Based on these outputs, one can begin to understand how the system should be set up, that is, what input values tend to outperform others. Input values can range from simple quantities representing the amount of machinery or manual labor required at a work station to more nonintuitive concepts such as probabilistic values governing the percentage of time a triggering mechanism should be fired. Although simulation itself can not be used to verify with 100 percent certainty that any given set of inputs is "best," through the generation of a significant volume of output it is possible to hypothesize that a near-optimal set of values has been found. Various statistical techniques are often employed together with simulation to generate confidence bounds on near-optimal solutions, providing reasonable assurance that they will perform well in the real world.

Due to these features, simulation has become increasingly popular during the 1990s. The increase in computing speed and the ability of technology to handle massive volumes of data have enhanced its popularity. While analytical techniques are still widely employed in many fields and are predominant in the engineering sciences, many of their shortcomings become apparent when one considers how difficult it is to determine optimal solutions analytically for a model which is highly representative of a complex system. Ordinarily, decision makers find themselves making significant concessions between proposed optimal solutions for models which do not truly represent the system being modeled, and near-optimal solutions for models which are more representative of the system being studied. Neither choice is a panacea, both cases pose a dilemma. Whereas analytical models are employed with great success in fields such as electrical engineering, physics, and chemistry, the degree of uncertainty and irrationality presented by human nature make it very difficult to determine if a given analytical model is truly representing what is happening in the real world. More often it is the case that a given model yields solutions to a would-be perfect and rational world, which unfortunately is not the world we currently inhabit.

Hence, simulation becomes a valuable modeling tool. A good programmer with corresponding analytical, project management, and communication skills can construct and analyze a model that represents the system under study with great accuracy and consider the impact that various input values have on the behavior of the system as a whole.

It is the purpose of this book to illustrate how simulation can be used to study some important real-world problems in both the manufacturing and the service sector. While the book provides an in-depth look at how the simulation process is used within these contexts, bear in mind that any book can only hope to skim the surface regarding the depth, richness, and applicability of simulation as a tool of choice for decision makers worldwide.

A discussion of the general approach one takes when conceptualizing how a simulation model may be used begins our journey. Following this, attention is turned to the formal development of a simulation project. From there specific applications for simulation are examined. While no expectations are set regarding the level of expertise one may anticipate absorbing as they peruse this material, it is the hope of the authors that an appreciation of the art of simulation develops as the pages of this book are turned. To begin our journey, consider some questions commonly encountered within the field of simulation.

SOME BASIC QUESTIONS

Question 1: Why are simulation models necessary?
Response: Outside of the reasons cited earlier, simulation models are needed for the following three reasons:

1. Experimentation with the real system under study would be disruptive. Collection of data and/or observation of the process could certainly lead to inefficiencies in the workplace. Furthermore, changes in the inputs (those variables whose values are to be changed in order to study the effect they have on the behavior of the system) may be impractical and perhaps impossible to manipulate under real conditions.
2. Inputs to the process may involve persons at all levels of the operation, who may be inaccessible or whose coordination in a real-time study is difficult to obtain.
3. Experimentation on a real system would not be cost effective.

Question 2: When should a simulation project be considered?
Response: The most obvious reason would be that some aspect of a manufacturing process appears to be malfunctioning.[1] In this instance simulation can provide sufficient data so that an assessment can be made as to (1) whether or not a malfunction exists, and (2) where the malfunction might be. Keep in mind that the results of many (perhaps thousands) of simulated results are usually very reliable, and if the results differ significantly from those observed in the workplace, the probability is high that a malfunction does indeed exist.

Another common use for simulation involves the design of a new system. Simulation allows for results regarding effectiveness to be determined prior to making any capital investment on potential equipment purchases, facility design decisions, or changes in operating personnel. The cost involved in generating a simulation study is negligible relative to the cost of redesigning a system which is already in place. Hence, it provides a cost-effective means of analyzing potential strategic and tactical level decisions prior to any investment of time, money, and/or other scarce resources.

Question 3: Why has the use of simulation increased over the last decade?
Response: First, decreases in computer-related costs have made simulation a more desirable modeling tool. In the days of the mainframe, simulation was usually a last resort.

Second, the increase in animation software now allows simulation to be conducted in conjunction with visual decision-support tools. For example, animation of the human form allows visual studies to be conducted regarding simulated effects of weightlessness, medical diagnoses, and muscular and cardiovascular effects associated with various exercise and dietary programs.

Third, the streamlining of simulation software, more intuitive interfaces, and less complicated programming languages have contributed to the increased popularity of simulation. Also, greater processing capability and speed have allowed simulation to be used in environments involving more complex processes. Simultaneously, the decrease in storage space (in terms of physical space, not byte space) required to use simulation has allowed it to be removed from the mainframe to the desktop environment and ultimately to the laptop environment.

Lastly, the increased emphasis on cost reduction in the workplace has increased the need for analyzing the effects of proposed changes on productivity in the workplace. As mentioned before, experimenting with these changes directly in the workplace is highly inefficient and is not cost-effective. Simulation provides a quick and relatively simple way to experiment with a multitude of proposed changes in order to determine those which appear to have built-in efficiencies.

Question 4: What are the basic requirements for a simulation project?
Response: The only requirement is that the process under study involves the flow of materials through stations which are governed by both internal and external influences.[2] However, in a simulation project, it is desirable

(although not necessary) to be studying a process which (1) has high visibility, (2) can be modeled accurately via a simulation model, (3) has no alternate means of solution which are relatively straightforward, and (4) allows for team-oriented decisions.

Many simulation models also include elements of random behavior. In addition, there generally exist dynamic interactions between man and machine. Both of these considerations provide volatility which can be observed and monitored through a simulation study, especially in the observation of changes made to the system, commonly referred to as "bumps." Consequently, a simulation model helps transform a high-risk idea into a low-risk solution.

In summary, almost any system can be simulated in order to observe its behavior. The above characteristics simply define the type of system which is more amenable to study.

PROFILING THE SIMULATION TEAM

Ordinarily, individuals have varying perspectives regarding the usefulness of simulation as a modeling tool. In order to categorize each individual, a six-step scale may be utilized. Six categories outlined and briefly discussed are:

- *Enthusiast:* a firm believer in simulation as a management tool that can help solve all problems basic to a manufacturing operation. While not exactly a fanatic, the enthusiast approaches his work with a vigor not found in the subsequent classes.

- *Visionary:* similar to the enthusiast, also believes that simulation is a valuable management tool that may assist management in seeking solutions to problems that may exist in a manufacturing operation. But while the enthusiast is more likely to jump headlong into simulating the problem at hand, the visionary proceeds a bit more slowly, trying to envision *how* simulation may assist management prior to committing resources to the simulation process.

- *Pragmatist:* knows about simulation and is willing to use it as a modeling tool only if it can assist in solving the day-to-day problems encountered in a manufacturing operation. A pragmatist is more likely to consider other analytical methodologies, if they appear tractable in solving these problems. While appearing more circumspect then the preceding classes, the energy of the pragmatist wanes in comparison to the visionary and the enthusiast.

- *Conservative:* is aware of simulation but needs to be shown how simulation can assist management as a decision-support tool in solving problems related to manufacturing operations. The conservative will ordinarily stop, look, and listen prior to crossing the track leading to simulation as a methodology of choice.

- *Laggard:* has heard of simulation but can not envision how it can possibly be utilized to solve problems arising in a manufacturing operation. Individuals in this class ordinarily resort to either (1) using analytical schemes which find solutions to models which represent similar problems to the one being encountered or (2) utilize heuristics, or rules of thumb, if they do not have the required expertise to employ analytical models. While the laggard will ordinarily turn his back to the idea of simulation, he may be easily swayed to the simulation cause through logical reasoning.

- *Dullard:* has never heard of simulation, has no interest in hearing about simulation, and is opposed to trying to use it in solving manufacturing-oriented problems. While almost everyone believes they are not in this class, a significant percentage of managers do fall prey to this type of thinking. Individuals in this group are normally anchored on old-school approaches which have traditionally provided reasonable solutions to problems, and are consequently risk averse towards utilizing or experimenting with new approaches to solve new problems. Unfortunately, the increased complexities in manufacturing operations in the latter part of the twentieth century dictates newer, more sophisticated methodologies in deriving optimal or near-optimal solutions, while rendering many old methodologies obsolete.

When undertaking a simulation project it is ideal to have a representative sample from all the aforementioned types, with the exception of the dullards. Enthusiasts and visionaries provide the energy required to pursue the simulation project with full vigor. Pragmatists and conservatives provide the group with a devil's advocate and will support alternate methodologies, suggest alternate approaches, or simply note shortcomings in the simulation model which visionaries and enthusiasts may overlook. Even the laggard can contribute to the extent that he must be swayed by logic. By educating the laggard and teaching him how the simulation model can be utilized, all members of the group reinforce their belief that the model will indeed be effective. If difficulties are encountered in providing the laggard with sufficient rationale for using the simulation model, then the team may need to reconsider the project, as well as the assumptions under which they are working. Consequently, all members of the simulation team serve a unique purpose, and a good cross-section provides the best balance for the simulation team.

While working together, the simulation team must understand that benefits from a simulation model are not automatic. Modeling the system correctly requires forethought on the part of management as to (1) how the system should be modeled, (2) what parameters are flexible, and (3) the extent of flexibility which should be built in.

In utilizing simulation, an immediate hidden benefit is the ability to step back and view the system as a whole, while examining each facet of the operation. In practice, there exists an overwhelming tendency to simply add people or machinery when a problem is encountered. However, a simulation model allows management to review the nuances of a given system, and realize the potential efficiencies which can be achieved through the effective utilization of existing resources rather than the addition of new ones. While traditional inertia exists in management, increasing reluctance to implement change, simulation allows management to perform a "what-if" analysis in a risk free environment at minimal cost.

In summary, for a simulation model to be effectively implemented, it requires a heterogeneous group, all willing to work together as open-minded individuals. Each person has to believe that the simulated improvements to the system brought about by simulated changes will result in real improvements to the system when the real changes are made to the system.

THE STEPS INVOLVED IN A SIMULATION STUDY

In order to successfully undertake a simulation project it is necessary, as with other actions in life, to have a specific plan of attack. In general, failing to plan is planning to fail; so it is in a simulation project. Failure to plan may lead to either overlooking important facets of a project, not gathering all the necessary or relevant data, or not consulting all individuals who are conversant with the problem being studied. To combat this, the following steps summarize a planning procedure considered standard in organizing and developing a meaningful simulation study.[3]

Step 1. Problem Formulation and a Plan of Action

There are several aspects involved in the formulation and plan of action. First, one must have an overall objective in mind. For example, why is the simulation being pursued? What does one hope to gain from the results of the simulation?

At this point one must be careful not to prematurely determine what numerical results might be expected, as this could lead to a systematic bias both in the collection of data and the interpretation of results. One must identify any performance problems that exist in the present system, be they utilization of workers or equipment, wait times for product flaws, or how long it takes to get a unit of product through the system. How is the model to be used? Where are the performance problems in the system? For example, is worker or equipment utilization not up to standard? Does it take too long to produce a unit of product? Is product throughput too long?

The system being studied should be delineated and an appropriate list of required resources should be drawn up, including such factors as personnel, time, and hard materials.

Step 2. Data Collection and Model Development

Following the initial plan, extensive information must be gathered regarding the system's operating procedures and the logic that controls these procedures. How are various subsystems interconnected? How does work flow through the system? What parameters effect the model's operation, and which of these are controllable by management? The responses to these questions concern what might be titled endogenous information. In addition to this information, exogenous information must also be gathered. For example, what are the underlying probability distributions for random variables in the problem? What is the range of values assigned to the system parameters? All this information is put into our assumptions document, which establishes the basic conditions for the model of the system.

Additional data must be gathered relating the values of all inputs and the corresponding performance data for the system under study. This data will be used to compare the simulation model with the actual or anticipated performance of the system. Only when the model is deemed representative of the system under study can it be used to further the analysis by altering some of the inputs and/or decision variables. The complexity of the model should also be determined at this point, and is based on the objective, available data, and credibility of concerns, which involves generating feedback from various team members regarding which items should and should not be included in the model.

Step 3. Testing the Validity of the Conceptual Model

Prior to coding the simulation model, all parties meet to discuss the information presented in the assumptions document. At this point each member of the simulation team needs to take ownership of the model and cite weaknesses or limitations involved in the assumptions or the scope of the conceptual model as suggested. Working as a team, all suggestions are reviewed and the assumptions document modified to reflect those views which may have been overlooked earlier. This review also provides another opportunity to look at the level of complexity and reach an agreement regarding the details to be included or not included.

Step 4. Computer Code Development and Formal Model Verification

At this point, the coding procedure begins. Various alternatives are available for this step. A specific simulation may be coded in a general all-purpose programming language, a specific simulation software, or by using a simulator. The appropriate choice is predicated on the level of expertise that is available among the members of the simulation team. Once the code is constructed, the verification process is begun. One checks that the model generates output for different levels of inputs and that general relationships between components of the system (workstations, people, machinery) are upheld. It is necessary to know that all logical operations of the model are performing as intended.

Step 5. Pilot Runs and Validation of the Formal Model

While the conceptual model must pass validation in step 3, the formal model is tested here. In general, one needs to determine that preliminary results generated by the model are reasonable. At this stage one may also incorporate animation to enhance the credibility of the model and expose any obvious inconsistencies.

During validation, one must ensure that the model's outputs are indicative of results generated by the real-world system. One method involves utilizing the data collected from the real-world system. Inputs are fixed, and the outputs from the model are compared to the observed outputs in the actual system.

To validate the model all the outputs are reviewed with those persons most closely allied with the real system. If the simulation involves a proposed design for a system not yet in place, then the system's output must be discussed with those individuals responsible for designing the system, or others who are familiar with results from systems similar to the one being considered. Once the results generated by the simulation are validated, the model can be used to analyze the behavior of the system when inputs are changed.

Step 6. Experimental Testing

The major thrust behind the development of a simulation lies in its ability to illustrate the impact that changes, or "bumps," in a system's parameters will have on the output values. Critical decisions regarding real-world parameters are often made after this stage.

This is also the time when decisions must be made regarding how many independent runs of the simulation will be required before the mean values of the output are deemed reliable. Together with this decision is that of determining the length of time prescribed for each simulation run. A simulation which is run over too short a period of time does not have time to reach equilibrium, while a simulation which runs longer than required wastes valuable time.

In response to these issues, the simulation team needs to determine if the system should run long enough to reach "steady state," or equilibrium, before the collection of statistics occurs. This is desirable if one does not want the effects of initial conditions to influence the output of the model. For instance, if when monitoring the queuing process at an inspection station, one begins with a fixed initial queue representative of shut down the previous night, the output should not be influenced by the initial condition, if the results are to be indicative of those results which one would obtain if beginning the simulation at a random point of time during the day. However, if the simulation was designed to actually monitor the behavior of the system beginning at startup time, that is, the first day of system installation, then the simulation team would want the initial condition incorporated into the model.

When changing values of inputs in order to understand their impact on outputs, each change should be made sequentially, so that the effects of each can be isolated and can be independent of one another. However, if two inputs have any dependence on one another, then sequential changes are not sufficient. In this case, one must first change the value of the first input and collect output results. Then that input must be reverted to its initial value at which time the value of the second input is changed, and new output results gathered.

For example, many automated materials handling systems now incorporate automatic guided vehicle (AGV) systems. If an AGV system were being monitored for throughput and we desired to test the speed of the AGVs versus adding additional AGVs to the system, we would need to be certain that any system parameters monitored were not influenced by other changes which have been made. For instance, if the throughput at stage X in a manufacturing process were monitored, its throughput would be partially dependent upon the flow of materials into the vehicle's cell. If a prior change increased the flow of materials into this cell (perhaps by adding an AGV or changing the speed in an upstream cell in the manufacturing process) then we might anticipate that the throughput in stage X might be biased. If the speed of the vehicles in stage X are changed first, and the resulting impact upon throughput noted, when an additional vehicle is introduced, its impact may be different at the new speed opposed to the initial speed. It would be better to check the effects of adding an AGV to stage X under the conditions that all other attributes of the system have been unaltered, so that any potential change in throughput at this stage is only impacted by the specific change being explored within the manufacturing cell being observed.

Step 7. Analysis of Simulated Output Data

The use of statistical analysis provides credibility for the model generated output. By comparing simulated results for the base model versus actual results, confidence intervals and levels of statistical accuracy can be determined. These statistical results can then be extended and compared to those results generated through "bumps" in the system to obtain a richer sensitivity for the true levels of the output values and the degree of variation in each. Time plots and other graphs are also used to aid the understanding of output data.

Depending on the actual design of the model, more information may be determined from the simulation model (by analyzing various "bumps") than can be reasonably determined from the real-world system. The abundance of information often leads to (1) the consideration of additional "bumps" and (2) creative insight regarding new design features which would not have been thought of without the output data garnered through the simulation process.

Step 8. Documentation, Presentation, and Implementation

Once all the "experts" have sanctioned the formal model as providing reasonable and appropriate results (after extensive review of the output data), the model is documented as being a viable representation of the system under study. Pertinent results are then presented, particularly as they apply to the "bumps" in the system. These results lay the groundwork for changes to be implemented in the real-world system.

Once these proposed changes have been implemented, and the system again returns to equilibrium, comparison of the simulation output can be compared to the real-world values to further reinforce the simulation as being representative of the system under study. Should these proposed changes yield results differing from those generated from the simulation, an intense examination of the simulation model most be undertaken, as well as of the real-world system. This examination must uncover the reason for the discrepancy. Prior to jumping to conclusions, however, adequate time must be allowed for the system to adjust to the newly implemented changes. Changes in machinery, assignments, work schedules, and manpower ordinarily require significant adjustment time. Work studies and the effect of learning curves can often assist in determining how much adjustment time is required before a system achieves steady-state after the implementation of changes.

At this stage the simulation is complete. It is hoped that all objectives discussed initially have been achieved. The assemblage of a good simulation team with well-defined objectives, together with the adherence to the steps discussed above, ordinarily lead to meaningful results which increase the operating efficiency of any organization.

BENEFITS, DRAWBACKS, AND MYTHS IN THE SIMULATION WORLD

Undertaking a simulation project involves both derived benefits and drawbacks. While some may disagree, it is the contention here that the benefits far outweigh the drawbacks. Explicitly determining an exhaustive list of benefits and drawbacks would be an impossible task, especially considering that both supporters and nonsupporters would not universally agree on all items. However, there are some generalities which would stand out as well accepted in their respective categories. Five such generalities are listed for both benefits and drawbacks. To begin, consider the following benefits:

1. Modeling a real-world system using simulation forces the users and, inevitably, the organization to understand the role that each component plays in a system and the specific interaction between each of them.

2. The creation of a simulation team encourages creative thinking, group thinking, and teamwork. It creates an atmosphere of positivism and promotes cooperation among a diverse set of individuals.

3. The development of a simulation model helps isolate operational parameters which can be either controlled or not controlled. Further, it allows for the actual impact of each parameter upon the others in the system and records the system's behavior under these circumstances providing greater understanding of the system.

4. The output of the model demonstrates to management what resources may be needed and how existing resources may be efficiently allocated. The effect of straying from the suggested allocation can also be studied in order to understand the importance that each system resource has regarding the behavior of the system as a whole.

5. It allows, through exhaustive runs, the determination of optimal or near-optimal solutions for what otherwise may be an intractable problem to solve analytically. Where rules of thumb and heuristics are commonly employed, simulation provides a strong decision support tool from which reasonable solutions can not only be suggested, but tested and analyzed as well.

Consider now a list of potential drawbacks:

1. The required time in the development of a representative simulation model may be extensive, especially when data is difficult
   to obtain.

2. There may exist groups of individuals (exogenous to the simulation
   team, but present in the hierarchy of management) who have a
   natural resistance to both the development and the validity of results
   derived from a simulation model. This may subsequently increase
   tension and lower morale within an organization while imposing
   barriers to creative thinking and continuous progress toward the
   ultimate aim of the project itself.

3. In the process of building, running, and analyzing a simulation
   model there may be surprises which are both positive and negative,
   with potential side effects such as increasing fear and tension, and
   heightening risk aversion. This could adversely affect the behavior
   of the organization psychologically and be translated into other
   losses over a period of time.

4. The model is only as good as its developers. Finding and assembling
   a strong simulation team is a difficult task, and the level of expertise
   of the team is not well-judged internally. Obtaining objective meas-
   urements from outsiders regarding the quality of the simulation
   team is also unlikely.

5. While simulation offers good near-optimal solutions, the degree of
   precision in estimating the optimal solution may not be within the
   tolerance desired by management, whereas an analytical model may
   be preferable, if available.

While not universally accepted, simulation has increased in popularity,
and in those instances where simulation does not receive compelling
support, it is still maintained as a support tool to reinforce alternate means
of solutions. Why simulation is not utilized to a greater extent remains an
open question. Perhaps some of the reasons can be found in some common
myths associated with simulation. Consider the following:

- *Myth 1: Simulation projects must be difficult.* While some simulation
  models are very complex, any process which involves the flow of

material subject to both internal and external influences can be simulated.

- *Myth 2: 80 percent of simulation modeling is encompassed in formal model building.* There are many analytical minds which would have us believe this, but a good simulation team ordinarily allocates more time to accumulating data and developing the conceptual model, from which the formal model is derived and coded.

- *Myth 3: Simulation software training is sufficient preparation for model building.* While beneficial, it serves as a necessary condition for a successful simulation experience but not a sufficient one.

- *Myth 4: It is sufficient to perform a simulation with one set of input values.* If this were sufficient, there would be no need for simulation. The purpose of simulation is to study the impact of changing input values and the incorporation of uncertainty and variability among both internal and external influences.

- *Myth 5: Computer programmers make effective simulationists.* Again, good programming skills are a necessary condition, but certainly not a sufficient one. Other important skills involve statistical analysis, project management, and good communication.

- *Myth 6: Simulation should be introduced to the organization by modeling the whole system.* While certainly an ambitious route, most systems are too complex to be modeled in their entirety. Even when feasible, the abundance of information is more likely to create a negative perception of the process among groups of individuals unfamiliar with the simulation. Preferably, a small subsystem should be modeled, accompanied by a rigorous set of alternative input values, a strong statistical analysis, and forceful recommendations.

- *Myth 7: The greater the amount of information contained in the model, the stronger the simulation model.* In actuality too much information drags down the model and clouds the issues of importance with irrelevant detail. A good model contains only those elements which have a bearing on the behavior of the system over time. All others need not apply.

- *Myth 8: Good animation implies that the system will work well.* While attractive intuitively, this is far from true. Animation is only a byproduct of simulation outputs. In order to verify that simulation outputs are truly what they appear to be, good statistical analysis must be performed to illustrate how distortions in the output and animation may take place, regardless of how infrequent they may be.

- *Myth 9: I ran the model once, and here are the results.* The strength of simulation lies in its ability to understand the variability of output, even for fixed levels of inputs. One simulation run is simply a single random observation of a process subject to fluctuation. Multiple runs exacerbate a smoothing effect similar to concepts involved in statistical sampling. Never put much credence in results generated from few simulation results.

- *Myth 10: Up on the top of the mountain lies the prophetic simulation guru.* Simulation is a developing field. Some individuals have naturally adaptive abilities which enhance their opportunity to grasp the fundamentals of simulation more quickly than others. Even so, simulation is a decision support tool which can be understood and utilized by people in all fields. The only requirement is time. We hope that the lessons given in subsequent chapters alleviate any fear of simulation modeling and illustrate how anyone can utilize simulation to their benefit as a valuable aid in the decision-making process.

To continue, Chapter 2 explores the first three steps involved in a simulation project: problem formulation and a plan of action, data collection and model development, and testing the validity of the conceptual model.

NOTES

1. While service processes may also be included, for purposes of clarity, references in this chapter are focused on manufacturing-oriented issues.

2. It must be noted that the concept of materials may be extended to include people, as well. For example, work in the health sector may involve the flow of patients through a radiology department.

3. The steps are taken from A. M. Law and M. G. McComas, 1991, Secrets of successful simulation studies, in *Conference proceedings of the 1991 winter simulation conference*, edited by B. Nelson, W. Kelton, and G. Clark, pp. 21–27, Phoenix, Arizona.

2

The Simulation Project: Observing the Basic Steps

In this chapter the philosophy presented in Chapter 1 is applied to a prototype simulation. The development of a dialogue between two individuals involved in exploring how simulation can benefit an operation under study provides insights regarding the types of questions which must be asked in preparing for a simulation.

The particular problem to be investigated involves the operation of a transfer depot which has two major concerns: (1) How many forklift trucks are needed to have an efficient operation? and (2) How large a volume can be handled at this depot? To proceed, the two principals of the dialogue, namely, Warren Harcourt, who is the modeler for SIMUTECH, Inc., and Samuel Ainsworth, the manager of the transfer depot meet for the first time in Samuel Ainsworth's office. Following the presentation of this dialogue, a few points made to highlight certain aspects of their discussion.

SAM: Good morning Warren, feel free to take a seat at the conference table. Can we get you a cup of coffee?

WARREN: If you have the low test, that would be great. I prefer mine black.

Sam relays this information to his assistant while both individuals take seats at the table.

SAM: I certainly hope your team at SIMUTECH can help us out.

WARREN: We'll certainly give it our best. Perhaps we can begin by taking a look at the blueprint that I suggested you have ready when we arranged this meeting?

Sam produces a blueprint of the facility, spreading it out across the table at which they are seated. (An abbreviated version of this blueprint is provided in Appendix 2.1.)

WARREN: Tell me a little bit about how you're currently using the depot.

SAM: [*with a chuckle in his voice*] Just how much time do you have, Warren? As you can see from the blueprint we have fourteen bays on either side of the facility. Each bay is approximately twenty-feet wide. One side of the facility is used for incoming vehicles, the other for outgoing. We might want to consider changing this design, if you feel that an alternative arrangement would be beneficial.

WARREN: [*always looking for an opportunity to find more work*] If you would like to consider that we will be glad to accommodate you, but that wasn't part of the original contract as arranged. I'm afraid an additional fee would be assessed for that service.

SAM: Well, once we get moving on the overall project, I might be able to arrange funds to be transferred for that purpose. Either way, let me show you a few things on this blueprint. On each side of the depot, the last four bays, numbered eleven through fourteen, are reserved for our short-haul local pickup and delivery trucks, which I'll just refer to as short-haulers. We allocate only four bays because we have only four short-haul trucks. However, one thing we're concerned about is the potential change in our transfer mix. It may be that we should allocate more or less than four bays to accommodate these potential changes. Another thing, if the business picks up we may want to consider enlarging the whole depot. Sorry, Warren, I seem to be getting sidetracked.

WARREN: That's okay, Sam. Your thoughts create additional avenues for consideration. We can simulate several of these possibilities later on and try to understand the effect they would have on the efficiency of your operations. Let me ask you about the trucks arriving on the incoming side of the depot.

SAM: Well, the last four bays are allocated to the short-haulers as I mentioned, while the other ten bays are reserved for the overland trailers, which I'll refer to as long-haulers. Occasionally, we use one of the four short-haul bays for an overland trailer as well.

WARREN: Does this occur with sufficient frequency for consideration in the simulation?

SAM: It depends on what you mean by "sufficient frequency"?

WARREN: Daily? Twice a week? Once every two weeks? You tell me.

SAM: To tell you the truth, I really don't know. I have seen it on occasion, but maybe it isn't often enough to worry about at this point.

WARREN: In that case we'll consider it as another potential extension to the model which can be considered afterwards. It seems that the impact of this phenomenon isn't significant enough to merit its inclusion, at least initially.

SAM: Fine by me, you're the boss

WARREN: [*interrupting*] No, Sam, that's not true. Admittedly we do the simulation, but the elements that enter into the model are the things that *you* believe impact your operation. It's important for you to observe the operation from a bird's eye view and suggest everything that might possibly effect the efficiency and operation at your depot. If we build an exhaustive list we can work backwards and remove items deemed unnecessary. Whatever is left can be modeled in the initial phase of our study. Better to have more information than not enough.

SAM: Sounds good, Warren.

WARREN: Okay, now, let's get back to the incoming side of the depot.

SAM: All right. When overland trailers arrive at the depot, they're always fully loaded with pallets. Each truck accommodates up to twenty-eight pallets, stacked two pallets wide, two pallets high and seven ranks deep.

WARREN: How often do these trucks arrive?

SAM: Well, that depends on the time of day.

WARREN: Do the arrival rates vary enough for us to include them in the model?

SAM: I think so, but let me describe it in more detail before we make a decision. The peak load time for arrivals occurs during the 8 A.M. to 4 P.M. shift, the first shift. Trucks arrive at the rate of about one per hour.

WARREN: [*interrupting again*] Is there any variation in that rate or can we simply have long-haul trucks arriving every hour and be done with it?

SAM: I would guess that although on average one truck arrives per hour, the actual arrival time for the trucks varies between forty-five minutes and one hour and fifteen minutes. No one time within the shift seems more likely than any other.

WARREN: That's an important point, Sam. That tells us that the arrival process follows what is referred to as a uniform, or equally likely, distribution. The mean time between arrivals are an hour, varying up or down by a maximum of fifteen minutes.

SAM: I think I know what you mean by that but let me just explain it as I remember it. Essentially a truck could arrive in forty-five minutes, forty-six minutes, and all the way up to seventy-five minutes where each time would be equally likely.

WARREN: Exactly, Sam. As a matter of fact, we need not limit the arrival times to whole minutes either. We could have a time between arrivals of 47.64 minutes. The simulation language we'll propose for this project has what is known as a floating point decimal, thus, any time between forty-five and seventy-five minutes, whole or not, is equally likely. What about the remainder of the day?

SAM: Between 4 P.M. and midnight, the second shift, trucks arrive in the same fashion as we just discussed, except they come in on average every hour and a half, give or take thirty minutes.

WARREN: Do you mean that the time between any two successive arrivals is equally likely between sixty and one hundred twenty minutes?

SAM: That's right. During the third shift, between midnight and 8 A.M., trucks don't arrive very frequently at all. I'd say, maybe one every two hours on average, equally distributed with a range of plus or minus forty-five minutes.

WARREN: Is it true that these overnight arrivals occur with the same frequency through the whole shift, Sam? Is it possible that more of them tend to arrive closer to daybreak, when you're approaching your peak load period?

SAM: Occasionally we start picking up increased arrivals near daybreak, but if I remember the logs correctly they've been spread out pretty evenly throughout the night. Let's leave it that way.

WARREN: All right. I ask because arrival processes can be tricky. For instance, if unscheduled arrivals occur randomly throughout a period at a certain mean rate, the arrival process follows what is commonly referred to as a Poisson process. It doesn't appear that we have that here, but we have to be certain so that the simulation model represents the real-world system as closely as possible.

SAM: There's clearly some good sense there.

WARREN: What about the arrivals for local trucks?

SAM: Arrivals for those work differently. Local trucks always depart at 8 A.M. on the button with whatever has been loaded on them by the end of the third shift. Each of these trucks is gone anywhere from an hour and fifteen minutes to two hours and thirty minutes. While they're out, they're routed to make pickups as well as deliveries. Consequently, when they return, they might have anywhere between four and twelve pallets loaded on them.

WARREN: It sounds like those local trucks are going to be returning anytime during the first shift depending on how long they have been gone. Is that the way it works, Sam?

SAM: Exactly the way it works.

WARREN: [*doing some quick figuring*] Then we could establish an arrival pattern for these trucks to be an average of one hundred twelve minutes plus or minus thirty-eight minutes, that would get us the minimum and maximum time that you indicated that a truck would be out. We'll also treat that as a uniform distribution unless you have more specific figures.

SAM: Let's go with it that way, we can always change it later if it doesn't look right. Can we do that?

WARREN: We will check it in the verification process and see what it looks like. We'll also put the time in a table and see what the distribution looks like when we run it. Do you have any specifics on the number of pallets that are on these trucks?

SAM: Funny you should ask that.

Sam produces a computer printout specifying probability distributions for the number of pallets on short haulers which have completed their pickups and deliveries, as well as the disposition for contents on both long and short haulers. (A copy of Sam's printout is provided in Appendix 2.2 at the end of this chapter.)

SAM: Will this distribution be sufficient for modeling purposes?

WARREN: You bet! In fact, even if we model each short-hauler independently, according to this distribution the overall percentage of arrivals containing each possible number of pallets will still conform to this distribution, provided that we allow the simulation to run for a sufficient amount of time. [*Pausing*] Is there anything else I should know about the trucks? Do they make more than one trip per day?

SAM: I thought you might ask that. The fact is, each short-hauler does make an additional trip each day. All trucks leave when loaded with twelve pallets. If a truck does not have a full load, we still send it out at 1 p.m. That is the only time we send one out with less than six pallets. We do that to avoid overtime, which the drivers get if they're out after 4 p.m. By the way, we sort all the incoming material according to their destination, but we'll get to that later. When the trucks have returned from their second trip, we unload them. Following that, each truck receives a maintenance check, which takes anywhere from twenty to thirty minutes, gets a refueling, and is then put in place for overnight loading at one of the available short-haul bays. The choice of bay is random, although limited to the four short-haul bays. The loading process for the short-haulers' first trip out the next morning will be similar to that of the long-haulers, but we can pick that up when we check the outgoing side of the depot.

WARREN: One more question regarding the second trip for the local trucks. Since some of them leave not fully loaded, we can decrease the sojourn, or trip time for these trucks. Maybe we can assume that the trip time distribution is halved for trucks leaving for their second trip with six pallets or less?

SAM: That sounds fine to me.

WARREN: Do we need to incorporate a time for refueling?

SAM: I would guess somewhere between four and eight minutes, uniformly distributed. Let me mention that for long-haulers, similar operations apply. Times, as expected, are a bit longer, however. I'd say anywhere from one hour to one hour and fifteen minutes to perform maintenance on these vehicles and then somewhere between eight and twelve minutes for refueling. Once all of that is done the long-hauler is moved to the outgoing side of the depot and parked in the empty bay currently holding the greatest number of waiting pallets.

WARREN: Does it take any time to position these vehicles at either the incoming or outgoing dock?

SAM: When a vehicle pulls out of the depot the time is negligible, but positioning the vehicles when parking takes a bit of time. Let's say three minutes plus or minus one minute, that is, between two and four minutes uniformly distributed for the short-haulers

WARREN: [*Interrupting once more*] I've got it.

SAM: and five minutes plus or minus two minutes for the long-haulers, obviously the big babies need a little more time. By the way, we might incorporate a bit of time for opening up the incoming vehicles and closing up the outgoing ones.

WARREN: How much time would that account for?

SAM: Probably two minutes tops, as short as one minute on occasion. Let's just approximate between one and two with a mean smack in the middle, at ninety seconds.

WARREN: Sounds good to me, Sam. You really seem to be getting the feel for this, you know, stepping back and providing all the information which is relevant to the operation of the depot. A simulation model only performs realistically when all salient elements get incorporated. Any other items dealing with the movement of the vehicles?

SAM: Let me think. [*Sam muses out loud*] Arrivals, parking, removal, maintenance, refueling, and departure. I think we've got it all, Warren, except for the positioning of material when it's unloaded from the trucks.

WARREN: Okay, first maybe you can review the unloading operation for the long-haulers with me? How is that handled?

SAM: Basically we unload the contents of each vehicle and then reload it into another. You can see from our blueprint that each outgoing long-haul bay is inked with a predetermined destination. We allocate one bay to each of our ten shipping areas. As pallets are unloaded at incoming bays they're either loaded onto a vehicle, if one is waiting at the appropriate bay, or stacked on the floor at the appropriate bay of the loading dock until a vehicle parks there. By the way, Warren, we deliver to four local areas as well, so that each short-haul vehicle delivers exclusively to one area. We set aside one short-haul bay at the outgoing dock for each of these areas.

WARREN: Do you always allocate exactly one bay per destination area, or do you sometimes allocate two bays for the same destination. This would allow you to fill two trucks headed for the same destination without re-handling the pallet twice; once when unloading it and setting it on the floor, and again when moving it from the floor to the vehicle when it pulls in.

SAM: That's an interesting idea, Warren. Actually we never change the distribution of outgoing bays. We simply continue to load pallets at the appropriate single bay, and if overflow exists we just keep piling it up until the next vehicle pulls in.

WARREN: In that case, Sam, let's consider multiple bays for one destination as a possible "what-if," or extension, to the basic model. While I don't particularly care to create more work than necessary, my responsibilities as a simulationist include pointing out all opportunities or refinements which may contribute to the efficient operation of your business. The best part of it is that you can test all these ideas prior to implementing them, without any cost of capital, to see the effects that they'll have on the behavior of your operation. Anyway, I assume the pallets on an incoming long-hauler are ordinarily not all destined for one location?

SAM: Correct. If that were the case there would be no need to stop at the depot. Take another look at the information I've given you. Where is that printout? [*Sam fumbles through some papers and finally pulls out the printout referred to earlier*] Here it is. I've kept a log of the contents of the long-haulers over the last month in anticipation of this meeting. Even though I had a good idea of the distribution of pallets beforehand I thought this data would provide supporting evidence, which it did. Here, take another look.

WARREN: [*Warren surveys the information carefully*] Ten percent local, ten percent Columbus/Cincinnati, ten percent Indianapolis, and the rest [*Warren takes a moment*] I gather about 8.5 percent for each of the remaining eight locations, is that right?

SAM: On the button.

WARREN: I also see that any pallets unloaded for local delivery are distributed equally among the four local areas. That would mean that each short-hauler gets an equal percentage of the material unloaded from the long-haulers, namely, 25 percent.

SAM: Exactly.

WARREN: Let me look at the contents on the short-haulers. This would be the disposition of goods that the short-haulers bring back from their first trip?

SAM: That's right.

WARREN: Ten percent remain local, while the remainder is split up with 16 percent outgoing to Columbus/Cincinnati, 15 percent to Chicago and 10 percent to New York. The rest get evenly distributed. I guess that would be 7 percent to each of the other seven locations. These figures seem a bit too convenient Sam!

SAM: That's the truth, Warren. The figures just worked out that way!

WARREN: Easier for us, Sam. How about the stacking process in the short-haulers?

SAM: The same as the long-haulers, except they only get stacked three deep.

WARREN: And that's two high and two wide?

SAM: Yes.

WARREN: Great, Sam. I think we're getting there now. Next, I need to understand how the pallets are actually removed from one vehicle and transported to the outgoing side of the depot, which involves the forklift operations.

SAM: We schedule our forklift operations around the arrival of long-haul trucks. That normally means that four forklifts are in service between 8 A.M. and 4 P.M., with three during the second shift and two during the last shift. That coincides roughly with the rate of arrivals we discussed earlier. There are three additional forklifts, for a total of seven, but the three excess lifts are ordinarily tied up in maintenance or getting their batteries recharged. If we have a sudden unexpected breakdown we can usually press one of them into action so that we can run continuously.

WARREN: How about labor? Do the operators take breaks?

SAM: Not outside of their forty-five minute meal break, which we try to stagger as best we can. Usually operators will come and go for coffee or duck out to use the facilities now and again, but they don't have an official break. We have toyed with the idea of providing a formal fifteen minute break because we anticipate that each operator uses more time than that on our current informal basis.

WARREN: How do you think we should model that?

SAM: I'll tell you what, let's go with a forty-five minute meal break and a thirty minute knock off at the end of the shift to allow time for clean up and to get their forklift trucks on the chargers before they punch out. I'll let you decide how to get that into the model.

WARREN: All right. What can you tell me about the movement of the forklifts?

SAM: [*Sam slides another printout toward Warren*] Well, we have some pickup and deposit times, whether pallets are in the trucks or on the floor. We think the forklift takes about twenty seconds to travel from the incoming side of the bay to the outgoing side, and vice versa. For the most part our operators usually move across the dock before they move up or down to the appropriate loading bay. Remember to double that time since we have to travel back to get more pallets. Movement up and down the bay occurs at the rate of about five feet every two seconds.

(Information regarding pickup and deposit times can be found in Appendix 2.3 at the end of this chapter.)

WARREN: What about raising or lowering the forks?

SAM: Since all forklifts travel with their forks in the down position we've included the raising or lowering of the forks in the pickup and deposit times.

WARREN: And what about movement in and out of the trucks?

SAM: There's about an eight second increase or decrease each time we change one row. In other words, the distance which the forklift has to move in order to reach the respective four-by-four row in the truck adds or decreases the movement time by four seconds per row.

WARREN: I need a bit more clarification on the pallets that go into the short-haul trucks. Do they just get stacked on the dock during the day? Also, when are they loaded?

SAM: Let me sort this out, Warren. Let's begin with the second shift, which runs from 4 P.M. to midnight. Any pallets unloaded from the long-haulers for local delivery during that shift will get put right on the local truck if it has been parked after its maintenance check and gas-up time. Also, if there are any pallets on the floor, they too will be loaded. The dispatcher will have this information and will plan the delivery route according to the location of the pallets on the load. If an additional pallet is scheduled for a short-hauler after that point it gets loaded directly onto the short-hauler by the forklift carrying it. If there isn't room, we leave it on the floor at the appropriate bay. It would then be loaded onto a short-hauler after it returns from it's initial trip at 8 A.M. for delivery on the truck's second trip out during the afternoon. As for the actual procedure of placing them in the truck, it really doesn't add any modeling time outside of what we discussed earlier.

WARREN: O.K., let's move onto the first shift?

SAM: Once the trucks are out at 8 A.M. we continue to set the pallets on the floor at the appropriate local outgoing bays. When a truck has returned and is positioned on the left side for unloading, we unload the pallets picked up during that trip. They're either placed onto a short-hauler, if one is waiting, or stacked on the floor at the appropriate outgoing bay. If pallets are waiting to be loaded into a short-hauler, when a forklift transports a pallet to this truck's bay, it proceeds to load all stacked pallets there. We continue loading the short-haulers for their second trip in this manner until the short-hauler is full or it is 1 P.M., whichever comes first.

WARREN: [*appearing content with the volume of information obtained*] I think we can handle that. Is there anything else I should know about your operation?

SAM: Well, to clarify, let me just state that we only refuel and perform routine maintenance on the short-haulers after their second trip out, and not after each trip. Also, it occurs to me that when a lift picks up a pallet from the floor for loading, the operator has to turn the lift around which takes anywhere from thirty-five to fifty seconds. Outside of that we've covered most of the bases. What do you think?

WARREN: I think we've done a good job, but I do have a question regarding local pickups and deliveries.

SAM: O.K.

WARREN: I'll assume that whenever a drop-off is made a forklift is there to assist you. What happens if a location has a drop-off and a simultaneous pickup? What do you do about the reloading process?

SAM: That's a good question, Warren. Ordinarily the dispatcher considers that when planning the vehicle's route so we can avoid such a situation. If we run up against an unexpected pickup than we do a little jockeying, but the organization responsible at the pickup point ordinarily resets things in the truck accordingly.

WARREN: Well stated, Sam. Do you ever have pickups of partial pallets?

SAM: Up to now we haven't allowed for that, but some of our clients judge that we should. We would then consolidate these items in a palletizing operation in our shop. I've been resisting doing this because we're strictly a transfer depot and not a warehousing operation. However, to meet increased competition in the future I may need to consider providing this type of service.

WARREN: Perhaps we can simulate that after we've come up with some preliminary results regarding the current operations.

SAM: O.K., but first we should focus on the major issues at hand. Golly, I almost forgot about our yard tractor.

WARREN: What do you mean a "yard tractor"?

SAM: We have a pool of ten to twelve trailers sitting here in the yard. During the day shift we want to have the outgoing bays full all of the time so we don't have to double handle our pallets, something you had pointed out earlier. I should have mentioned this at that time, but it slipped my mind. All this simulation stuff is so new to me. Anyway, we have a yard tractor whose express purpose is moving trailers in and out of bays during the day shift on both sides of the depot.

WARREN: You're only going to do this on the day shift?

SAM: With fewer forklifts on the second and third shifts, we don't fill as many trailers so we'll just let the bays remain empty until the next day.

WARREN: What about incoming long-haulers during the second and third shifts?

SAM: We ask our drivers to park their trailers and then unhitch the rig and take it to maintenance. This way we don't have to wait on the outgoing side for a long-hauler to complete the maintenance and get gassed up before putting a trailer in the outgoing bay. During the day shift, when a long-hauler arrives the driver just drops the trailer and the yard tractor takes care of positioning it. The driver just takes his truck directly to maintenance.

WARREN: Sounds like all that information you gave me on maintenance and gassing up has no effect on the flow.

SAM: For the long-haulers that is true, but you still need to incorporate it for the short-haulers because getting them to the outgoing side is delayed by maintenance and gassing after the second trip.

WARREN: You don't have any other surprises for me, do you, Sam?

SAM: Not another thing, and I'm really sorry I didn't mention it before.

WARREN: What is important is the fact that we have the information and can incorporate it into the model. Now, there is one more thing we need to discuss. Needless to say, your operations here are on a twenty-four hour basis, so in a sense there's only been one official start-up. In other words, all filled trucks on the left side, all empty trucks on the right side and no pallets on the floor. Subsequent to that, every shift begins with work-in-process inventory, that is, pallets on the floor. For simulation purposes, the model must begin somewhere. We have two alternatives. One is to start "at the beginning" as just described, and let the model run through approximately five days worth of time, at which point we can assume that the system is in equilibrium, or steady-state. From that point on we could begin the collection of statistics. The other alternative involves initializing the model at some agreed upon set of values. We could start at a set time, say 8 A.M., and have some pallets on the floor, some partially unloaded trucks, some partially loaded trucks, and four forklifts that begin work at 8 A.M. at some assigned position. What's your preference?

SAM: I'm not sure, Warren, simulation isn't my forte. Tell me, based on your experience, what's better?

WARREN: There isn't really any clear-cut set of rules to follow, both approaches are reasonable. My preference might be to initialize the model and go from there. Let me take this information we've discussed back to my office and work up some initializing conditions. I'll fax them over to you, and then you and your team can review them and see if they appear realistic. At that time you can make any alterations or changes you feel are appropriate and send them back to me.

SAM: I hope this won't affect the completion time for our work?

WARREN: No, I doubt it will, Sam. I can have this material to you within a day, tomorrow morning at the latest. How's that?

SAM: That's fine, Warren. Feel free to give me a ring if you need additional information.

WARREN: Will do, Sam.

SAM: How long do you estimate it will be before you have an initial model up and running?

WARREN: We initially agreed to a month, and I'm confident we'll meet that deadline. In two weeks I want to get together with you to take a look at the operation of the model for the day shift only. If that is okay, it will be easy enough to extend it to the second and third shifts. I'll supply you with my assumptions list and some basic outputs. We can verify the workings of the model and validate the model by reviewing the outputs. After that, we will add the other two shifts and we can begin examining several of the "bumps," or "what-if" situations we discussed. By the way, can I have a copy of these blueprints?

SAM: Sure you can, I'll get copies for you on the way out. I think we're off to a good start and I look forward to receiving your fax. We'll look it over right away and I'll get in touch regardless of the result of our inspection. Thanks for helping us out, Warren.

WARREN: Thank you, Sam, for giving us the opportunity to show you what simulation is, and how it can assist you in your operations.

Warren's fax is shown in Appendix 2.3 at the end of this chapter. The initialized conditions were immediately approved by Sam and his team. Warren also called Sam the following day with regard to weekend operations. Sam indicated that the depot closed down at the end of the second shift on Friday (midnight) and began operations again with the third shift on Monday morning. Sam and his team also noted that the initialized conditions seemed appropriate for this schedule and could represent the initialized conditions for the beginning of the work week on Monday morning.

OBSERVATIONS FROM THE DIALOG

In reviewing the dialogue between Sam and Warren, one dominant theme is present: both Sam and Warren attempt to seek out and explore every facet of the operation that affects the system's behavior in a significant way. Many times Warren asked Sam to expand upon concepts and provide meaningful insights regarding the operation of the depot. Also, Warren requested that Sam represent as accurately as possible any numerical evaluations which Affect the operation. When topics were suggested by Sam, Warren did his best to verify that these facets of the operation were indeed important, and to determine whether these functions should be part of the basic model or part of the "what-ifs" to be examined later on.

On other occasions, Warren, drawing on his experience, suggested items that Sam had not even considered. Often those who are intimately involved in the operations of an organization fail to see everything that is going on because (1) they take so much for granted and (2) many functions involved in the operation become commonplace and go unnoticed, like the information about the yard tractor, a critical element in the flow that the simulation is to emulate. In order for a simulation model to properly emulate a system being investigated there must exist a free and thorough exchange of information, as evidenced in the dialogue presented above.

In many organizations existing operations are representative of an evolutionary process. Generally, drastic changes are not implemented within a system as often as other smaller changes; that is, those which are aimed to solve or circumvent specific problems. Eventually these small changes become customary, at which time newer, more innovative changes are suggested. This phenomenon exacerbates the need to break operations down into components and address each facet of the operation uniquely. As each function, or component, of the operation is analyzed, and small "bumps" are considered, and perhaps added to the system, greater efficiencies can be uncovered. While at first, some explanations may be wanting for these improved efficiencies, answers evolve slowly over time as the process becomes further understood. One of the goals of simulation is to assist in this evolutionary process by uncovering some of these small changes which may eventually lead to the restructuring of a system.

One last observation in the dialogue between Warren and Sam is the effort by Warren to help Sam feel in control of the simulation, and take part ownership in the model. Initially Sam was enthusiastic regarding the impact that simulation might have on existing operations at the transfer depot, otherwise he would not have hired SIMUTECH to begin with. However, Warren continually involves Sam in all decisions, and lets Sam assume great responsibility in designing the theoretical model from which the formal model will be developed. The greater the responsibility placed in the hands of the end user, the more enthusiastically the results will be received, be they optimistic or pessimistic. If genuine enthusiasm and optimism does not exist, this blocks the creative process necessary to institute the continuous improvement philosophy which is critical in updating, proposing, and evaluating incremental changes in the simulation model which ultimately affects the actual implementation of innovative ideas.

The dialogue and informal model presented in this chapter is further explored in Chapter 3, where the formal model for the transfer depot is presented and analyzed. For now, it is sufficient to say that understanding how the initial steps of a simulation process evolve is a critical part in building and designing a functional, reliable simulation model. It is hoped that the dialogue between Sam and Warren illustrates how a meaningful and well-developed concept can begin, and how the initial steps of a simulation project can be approached.

Appendix 2.1
Layout for the Transfer Depot

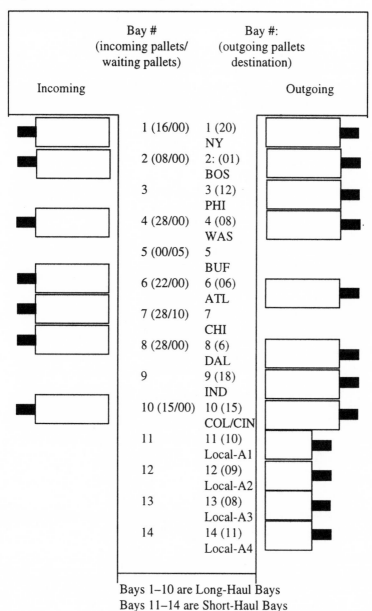

Bays 1–10 are Long-Haul Bays
Bays 11–14 are Short-Haul Bays

Appendix 2.2
Incoming/Outgoing Distributions

Distribution of Pallets on Short-Haul Trailers	
Number of Pallets	*Probability*
4	0.06
5	0.10
6	0.14
7	0.24
8	0.18
9	0.10
10	0.08
11	0.06
12	0.04

Disposition of the Contents of Long-Haul Trailers That Arrive at the Depot

Destination	*Probability*
Local	0.10*
Columbus-Cincinnati	0.10
Indianapolis	0.10

The remaining eight locations (Buffalo, New York, Philadelphia, Washington, Atlanta, Chicago, Boston, and Dallas) are equiprobable.

Disposition of the Contents of Long-Haul Trailers That Arrive at the Depot

Destination	*Probability*
Local	0.10*
Columbus-Cincinnati	0.16
Chicago	0.15
New York	0.10

The remaining seven locations (Buffalo, Indianapolis, Boston, Philadelphia, Washington, Atlanta, and Dallas) are equiprobable.

* The four local areas are equiprobable.

Appendix 2.3
Activity Times and Disposition of Bays

Activity Times	
Activity	*Time*
Pick-up pallet in truck	40 ± 10 seconds
Pick-up pallet from floor	35 ± 7.5 seconds
Deposit pallet in truck	40 ± 10 seconds
Deposit pallet on floor	35 ± 7.5 seconds

Initializing Conditions at the Beginning of the Third Shift

Bay	*Pallets Incoming*	*Pallets Waiting*	*Destination*	*Pallets Outgoing*
1	Trailer (16)		New York	Trailer (20)
2	Trailer (8)		Boston	Trailer (1)
3			Philadelphia	Trailer (12)
4	Trailer (28)		Washington	Trailer (8)
5		(5)	Buffalo	
6	Trailer (22)		Atlanta	Trailer (6)
7	Trailer (28)	(10)	Chicago	
8	Trailer (28)		Dallas	Trailer (6)
9			Indianapolis	Trailer (18)
10	Trailer (15)		Col-Cin	Trailer (15)
11			Local-A1	Vehicle (10)
12			Local-A2	Vehicle (9)
13			Local-A3	Vehicle (8)
14			Local-A4	Vehicle (11)

The four forklift trucks are ready to work as the shift begins. Each of the forklift trucks will be working in an incoming, partially loaded trailer (i.e., bays 1, 2, 6 and 10). After each trailer is emptied, the forklift truck will begin work on any trailer that is not at capacity. If there are none, work begins on the trailer that has been there the longest. This rule will apply for all shifts. The values in parenthesis represent the number of pallets to be unloaded, already loaded, or sitting on the floor, as evidenced by their location.

3

Modeling Truck Terminal
Transfer Operations

In Chapter 2, Samuel Ainsworth of The Rodgers Trucking Company met with Warren Harcourt of SIMUTECH, Inc. to discuss the operations of his truck transfer terminal. The intent of that dialogue was to provide as much information as possible about the operations so that a simulation model could be built that would effectively emulate the system. They hoped that the simulation would help (1) answer some questions that Sam had regarding the present operations at the terminal and (2) indicate where problems might arise in the future should there be an increase in truck arrivals.

At the end of their conversation, the two principal parties agreed to meet in order to discuss the results of the first runs of the model and the outputs for the first shift of the operation. Although no dialogue is presented between Warren and Sam as done before, we provide a discussion of the computer simulation model, its operation, and the outputs that were generated by the model for the first shift.

BUILDING THE MODEL

A simulation modeler is often faced with many subtleties and nuances that inherently take place in the system to be modeled that are not discussed in the initial meeting of the principals. Perhaps it would have been wise to have one of the forklift drivers present to actually discuss what happens on a typical day. Early runs of the simulation model indicate that problems exist pertaining to the loading of pallets on the short-haulers before the afternoon departure. Who loads the pallets on the floor and at what time if there is no specific pallet randomly assigned to that truck prior to the 1 P.M. departure? You may recall that the rule that was utilized was that the first forklift having a pallet for the truck would load all pallets that were sitting on the floor.

Does a forklift driver ever have to wait for another forklift driver to drop off a pallet either in a truck or on the floor before being able to off-load the pallet he is carrying? Information regarding interference was not discussed, and yet we would surmise that with pallets being assigned to outgoing trucks on a random basis, two forklifts might need to be in the same spot at the same time.

It seems likely that at the beginning of the first shift, the number of trucks with full loads could be anticipated to be fixed, but the number of pallets on trucks that have less than a full load is random and should not always be reflected as a fixed value. Likewise, the number of trucks on the outgoing side and the number of pallets on each, as well as those spots where pallets are located on the floor, should also be random. These numbers vary each day and should be reflected in the model.

When does an individual go to lunch? The model cannot just put the individual at lunch when the clock reaches a particular time. If that were done, the individual may be assigned to go to lunch when he is backing his forklift truck out of a trailer or when he is crossing from one side to the other. In a similar vein, does the model simply take the individual out of circulation at 4:30 P.M. when he is scheduled to cease work? Obviously, as noted before, that cannot be done if the driver is in the middle of an operation.

Sam had indicated that a local truck would leave on its second trip at 1 P.M. unless the truck was full before then. If this were to happen, it adds subtlety to the rule of having all four trucks leave at the same time as well as having forklifts put the pallets on the floor because the truck is full. Further, do the drivers always leave right after their lunch, or will the driver whose truck is filled ahead of time forego lunch to get on the road and start delivering his load?

Many of these sensitive issues relative to the real-time operations of the depot and inherently pertinent to the operation of the model were not discussed by Sam and Warren. Basically there are three choices that are available to the modeler in responding to these types of issues concerning the subtleties and nuances of the model: (1) they can be incorporated into the model in exactly the same manner as they would occur (2) averages when appropriate can be incorporated into the model, or (3) they can be ignored. If the model is to truly reflect what is happening in the terminal then the third alternative is the least likely of the three. However, even if choice three is selected, it is imperative that an assumptions document be prepared and shared between the two principals so that, in this case, Sam has the opportunity to sign off on the model operation and, in so doing, recognize that any of the results are predicated on this information. Thus, one of the first things that Warren will do prior to the first results meeting is to prepare the assumptions document.

THE ASSUMPTIONS DOCUMENT

The assumptions document is designed to provide all of the information that serves as the basis for the operation of the model. It can include basic information, such as input data as to speeds of equipment, completion duration, and distributions from which to sample; decision rules (for example, after the first pallet is deposited into a trailer, a check is made for pallets on the floor); or nuance rules (for example, each forklift driver waits until the back of the truck is cleared before moving into the truck). By spelling out as many of these items as possible and obtaining agreement from the principals, it is anticipated that the results will be more readily believed and accepted.

The modelers at SIMUTECH, Inc. have created an initial model that operates within a framework of the given information and the set of decision rules that were provided. Other rules have also been incorporated based on the experience of the modeler and also on the need to overcome problems that arose in the early stages of the modeling process. When these decisions are made, the completion of the model can move forward, but there is an awareness that the model is subject to revision based on the willingness of the principals to accept it under the present operating conditions. It is also understood that moving forward in this manner will alleviate the need to stop and call the principals each time a new decision rule is invoked. It should also be recognized that the assumptions document is not a fixed item but is subject to change by either the principals or the modeler as building the model progresses. This does not imply that factual information, such as conveyor speeds or completion times, can be changed arbitrarily. Rather, it implies that changes may occur as new information becomes available.

The proximate motivation for the meeting between Sam and Warren following the achievement of a working simulation model for the first shift is to review the assumptions document and to look at the results of the early simulation runs based on the model. An agreement by Sam at this stage will permit the development and incorporation of both second and third shift operations. The assumptions document prepared for The Rodgers Trucking Company is in Table 3.1.

Although the assumptions document is rather lengthy, it should be reviewed in detail when Warren and Sam meet. Warren must establish why an interference rule was put into effect for putting pallets into the trucks but not for placing pallets on the floor. Sam has to approve of the drivers' scheduled lunches and the idea of randomly generating pallet counts for the initial start-up. All of the pertinent times in the model will be reviewed, as well as the flows in the model to make sure that its operation does indeed emulate the flow of pallets in the transfer terminal. Using the output information derived from this initial simulation model will be helpful in supporting the assumptions document.

OUTPUTS FROM THE MODEL

Observing the initial outputs of the model provides the basic building block to substantiate the elements of the assumptions document and ultimately serve to validate the model. If something doesn't look right, perhaps it is the result of an incorrect item in the assumptions document. On the other hand, if the outputs are indicative of what is actually happening at the transfer terminal, the assumptions document is tacitly approved and the model is validated. Approval and validation are very critical steps in the simulation process. If the model reproduces reality, Sam will proudly take further ownership of the model and will be more receptive to the results and their interpretation when "what-ifs" are incorporated into the model.

There is no prescribed order for the presentation of the results. At this stage, Warren and his team are trying to ascertain whether the results from the initial simulation model do indeed represent the actual operations of the transfer terminal. This is accomplished by making multiple runs and then combining the results of the multiple runs to create averages, maximums, minimums, tables, matrices, or typical daily outputs, that is,

Table 3.1
Assumptions Document Prepared for The Rodgers Trucking Company by SIMUTECH, Inc.

Forklift Truck Operations

cross bay travel	40 seconds	
travel on bay side	2 seconds per five feet	
pickup pallet in truck	U(40, 10)	seconds
deposit pallet in truck	U(40, 10)	seconds
place pallet on floor	U(35, 7.5)	seconds
remove pallet from floor	U(35, 7.5)	seconds

Long-Haul Truck Arrival Rates

8:00 A.M. to 4:00 P.M.	U(45, 15)	minutes
4:00 P.M. to 12:00 A.M.	U(90, 60)	minutes
12:00 A.M. to 8:00 A.M.	U(120, 45)	minutes

Short-Haul Truck Arrival Rates

Truck returns to the depot are dependent on the length of time the truck is away from the depot. A.M. trip times are U(112.5, 37, 5), and the P.M. trips are .7U(112.5, 37, 5).

Yard Tractor Operations

The depot maintains a yard tractor for the express purpose of moving full trailers into and empty trailers out of the incoming bays, and removing full trailers from and moving empty trailers into the outgoing bays. This tractor operates only between 8:00 A.M. and 4:00 P.M.

Time to move into bay	U(5, 2)	minutes
Time to move out of bay	U(4, 1)	minutes
Time to move trailer from lot to bay	U(10, 4)	minutes

Model Initialization Rules

Incoming side:
7 trucks at positions 1, 2, 4, 6, 7, 8, and 10, where trucks at positions 4, 7, and 8 have 28 pallets and positions 1, 2, 6, and 10 have a randomly generated figure sampled from U(10.5, 6.5).

Outgoing side:
8 trucks at positions 1, 2, 3, 4, 6, 8, 9, and 10, where trucks at all positions have a randomly generated pallet figure sampled from U(10.5, 7.5).

4 local trucks at positions 11, 12, 13, and 14, where trucks at all four positions have a randomly generated pallet figure sampled from U(8.5, 3.5).

Pallets on the Floor

Located at positions 5 and 7, the number randomly generated from U(6, 3).

Table 3.1 (continued)

Surplus Empty Trailers

The model begins with 12 surplus empty trailers waiting to be moved to the outgoing side as bays become available.

Initial Starting Position

The model begins at 8:00 A.M. with four forklift operators moving to trucks on the incoming side at positions 1, 2, 6, and 10.

Other Distributions of Interest

The distribution of pallets on returning short-haulers:

Pallets	4	5	6	7	8	9	10	11	12
Occurrence %	.06	.10	.14	.24	.18	.10	.08	.06	.04

The distribution of the contents of long-haul trailers that arrive at the terminal:

Destination	Probability
Local	0.12
Columbus-Cincinnati	0.10
Indianapolis	0.10

The remaining 8 locations are equiprobable with probability 0.085.

The distribution of the contents of short-haul trailers that arrive at the terminal:

Destination	Probability
Local	0.10
Columbus-Cincinnati	0.16
Chicago	0.15
New York	0.10

The remaining 7 locations are equiprobable with probability 0.07.

Miscellaneous Data Pertinent to the Operation of the Model:

1. The model will operate with 4, 3, and 2 forklift drivers for the three shifts, respectively.
2. Forklift drivers will take a 45-minute break for lunch. In the first shift, two will go to lunch at 11:45 A.M. and the other two at 1:15 P.M. In the second shift, two will go at 7:45 P.M. and the third at 8:30 P.M. In the third shift, one will go at 3:45 A.M. and the other at 4:30 A.M.
3. Forklift drivers will stop work one-half hour before the end of their shift.
4. The yard tractor will maintain a full complement of trucks at the outgoing bays to minimize double handling of pallets.
5. Drivers of arriving trucks and outgoing trucks will, respectively, park and remove their trucks during the second and third shifts.

Table 3.1 (continued)

6. Long-haul trucks receive maintenance and fuel, but the operation is not critical to the model. Work is done while the trailer is on line.

7. An empty truck or a filled truck needs to have attention immediately after parking to secure its doors. The time to do this is U(3, 1).

8. The model is to be run in seconds. After acceptance of the assumptions document and the initial outputs, the model will be run for a period of five consecutive days.

9. The number of runs necessary to account for variability will be determined by the modeler.

10. A yard location is maintained for arriving long-haul trucks when there are no bays available.

11. A pool of empty trailers (12) is maintained to fill open bays on the outgoing side of the terminal.

Basic Rules of Operation Within the Model

1. A forklift truck removes a pallet from an incoming trailer, determines the destination, moves across the bay, travels on the outgoing side, and off-loads the pallet either into the truck or places it on the floor if no truck is available. The route is retraced and the process is repeated.

2. All local trucks depart from the terminal at 8:00 A.M. with initialized loads (first day only). The period away from the terminal is determined, and, as each truck returns, it is unloaded and moved to the outgoing side to be loaded for 1:00 P.M. departure. When a local truck returns a second time, it is unloaded, receives maintenance and fuel, and is placed back on the outgoing side for overnight loading.

3. Forklift drivers periodically check for the return of local trucks as they receive priority unloading. Once the local trucks are unloaded, the forklift drivers return to the operations that were in progress before the interruption.

4. Forklift drivers periodically check the time for their lunch break and, later in the day, for their quitting time.

5. The yard tractor moves arriving trailers into an open bay position always working from position one to ten. The order of entry into the docking area is maintained so that the earliest arrivals are always unloaded first.

Other Rules of Operation for the Model

1. Interference rules are in effect for entry into the outgoing trucks. A queue is established to gather results.

2. At 12:30 P.M. all local trucks are checked to ensure that any pallets on the floor are loaded.

3. All local trucks depart at 1:00 P.M. even if filled earlier.

anything possible that can provide Sam with the evidence necessary to decide whether or not the model is operating properly. Warren chose to start at the beginning, so to speak. These results are shown in Table 3.2.

The output results document presented above illustrates all of the pertinent information that has been derived from the analysis of the multiple runs. In addition to the factual information, Warren will add his own comments and observations regarding the information from these runs.

Observations Regarding the Output Results

The observations provided in this section parallel the output results which are shown in Table 3.2.

It would appear that the forklift operators cannot keep up with the flow of incoming trucks. However, it is anticipated that with the second and third shifts (i.e., a longer interarrival rate for incoming long-haul trailers with fewer forklift drivers and no local trucks to unload) incoming trucks will be taken care of, and a buildup will not be a problem. However, one can only be sure when the second and third shifts are added to the model. If a truck was empty as late as 3:38, it would appear that one of the forklift drivers was working past the 3:30 quitting time. This may or may not be true, but the last pallet in the truck was picked up before 3:30 and the added time has to do with closing up the truck, moving it out of the bay, and then recording the departure time.

In analyzing the removal of filled long-haul trucks and primarily their destinations (bay number represents destination), there is evidence that first-filled trailers follow the pattern of initialization. Only bays 19 and 21 begin without a trailer and with less pallets on the floor than would be represented on the eight partially filled trucks. Perhaps consideration should be given to having eight partially filled trucks for an initialized condition with randomly selected locations rather than fixed. It is also assumed that with a consecutive run of five days, the effect of the increased probabilities of pallets going to selected locations will be more evident.

The status of the bays at the end of the shift shows that the effort to keep all bays filled on the outgoing side is working well. On the incoming side, even though arrivals occur faster than the available capacity can empty the trailers, the average number of filled bays was 8.67. Also, of the twenty-seven runs only five yielded times for which all of the bays were filled. This resulted in arriving trailers being placed in a holding area where they waited for an average of forty minutes before being placed in an open bay.

A snapshot of the bays at the end of a typical day provides a good picture of how the model progresses. All ten bays of the incoming side are filled, and four of those trailers are partially filled, indicating that these are the trailers that are being emptied when the simulation terminates. There is also one local truck still at the dock, while the others have gone to maintenance or to be refueled. On the outgoing side there are seven bays that are filled with trailers. As the simulation ends, the yard tractor is in the process of retrieving an empty trailer to be placed in one of the vacant bays. No local trucks have completed their maintenance inspection and refueling as none appears on the outgoing side of the terminal.

The status of the bays is predicated on the ability of the yard tractor to move trailers in and out. Although the average utilization of the yard tractor was just slightly above 50 percent, no time was allotted in the model for the driver to go to lunch or take a break.

The information on interference as it pertains to the trailers indicates that there are occasions when two forklift trucks need to have access to the same truck at the same time. Although the maximum wait time for a forklift truck was fifty-one seconds, it is probably a good idea to maintain this check for interference in the model. The decision not to include an interference check for the pallets put on the floor was predicated on the basic decision to keep all bays filled, thus minimizing the number of pallets on the floor. In addition, with fewer forklift trucks during the second and third shifts, the probability of occurrence is greatly minimized even though more pallets can be expected to be put on the floor during those two shifts.

The average times to deliver allow the local trucks to return to the depot in midmorning for unloading and reloading, which is also true in the afternoon. It is the late returning trucks that create potential difficulties. One thing to keep in mind in reviewing the maximum figures is that these represent an average of all the maximum values for the twenty-seven runs. Consequently, individual times may be at the upper limit of the distribution of times. The average outgoing loads differ for A.M. and P.M., which indicates a shorter time to make P.M. deliveries. Incoming loads are basically the same for all categories for both time periods.

It is now up to Warren and Sam to resolve any discrepancies that may arise in their exchange of information regarding Sam's expectations and Warren's results. This meeting should adequately help to rectify any logic problems in the model as well as to clarify any of the factual information

Table 3.2
Results of the Simulated Runs Prepared for The Rodgers Trucking Company by SIMUTECH, Inc.

The simulation model, representing the first shift of the transfer terminal operations, was run for a total of twenty-seven days. The results that are presented below represent the average values for these runs, unless otherwise noted, for an eight hour period.

Long-Haul Trucks	Mean	Median	Maximum	Minimum
Number of arrivals	9.22	9.00	11.00	8.00
Number of empty removals	6.96	7.00	8.00	6.00
Number filled	7.28	7.00	9.00	6.00

A truck was empty as early as 9:02 and as late as 3:38.
A truck was filled as early as 9:39 and as late as 3:37.

Long-Haul Truck Status, at End of Shift	Mean	Median	Maximum	Minimum
Incoming	8.67	8.50	10.00	7.00
Outcoming	9.74	10.00	10.00	8.00

An Analysis of the Outgoing Side Trailers

Bay	Number of trucks filled during the 27 runs
1	19
2	21
3	16
4	19
5	9
6	15
7	17
8	21
9	21
10	24

Table 3.2 (continued)

Status of the Bays at the End of a Typical Day

Incoming Side				*Outgoing Side*		
Bay	Truck?	Pallets	Floor Pallets	Pallets	Truck?	Bay
1	X	28		9	X	1
2	X	28		3	X	2
3	X	7		6	X	3
4	X	28		11	X	4
5	X	21	1	5		
6	X	23		24	X	6
7	X	28		7		
8	X	28		3	X	8
9	X	20		27	X	9
10	X	28	3	10		
11		3		11		
12	X	1	1	12		
13		6		13		
14		3		14		

Yard Tractor Information	**Mean**	**Maximum**	**Minimum**
Utilization	0.58	0.65	0.46
Trailers moved	31.00	34.00	26.00
Mean time per engagement (sec)	538.51	575.77	503.72

Interference for the Forklift Trucks

Outgoing Bay	*Maximum in Line*	*Average Entries*	*No Wait Entries*	*Percentage No Wait*	*Wait Time (seconds)*
1	1.00	16.41	15.56	95.34	19.30
2	1.00	17.11	16.00	94.43	22.99
3	1.00	16.04	15.63	97.76	17.14
4	1.04	16.82	15.82	94.52	31.76
5	1.07	21.00	19.26	92.50	51.15
6	1.00	16.89	16.19	96.29	29.99
7	1.11	19.96	18.26	91.90	39.21
8	1.00	16.89	16.26	96.38	20.01
9	1.04	19.96	19.00	95.08	34.71

Table 3.2 (continued)

Outgoing Bay	Maximum in Line	Average Entries	No Wait Entries	Percentage No Wait	Wait Time (seconds)
10	1.07	17.89	16.37	92.10	43.32
11	1.00	5.00	4.89	98.63	2.71
12	1.00	5.00	4.70	94.94	5.32
13	1.00	5.00	4.83	94.89	5.76
14	1.00	5.63	5.30	95.64	6.75

Local Trucks Information

A.M./P.M.	Truck	Mean	Maximum	Minimum
A. Length of Trips (minutes)				
A.M.		111.89	149.60	75.95
P.M.		80.01	104.95	52.57
B. Load Size–Outgoing (# of pallets)				
A.M.	1	7.76	11.00	8.00
	2	8.65	11.00	8.00
	3	8.47	11.00	10.00
	4	7.65	11.00	6.00
P.M.	1	4.76	8.00	2.00
	2	4.82	8.00	2.00
	3	5.35	10.00	1.00
	4	4.35	6.00	2.00
C. Load Size–Ingoing (# of pallets)				
A.M.	1	7.13	11.00	4.00
	2	7.25	11.00	4.00
	3	7.71	12.00	4.00
	4	7.58	12.00	4.00
P.M.	1	7.67	12.00	4.00
	2	7.58	11.00	4.00
	3	7.71	12.00	4.00
	4	7.46	12.00	4.00

that has been incorporated. In addition, it is the last time that modest changes can be made to the model and not be reflected as a "what-if."

It is to be hoped that after this meeting, Warren can add the second and the third shift to the model and then begin to make multiple five-day runs to provide a final set of results for the base model. From that point on, parameters in the model can be changed to reflect "what-if" scenarios that Sam would like to include.

Appendix 3.1
Simulation Code

Here, and following all remaining chapters, the simulation code used for the basic model utilized within the body of the chapter will be presented in its entirety in an appendix. Commentary will appear, as needed, in order to explain the material.

```
SIMULATE
    REALLOCATE FAC,65,HSV,60
    UNLIST
    NOXREF
********************************************************************************
*   THIS MODEL CREATES THE FLOW OF PALLETS THROUGH
*   A TRUCKING DEPOT EQUIPPED TO HANDLE 10
*   INCOMING TRAILERS AND 10 OUT-GOING TRAILERS. IN
*   ADDITION THERE IS SPACE TO HANDLE 4 SHORT HAUL
*   TRUCKS FOR BOTH THE INCOMING AND OUTGOING
*   SIDES. THIS MODEL IS INITIALIZED WITH TRUCKS ON
*   BOTH SIDES OF THE TERMINAL AND PALLET
*   QUANTITIES ON THE TRAILERS RANDOMLY
*   GENERATED. THE GOAL OF THE SIMULATION IS TO
*   VALIDATE THE NUMBER OF FORK-LIFT TRUCKS USED
*   DURING THE FIRST SHIFT AND TO OBSERVE THE
*   OUTPUT OF THE MODEL.
********************************************************************************
*   CREATION OF FUNCTIONS, VARIABLE, MATRICIES, TABLES, ETC.
********************************************************************************
SVAL FUNCTION PH1,D21
1,2/2,4/4,6/6,7/7,8/8,10/10,15/15,16/16,17/17,18/18,20/20,22/22,23
23,24/24,25/25,26/26,27/27,28/28,33/33,35/35,37
LOAD FUNCTION PH1,E21
1,FN(PICK1)/2,FN(PICK1)/4,28/6,FN(PICK1)/7,28/8,28/10,FN(PICK1)
15,FN(PICK2)/16,FN(PICK2)/17,FN(PICK2)/18,FN(PICK2)/20,FN(PICK2)
22,FN(PICK2)/23,FN(PICK2)/24,FN(PICK2)/25,FN(PICK3)/26,FN(PICK3)
27,FN(PICK3)/28,FN(PICK3)/33,FN(PICK4)/35,FN(PICK4)
PICK1 FUNCTION RN1,C2
0.0,10/1.0,23
PICK2 FUNCTION RN1,C2
0.0,3/1.0,18
```

PICK3 FUNCTION RN1,C2
0.0,5/1.0,12
PICK4 FUNCTION RN1,C2
0.0,3/1.0,9
LOTRK FUNCTION PH2,D4   PICKS UP LOADING DOCK NUMBER
1,25/2,26/3,27/4,28
INITL FUNCTION PH1,D3   SETS ORDER AFTER FIRST FOUR
1,4/2,7/3,8
TLOAD FUNCTION RN1,D14
0.03,25/0.06,26/0.09,27/0.12,28/0.22,24/0.32,23/0.405,15/0.49,16/0.575,17
0.66,18/0.745,19/0.83,20/0.915,21/1.0,22
LLOAD FUNCTION RN1,D14
0.025,25/0.05,26/0.075,27/0.1,28/0.26,24/0.41,21/0.51,15/0.58,16/0.65,17
0.72,18/0.79,19/0.86,20/0.93,22/1.0,23
WHBAY FUNCTION PH1,D4
30,1/31,2/32,6/33,10
WHFAC FUNCTION PH3,D4
1,30/2,31/3,32/4,33
TIER FUNCTION PH3,D28
1,6/2,6/3,6/4,6/5,5/6,5/7,5/8,5/9,4/10,4/11,4/12,4/13,3/14,3/15,3/16,3
17,2/18,2/19,2/20,2/21,1/22,1/23,1/24,1/25,0/26,0/27,0/28,0
FLRCT FUNCTION PH6,D14
15,29/16,30/17,31/18,32/19,33/20,34/21,35/22,36/23,37/24,38/25,39/26,40
27,41/28,42
COMPR FUNCTION PH6,D14
15,1/16,2/17,3/18,4/19,5/20,6/21,7/22,8/23,9/24,10/25,11/26,12/27,13/28,14
SPACE FUNCTION PH6,D14
15,50/16,51/17,52/18,53/19,54/20,55/21,56/22,57/23,58/24,59/25,60/26,61
27,62/28,63
OPPOS FUNCTION PH7,D4
39,25/40,26/41,27/42,28
LTIER FUNCTION PH3,D12
1,2/2,2/3,2/4,2/5,1/6,1/7,1/8,1/9,0/10,0/11,0/12,0
LOCCK FUNCTION PH2,D4
11,50/12,51/13,52/14,53
BAYOT FUNCTION PH2,D4
11,25/12,26/13,27/14,28
LOCIN FUNCTION PH1,D4
30,11/31,12/32,13/33,14

```
TRKLO FUNCTION PH1,D4            PICKS UP LOADING DOCK NUMBER
1,25/2,26/3,27/4,28
IBLOC FUNCTION PH3,D4
25,11/26,12/27,13/28,14
LOCCT FUNCTION RN1,D9
0.06,4/0.16,5/0.3,6/0.54,7/0.72,8/0.82,9/0.9,10/0.96,11/1.0,12
GONE  FUNCTION RN1,C2
0.0,4500/1.0,9000
SIGNL FUNCTION PH1,D4
11,50/12,51/13,52/14,53
XTRVL FVARIABLE (((ABS(PH8-PH6))*20)/5)*2
ITRVL FVARIABLE ((((ABS(PH4-PH2))*20)/5)*2)+.5 AISLE TVL TIME IN
OTRVL FVARIABLE ((((ABS(FN(COMPR)-PH2))*20)/5)*2)+.5 AISLE TVL TIME OUT
1  BVARIABLE BV2'E'1+BV3'E'1
2  BVARIABLE (XH50'E'1*PH1'E'30)+(XH51'E'1*PH1'E'31)
3  BVARIABLE (XH52'E'1*PH1'E'32)+(XH53'E'1*PH1'E'33)
4  BVARIABLE PH1'E'11+PH1'E'12+PH1'E'13+PH1'E'14
5  BVARIABLE XH39'NE'0+XH40'NE'0+XH41'NE'0+XH42'NE'0
6  BVARIABLE BV7'E'1+BV8'E'1
7  BVARIABLE F15'E'0+F16'E'0+F17'E'0+F18'E'0+F19'E'0
8  BVARIABLE F20'E'0+F21'E'0+F22'E'0+F23'E'0+F24'E'0
9  BVARIABLE PH1'E'30+PH1'E'31
1  MATRIX  MH,42,5               MATRIX FOR PALLET COUNT
2  MATRIX  MH,5,3                MATRIX FOR INCOMING TRUCK COUNT
3  MATRIX  MH,28,2               MATRIX FOR LOCAL OUT PALLET COUNT
4  MATRIX  MH,2,10               MATRIX FOR NEXT AVAILABLE DOCK
5  MATRIX  MH,4,4                MATRIX FOR LOCAL IN PALLET COUNT
1  MATRIX  X,20,10               MATRIX FOR LOAD COMPLETE TIME
2  MATRIX  X,4,4                 MATRIX FOR LOCAL DEPART TIME
3  MATRIX  X,20,10               MATRIX FOR LOAD EMPTY TIME
4  MATRIX  X,4,4                 MATRIX FOR LOCAL RETURN TIME
5  MATRIX  X,4,4                 MATRIX FOR LOCAL TRIP TIME
LOCTM TABLE  PL1,6200,500,11     TABLE RECORDS TRIP TIME
   STORAGE S(MAINT),4
****************************************************************************
*  THIS IS THE INITIALIZATION SECTION OF THE MODEL
****************************************************************************
   RMULT 731137
   INTEGER &COLCT,&COLC2         DEFINE SOME PARAMETERS
```

```
      INTEGER  &COLMN              DEFINE SOME PARAMETERS
      INTEGER  &MEAN,&MOD          DEFINE SOME PARAMETERS
      INTEGER  &P.M.CLK,&QTCLK     DEFINE SOME PARAMETERS
      INTEGER  &SHFT1,&LNCH1,&LNCH2          DEFINE SOME PARAMETERS
      GENERATE ,,,1,,12PH,3PL      CREATE A MASTER TRANSACTION
      BLET  &P.M.CLK=16200         SET THE P.M. CLOCK
      BLET  &SHFT1=28800           SET THE P.M. CLOCK
      BLET  &QTCLK=27000           SET THE P.M. CLOCK
      BLET  &LNCH1=13500           SET THE FIRST LUNCH CLOCK
      BLET  &LNCH2=18450           SET THE FIRST LUNCH CLOCK
RED10 ASSIGN 1+,1,H               PICK-UP COLUMN COUNTER
      MSAVEVALUE 4,1,PH1,FN(INITL),H         PUT INFO IN MATRIX
      TEST E  PH1,3,RED10          GO GET THE NEXT ONE
      ASSIGN  1,1,H                RESET PARAMETER ONE
PUCE1 SAVEVALUE PH1,FN(LOAD),H              SETS INITIAL LOADING
      SPLIT  1,RED3                SEND IN THE TRUCK
      ASSIGN  1,FN(SVAL),H         RESET THE PARAMETER
      TEST E  PH1,37,PUCE1         SEND TO DO THE NEXT LOADING
RED6  TEST NE N(RED3),20,RED7     LAST RANSACTION?
      TERMINATE
RED7  SPLIT  3,RED8,2PH           SETS UP FOR THE FOUR LOCAL TRUCKS
RED8  ASSIGN  1,FN(LOTRK),H       PICKS UP A BAY NUMBER
      SEIZE  PH1                   TAKES UP A POSITION AT DOCK
      TRANSFER  ,RED9              SEND TO BLOCK FOR HOLDING
RED3  TEST LE PH1,10,RED4         SEPARATE OUT INCOMING
      SEIZE  PH1                   TAKE POSITION AT THE DOCK
      TRANSFER  ,RED5              SEND TO PROPER LINK BLOCK
RED4  TEST LE PH1,24,RED6         SEPARATE OUT OUTGOING
      SEIZE  PH1                   TAKE POSITION AT THE DOCK
RED9  LINK   LOAD,FIFO            HOLD TRAILERS BEING LOADED
*****************************************************************************
*   CREATE THE INCOMING TRAILER PORTION OF THE MODEL
*****************************************************************************
      GENERATE ,,,1                SEND IN A MASTER TRANSACTION
RED1  BLET  &MEAN=2700            SET MEAN
      BLET  &MOD=900              SET MOD
      SAVEVALUE 43+,1,H           SET UP A ROW COUNTER
      SAVEVALUE 44,1,H            SET UP A COLUMN COUNTER
      ADVANCE 28800              LET FIRST SHIFT PASS
```

```
    BLET   &MEAN=5400            SET MEAN
    BLET   &MOD=1800             SET MOD
    SAVEVALUE 44+,1,H            SET UP A COLUMN COUNTER
    ADVANCE 28800               LET SECOND SHIFT PASS
    BLET   &MEAN=7200            SET MEAN
    BLET   &MOD=2640             SET MOD
    SAVEVALUE 44+,1,H            SET UP A COLUMN COUNTER
    ADVANCE 28800               LET THIRD SHIFT PASS
    TEST E  XH43,1,RED1          HAVE FIVE DAYS PASSED
    TERMINATE 1
   GENERATE  &MEAN,&MOD,,,,9PH,3PL        CREATES A MASTER
                                          TRANSACTION
    MSAVEVALUE 2+,XH43,XH44,1,H  COUNTS TRUCKS BY TIME PERIOD
RED12 SELECT E  1PH,1,10,0,XH,RED2        IS THERE A DOCK OPEN?
    TEST E  PH7,0,RED13          IS THIS A WAITING TRAILER?
    SEIZE  34                    TAKE POSITION TO MOVE IN
    ADVANCE 300,120             TIME TO MOVE INTO THE DOCK
    RELEASE 34                  POSITIONING COMPLETE
RED13 SAVEVALUE PH1,28,H         PUTS TOTAL IN THE SAVEVALUE
    SEIZE  PH1                   TAKE POSITION AT THE DOCK
RED11 ASSIGN  2+,1,H             SET UP A COUNTER
    TEST E  MH4(1,PH2),0,RED11   IS THE COUNTER BLANK?
    MSAVEVALUE 4,1,PH2,PH1,H     PUT THE NUMBER IN A MATRIX
    ASSIGN  2,0,H                ZERO OUT THE COUNTER
RED5 PRIORITY 5                  GIVE TRANSACTION HIGHER PRIORITY
    LINK   DOCKS,1PH             HOLDS ALL OVERLAND TRAILERS AT DOCK
RED2 LINK   WAIT,FIFO            HOLDS ALL TRUCKS NEEDING A DOCK
*****************************************************************************
*   THE FORKLIFT TRUCK PORTION OF THE MODEL
*****************************************************************************
    GENERATE ,,,1               CREATE MASTER TRANSACTION
    SAVEVALUE 46,1,H            SETS UP A COUNTER
    SAVEVALUE 48,1,H            SETS UP A COUNTER
    SAVEVALUE 49,1,H            SETS UP A COUNTER
    BLET   &COLMN=1             SET INITIAL COLUMN NUMBER
    SPLIT  3,BLU5,3             SET UP FOR FOUR FORKLIFT TRUCKS
BLU5 ASSIGN  1,FN(WHFAC),H       ASSIGN A FACILITY
    SEIZE  PH1                   PUT THE FORKLIFT INTO ACTION
    ASSIGN  4,0,H                PICK UP BASE LOCATION
```

```
       ASSIGN  2,FN(WHBAY),H          PICK UP WORK BAY LOCATION
BLU4 ADVANCE V(ITRVL)                 TIME TO MOVE ON THE INCOMING SIDE
       ASSIGN  3,XH(PH2),H            PICK UP PALLET COUNT
       ASSIGN  5,FN(TIER),H           HOW FAR BACK IS NEXT PALLET?
       ADVANCE (PH5*8)                TIME TO MOVE INTO THE TRUCK
       ADVANCE 40,10                  TIME TO PICK-UP THE PALLET
       SAVEVALUE PH2-,1,H             REDUCE THE COUNT ON TRAILER
       MSAVEVALUE 1+,PH2,&COLMN,1,H          COUNT THE PALLETS REMOVED
       ADVANCE (PH5*8)                TIME TO MOVE OUT OF THE TRUCK
       TEST NE XH(PH2),0,BLU1         IS THE TRUCK EMPTY?
       ASSIGN  6,FN(TLOAD),H          PICK UP DESTINATION CODE
       ADVANCE 40                     CROSS BAY TRAVEL TIME
       ADVANCE V(OTRVL)               TIME TO MOVE ON OUTGOING SIDE
BLU8 TEST E  F(PH6),1,BLU2            IS THERE A TRUCK AT THIS LOCATION?
       QUEUE  PH6                     IS THE FACILITY FREE?
       SEIZE  FN(SPACE)               TAKE POSITION AT BACK OF TRUCK
       DEPART  PH6                    GET OUT OF THE WAITING LINE
       ASSIGN  3,XH(PH6),H            PICK UP PALLET COUNT AT OUT BAY LOC
       TEST LE PH6,24,BLU9            IS THIS FOR A LOCAL TRUCK?
       ASSIGN  5,FN(TIER),H           DETERMINE THE SET DOWN LOC
BLU10 ADVANCE (PH5*8)                 TIME TO MOVE INTO TRAILER
       ADVANCE 40,10                  TIME TO PUT PALLET IN TRUCK
       SAVEVALUE PH6+,1,H             ADD TO THE COUNT IN THE TRUCK
       MSAVEVALUE 1+,PH6,&COLMN,1,H          COUNT THE PALLETS ENTERED
                                              ON TRUCK
       ADVANCE (PH5*8)                TIME TO MOVE OUT OF TRAILER
       RELEASE FN(SPACE)              FREE UP THE POSITION BEHIND
       THE TRUCK
       TEST NE XH(PH6),28,BLU3        IS THE TRUCK FULLY LOADED?
       TEST NE PH3,0,BLU14            IS THIS THE FIRST ONE ON THE TRUCK?
BLU6 TRANSFER ,BLU26                  GO CHECK FOR LUNCH
BLU27 TEST LE C1,&QTCLK,BLU25 IS IT TIME TO QUIT?
       TEST GE C1,&P.M.CLK,BLU23      IS IT AFTER ONE P.M.?
       BLET   &P.M.CLK=&P.M.CLK+28800        UPDATE SIGNAL CLOCK
       TEST E  BV5,1,BLU23            ARE THERE PALLETS NOT ON TRUCK?
       ASSIGN  8,PH6,H                SAVE THE PRESENT LOCATION
       SELECT MAX 7,39,42,,XH         WHICH TRUCK NEEDS TO BE
                                      LOADED?
       ASSIGN  6,FN(OPPOS),H          PICK UP THE PROPER
```

```
        ADVANCE  V(XTRVL)            TIME TO MOVE IN THE AISLE
        TRANSFER ,BLU15             SEND TO DO THE LOADING JOB
BLU23 ADVANCE  V(OTRVL)            TIME TO MOVE ON OUTGOING
SIDE
        ADVANCE  40                CROSS BAY TRAVEL
        TEST NE BV1,1,GRN1         HAS A LOCAL TRUCK RETURNED?
        TRANSFER ,BLU4             SEND BACK FOR ANOTHER ROUTINE
BLU1  UNLINK E DOCKS,BLU7,1,1PH,PH2       PICK TRUCK TO REMOVE FROM
                                          DOCK
        ADVANCE  40                TRAVEL CROSS BAY
        ASSIGN  6,FN(TLOAD),H      PICK UP DESTINATION CODE
        ADVANCE  V(OTRVL)          TIME TO MOVE ON OUTGOING SIDE
        ASSIGN  2,MH4(1,1),H       PICKS UP THE NEXT BAY TO UNLOAD
RESET MSAVEVALUE 4,1,XH49,MH4(1,(XH49+1)),H  MOVE UP THE VALUE
        SAVEVALUE 49+,1,H          BUMP THE COUNTER
        TEST E  MH4(1,XH49),0,RESET  AS THE RESET PROCESS COMPLETE
        SAVEVALUE 49,1,H           RESET THE COUNTER
        TRANSFER ,BLU8             SEND TO FORKLIFT FLOW ROUTINE
BLU2  ASSIGN  8,FN(FLRCT),H       DETERMINE THE FLOOR LOCATION
        SAVEVALUE PH8+,1,H         ADD TO THE COUNT ON THE FLOOR
        MSAVEVALUE 1+,PH8,&COLMN,1,H       COUNT THE PALLETS SET ON
                                           TO THE FLOOR
        ADVANCE  30,7.5            TIME TO PUT THE PALLET ON THE FLOOR
        TRANSFER ,BLU6             SEND TO FINISH OUTGOING SIDE ROUTINE
BLU3  UNLINK E LOAD,BLU13,1,1PH,PH6       PICK TRUCK TO LEAVE DOCK
        TRANSFER ,BLU6             SEND FORKLIFT ON ITS WAY
BLU13 SAVEVALUE PH1,0,H           RESET THE PALLET COUNTER
        RELEASE PH1                FREE UP THE LOADING BAY
        ADVANCE  180,60            TIME TO CLOSE UP THE BACK
        TEST LE C1,&SHFT1,BLU24    IS IT STILL THE FIRST SHIFT?
        LOGIC R RMOVE              SIGNAL FOR THE YARD TRACTOR
BLU24 MSAVEVALUE 1,XH48,1,C1,MX            PUT A TIME IN THE MATRIX
        MSAVEVALUE 1,XH48,2,PH1,MX  PUT THE DOCK IN A MATRIX
        SAVEVALUE 48+,1,H          ADD TO THE ROW COUNTER
        TERMINATE                  REMOVE TRANSACTION FROM THE MODEL
BLU9  ASSIGN  5,FN(LTIER),H       DETERMINE THE SET DOWN LOC
        TRANSFER ,BLU10           SEND BACK TO DROP OFF THE PALLET
BLU25 ASSIGN  2,0,H               SET PARAMETER TO LEAVE DEPOT
        ADVANCE  V(OTRVL)          TIME TO MOVE TO BATTERY AREA
```

```
 RELEASE PH1                          FREE UP THE FORKLIFT
 FUNAVAIL PH1                         MAKE THE FACILITY UNAVAILABLE
 TERMINATE                            REMOVE THE TRANSACTION
BLU26 TEST E  BV9,1,BLU29             IS THIS AN EARLY LUNCH PERSON?
 TEST GE  C1,&LNCH1,BLU27             IS IT LUNCH TIME YET?
 TEST E  N(BLU28),1,BLU28             IS THIS SECOND EARLY LUNCH PERSON?
 BLET   &LNCH1=&LNCH1+28880           UP DATE FOR TOMORROW
BLU28 RELEASE PH1                     TAKE A LUNCH BREAK
 FUNAVAIL PH1                         TAKE FORKLIFT OUT OF SERVICE
 ADVANCE 2700                         TIME FOR LUNCH
 FAVAIL PH1                           PUT FORKLIFT BACK IN SERVICE
 SEIZE PH1                            GO BACK TO WORK
 TRANSFER ,BLU27                      GO BACK TO REGULAR ROUTINE
BLU29 TEST GE C1,&LNCH2,BLU27         IS IT LUNCH TIME YET?
 TEST E  N(BLU30),1,BLU30             IS THIS SECOND EARLY LUNCH PERSON?
 BLET   &LNCH2=&LNCH2+28880           UP DATE FOR TOMORROW
BLU30 RELEASE PH1                     TAKE A LUNCH BREAK
 FUNAVAIL PH1                         TAKE FORKLIFT OUT OF SERVICE
 ADVANCE 2700                         TIME FOR LUNCH
 FAVAIL PH1                           PUT FORKLIFT BACK IN SERVICE
 SEIZE PH1                            GO BACK TO WORK
 TRANSFER ,BLU27                      GO BACK TO REGULAR ROUTINE
********************************************************************************
* LOADING FLOOR PALLETS PORTION OF THE MODEL
********************************************************************************
BLU14 TEST LE PH6,24,BLU15           IS THIS A LOCAL TRUCK?
 ASSIGN  8,FN(FLRCT),H               FIND THE FLOOR LOCATION
 TEST GE  XH(PH8),1,BLU6             ARE THERE PALLETS TO PICK UP?
BLU16 ADVANCE 30,7.5                 PICK PALLET OFF THE FLOOR
 SAVEVALUE PH8-,1,H                  REDUCE THE COUNT ON THE FLOOR
 ADVANCE 35,5                        TIME TO TURN AROUND
 ASSIGN  3,XH(PH6),H                 PICK UP COUNT ON TRUCK
 ASSIGN  5,FN(TIER),H                DETERMINE THE SET DOWN LOCATION
 QUEUE PH6                           GET IN LINE FOR THE TRUCK
 SEIZE FN(SPACE)                     TAKE POSITION AT BACK OF THE TRUCK
 DEPART PH6                          GET OUT OF THE WAITING LINE
 ADVANCE (PH5*8)                     TIME TO MOVE INTO THE TRAILER
 ADVANCE 40,10                       TIME TO PUT PALLET IN THE TRUCK
 SAVEVALUE PH6+,1,H                  ADD TO THE COUNT IN THE TRUCK
```

ADVANCE (PH5*8)	TIME TO MOVE OUT OF THE TRAILER
ADVANCE 35,5	TIME TO TURN AROUND
RELEASE FN(SPACE)	FREE UP THE POSITION AT BACK OF TRUCK
MSAVEVALUE 1+,PH6,&COLMN,1,H	COUNT THE PALLETS ENTERED ON TRUCK
TEST NE XH(PH6),28,BLU3	IS THE TRUCK FULLY LOADED?
TEST E XH(PH8),0,BLU16	ALL PALLETS REMOVED FROM THE FLOOR?
TRANSFER ,BLU6	GO BACK AND FINISH UNLOADING
BLU15 ASSIGN 8,FN(FLRCT),H	FIND THE FLOOR LOCATION
BLU22 ADVANCE 30,7.5	PICK PALLET OFF THE FLOOR
SAVEVALUE PH8-,1,H	REDUCE THE COUNT ON THE FLOOR
ASSIGN 3,XH(PH6),H	PICK UP COUNT ON TRUCK
ADVANCE 35,5	TIME TO TURN AROUND
ASSIGN 5,FN(LTIER),H	DETERMINE THE SET DOWN LOCATION
QUEUE PH6	GET IN LINE FOR THE TRUCK
SEIZE FN(SPACE)	TAKE POSITION AT BACK OF THE TRUCK
DEPART PH6	GET OUT OF THE WAITING LINE
ADVANCE (PH5*8)	TIME TO MOVE INTO THE TRAILER
ADVANCE 40,10	TIME TO PUT PALLET IN THE TRUCK
SAVEVALUE PH6+,1,H	ADD TO THE COUNT IN THE TRUCK
ADVANCE (PH5*8)	TIME TO MOVE OUT OF THE TRAILER
ADVANCE 35,5	TIME TO TURN AROUND
RELEASE FN(SPACE)	FREE SPACE AT BACK OF TRUCK
MSAVEVALUE 1+,PH6,&COLMN,1,H	COUNT THE PALLETS ENTERED ON TRUCK
TEST NE XH(PH6),12,BLU3	IS THE TRUCK FULLY LOADED?
TEST E XH(PH8),0,BLU22	ALL PALLETS REMOVED FROM THE FLOOR?
TRANSFER ,BLU6	GO BACK AND FINISH UNLOADING

```
******************************************************************************
*  TRANSFER INCOMING EMPTY TO OUTGOING SIDE PORTION OF THE MODEL
******************************************************************************
```

BLU7 RELEASE PH1	FREE UP THE DOCK SPACE
ADVANCE 180,30	PREPARE TRAILER FOR MOVING OUT
TEST NE BV4,1,BLU20	IS THIS A LOCAL TRUCK?
MSAVEVALUE 3,XH46,1,C1,MX	PUT A TIME IN THE MATRIX
MSAVEVALUE 3,XH46,2,PH1,MX	PUT THE DOCK IN A MATRIX
SAVEVALUE 46+,1,H	ADD TO THE ROW COUNTER
SEIZE 34	TAKE POSSESSION OF YARD TRACTOR
ADVANCE 180,30	MOVE THE TRUCK OUT OF THE BAY

```
        ADVANCE  300,120           MOVE TRAILER TO POOL AREA
        RELEASE  34               FREE UP THE YARD TRACTOR
        TEST GE  CH(WAIT),1,BLU11  ARE TRUCKS WAITING FOR DOCK SPACE?
        UNLINK   WAIT,BLU12,1       GET TRUCK FOR POSITIONING AT DOCK
BLU11 LINK   POOL,FIFO            PUT TRAILER INTO YARD POOL
BLU20 TEST E  PH12,1,BLU21         IS THIS THE FIRST TIME THROUGH?
        ASSIGN  2,PH1,H            REASSIGN THE 1ST PARAMETER
        ASSIGN  1,FN(BAYOT),H      WHICH BAY IS THE OUT BAY?
        SEIZE  34                 TAKE POSSESSION OF YARD TRACTOR
        ADVANCE  180,30            MOVE THE TRUCK OUT OF THE BAY
        ADVANCE  300,120           TIME TO POSITION TRAILER
        RELEASE  34               FREE UP THE YARD TRACTOR
        SEIZE  PH1                TAKE UP POSITION IN THE BAY
        LINK   LOAD,1PH           KEEP TRACK OF TRUCKS AT THE  DOCK
BLU21 ENTER  MAINT               HAVE THE MAINTENANCE DONE  ON TRUCK
        ADVANCE  1800,600          TIME TO DO THE MAINTENANCE
        LEAVE  MAINT              GET OUT OF THE MAINTENANCE  SHED
        QUEUE  GASUP              GET IN LINE TO GET GAS
        SEIZE  35                 PULL UP TO THE GAS PUMP
        DEPART  GASUP             GET OUT OF THE LINE TO GAS UP
        ADVANCE  300,120           TIME TO GAS UP THE VEHICLE
        RELEASE  35               FREE UP THE GAS PUMP
        ASSIGN  2,PH1,H            REASSIGN THE FIRST PARAMETER
        ASSIGN  1,FN(BAYOT),H      WHICH BAY IS THE OUT BAY?
        SEIZE  34                 TAKE UP POSITION TO MOVE IN
        ADVANCE  300,120           TIME TO POSITION TRAILER
        RELEASE  34               POSITIONING COMPLETE
        SEIZE  PH1                TAKE UP POSITION IN THE BAY
        LINK   LOAD,1PH           KEEP TRACK OF TRUCKS AT THE DOCK
BLU12 SEIZE  34                  ENGAGE THE YARD TRACTOR
        ADVANCE  600,240           TIME TO HITCH UP AND PUT IN POSITION
        RELEASE  34               FREE UP THE YARD TRACTOR
        ASSIGN  7,1,H             SET UP A MARKER
        TRANSFER  ,RED12          SEND TO THE DOCKING ROUTINE
********************************************************************************
*   UNLOADING FOR LOCAL TRUCKS PORTION OF THE MODEL
********************************************************************************
GRN1 ASSIGN  10,PH2,H            SAVE PRESENT DOCK LOCATION
        ASSIGN  4,PH2,H            SETS UP FOR IN SIDE TRAVEL
```

```
        ASSIGN  9,1,H                          SETS UP A FLAG
        ASSIGN  2,FN(LOCIN),H                  PICK UP THE LOCAL BAY LOCATION
GRN12 ADVANCE V(ITRVL)                         TIME TO MOVE ON THE INCOMING SIDE
        ASSIGN  3,XH(PH2),H                    PICK UP PALLET COUNT AT IN BAY LOC
        ASSIGN  5,FN(LTIER),H                  HOW FAR BACK IS THE NEXT PALLET
        ADVANCE (PH5*8)                        TIME TO MOVE INTO THE TRUCK
        ADVANCE 40,10                          TIME TO PICK UP THE PALLET
        SAVEVALUE PH2-,1,H                      REDUCE THE COUNT ON THE TRAILER
        MSAVEVALUE 1+,PH2,&COLMN,1,H                  COUNT THE PALLETS REMOVED
        ADVANCE (PH5*8)                        TIME TO MOVE OUT OF THE TRUCK
        TEST NE  XH(PH2),0,GRN2                IS THE TRUCK EMPTY?
        ASSIGN  6,FN(LLOAD),H                  PICK UP DESTINATION CODE
        ADVANCE 40                             CROSS BAY TRAVEL TIME
        ADVANCE V(OTRVL)                       TIME TO MOVE ON OUTGOING SIDE
GRN3  TEST E  F(PH6),1,GRN4                    IS THERE A TRUCK AT THIS LOCATION?
        ASSIGN  3,XH(PH6),H                    PICK UP PALLET COUNT AT OUT BAY LOC
        TEST LE  PH6,24,GRN6                   IS THIS FOR A LOCAL TRUCK?
        ASSIGN  5,FN(TIER),H                   DETERMINE THE SET DOWN LOCATION
GRN7  ADVANCE (PH5*8)                          TIME TO MOVE INTO THE TRAILER
        ADVANCE 40,10                          TIME TO PUT PALLET IN THE TRUCK
        SAVEVALUE PH6+,1,H                      ADD TO THE COUNT IN THE TRUCK
        MSAVEVALUE 1+,PH6,&COLMN,1,H                  COUNT THE PALLETS ENTERED
                                                      ON TRUCK
        ADVANCE (PH5*8)                        TIME TO MOVE OUT OF THE TRAILER
        TEST NE  XH(PH6),28,GRN8               IS THE TRUCK FULLY LOADED?
        TEST NE  PH3,0,GRN9                    IS THIS THE FIRST ONE ON THE TRUCK?
GRN5  TEST LE  C1,&QTCLK,BLU25  IS IT TIME TO QUIT?
        ADVANCE V(OTRVL)                       TIME TO MOVE ON OUTGOING SIDE
        ADVANCE 40                             CROSS BAY TRAVEL
        TEST E  PH9,0,GRN12                    IS WORK DONE HERE?
        TRANSFER ,BLU4                         SEND BACK FOR ANOTHER ROUTINE
GRN2  UNLINK E  DOCKS,BLU7,1,1PH,PH2                  PICK TRUCK TO  REMOVE FROM
                                                      DOCK
        SAVEVALUE FN(LOCCK),0,H                ZERO OUT THE CHECK DIGIT
        ADVANCE 40                             TRAVEL CROSS BAY
        ASSIGN  6,FN(TLOAD),H                  PICK UP DESTINATION CODE
        ADVANCE V(OTRVL)                       TIME TO MOVE ON OUTGOING SIDE
        ASSIGN  4,PH2,H                        REASSIGN THE OLD BAY
        ASSIGN  9,0,H                          ZERO OUT THE FLAG
```

```
      ASSIGN  2,PH10,H              REASSIGN THE OLD BAY LOCATION
      TRANSFER ,GRN3                SEND TO FORKLIFT FLOW ROUTINE
GRN4  ASSIGN  8,FN(FLRCT),H         DETERMINE THE FLOOR LOCATION
      SAVEVALUE PH8+,1,H            ADD TO THE COUNT ON THE FLOOR
      MSAVEVALUE 1+,PH8,&COLMN,1,H           COUNT THE PALLETS SET ONTO
                                             THE FLOOR
      ADVANCE 30,7.5                TIME TO PUT THE PALLET ON THE FLOOR
      TRANSFER ,GRN5                SEND TO FINISH OUTGOING SIDE ROUTINE
GRN6  ASSIGN  5,FN(LTIER),H         DETERMINE THE SET DOWN LOCATION
      TRANSFER ,GRN7                SEND BACK TO DROP OFF THE PALLET
GRN8  UNLINK E LOAD,BLU13,1,1PH,PH6    PICK TRUCK TO LEAVE DOCK
      TRANSFER ,GRN5                SEND FORKLIFT ON ITS WAY
GRN9  TEST LE PH6,24,GRN10          IS THIS A LOCAL TRUCK?
      ASSIGN  8,FN(FLRCT),H         FIND THE FLOOR LOCATION
      TEST GE  XH(PH8),1,GRN5       ARE THERE PALLETS TO PICK UP?
GRN11 ADVANCE 30,7.5                PICK PALLET OFF THE FLOOR
      SAVEVALUE PH8-,1,H            REDUCE THE COUNT ON THE FLOOR
      ASSIGN  3,XH(PH6),H           PICK UP COUNT ON TRUCK
      ADVANCE 35,5                  TIME TO TURN AROUND
      ASSIGN  5,FN(TIER),H          DETERMINE THE SET DOWN LOC
      QUEUE  PH6                    GET IN LINE FOR THE TRUCK
      SEIZE  FN(SPACE)              TAKE POSITION AT BACK OF THE TRUCK
      DEPART  PH6                   GET OUT OF THE WAITING LINE
      ADVANCE (PH5*8)               TIME TO MOVE OUT OF THE TRAILER
      ADVANCE 40,10                 TIME TO PUT PALLET IN THE TRUCK
      SAVEVALUE PH6+,1,H            ADD TO THE COUNT IN THE TRUCK
      ADVANCE (PH5*8)               TIME TO MOVE OUT OF THE RAILER
      ADVANCE 35,5                  TIME TO TURN AROUND
      RELEASE FN(SPACE)             LEAVE POSITION AT BACK OF THE TRUCK
      MSAVEVALUE 1+,PH6,&COLMN,1,H           COUNT THE PALLETS
                                             ENTERED ON TRUCK

      TEST NE  XH(PH6),28,GRN8      IS THE TRUCK FULLY LOADED?
      TEST E  XH(PH8),0,GRN11       ALL PALLETS REMOVED FROM THE FLOOR?
      TRANSFER ,GRN5                GO BACK AND FINISH UNLOADING
GRN10 ASSIGN  8,FN(FLRCT),H         FIND THE FLOOR LOCATION
      TEST NE  XH(PH6),0,GRN5       ARE THERE PALLETS TO PICK UP?
GRN13 ADVANCE 30,7.5                PICK PALLET OFF THE FLOOR
      SAVEVALUE PH8-,1,H            REDUCE THE COUNT ON THE FLOOR
      ASSIGN  3,XH(PH6),H           PICK UP COUNT ON TRUCK
```

```
      ADVANCE 35,5                    TIME TO TURN AROUND
      ASSIGN  5,FN(LTIER),H           DETERMINE THE SET DOWN LOCATION
      QUEUE  PH6                      GET IN LINE FOR THE TRUCK
      SEIZE  FN(SPACE)                TAKE POSITION AT BACK OF THE TRUCK
      DEPART  PH6                     GET OUT OF THE WAITING LINE
      ADVANCE (PH5*8)                 TIME TO MOVE INTO THE TRAILER
      ADVANCE 40,10                   TIME TO PUT PALLET IN THE TRUCK
      SAVEVALUE PH6+,1,H              ADD TO THE COUNT IN THE TRUCK
      ADVANCE (PH5*8)                 TIME TO MOVE OUT OF THE TRAILER
      ADVANCE 35,5                    TIME TO TURN AROUND
      RELEASE FN(SPACE)               LEAVE POSITION AT BACK OF THE TRUCK
      MSAVEVALUE 1+,PH6,&COLMN,1,H        COUNT THE PALLETS ENTERED
                                          ON TRUCK
      TEST NE  XH(PH6),12,GRN8        IS THE TRUCK FULLY LOADED?
      TEST E   XH(PH8),0,GRN13        ALL PALLETS REMOVED FROM THE FLOOR?
      TRANSFER ,GRN5                  GO BACK AND FINISH UNLOADING
**************************************************************************
*   CREATES THE LOCAL TRUCKS PORTION OF THE MODEL
**************************************************************************
      GENERATE ,,1,1,,12PH,3PL        CREATE A MASTER TRANSACTION
      BLET  &COLCT=1                  SET UP A COLUMN COUNTER
      BLET  &COLC2=1                  SET UP A COLUMN COUNTER
BLK2  ASSIGN  1+,1,H                  UPDATE A PARAMETER
      ASSIGN  2,FN(TRKLO),H           PICK PROPER BAY NUMBER
      UNLINK E LOAD,BLK1,1,1PH,PH2 PICK TRUCK TO LEAVE DOCK
      TEST E  PH1,4,BLK2              HAVE ALL FOUR BEEN RELEASED?
      TEST E  N(BLK2),4,BLK4          BYPASS THE SECOND TIME AROUND
      ASSIGN  1,0,H                   RESET PARAMETER
      ADVANCE 17999                   WAIT FOR TIME TO PASS
      BLET  &COLCT=&COLCT+1           UPDATE COLUMN COUNTER
      BLET  &COLC2=&COLC2+1           UPDATE COLUMN COUNTER
      TRANSFER ,BLK2                  SEND BACK TO RELEASE SECOND TRIP
BLK4  ADVANCE 10800                   LET TIME GO BY
      TERMINATE 1                     SHUT OFF THE SIMULATION
BLK1  RELEASE PH1                     FREE UP THE BAY SPACE
      MSAVEVALUE 3+,PH1,&COLCT,XH(PH1),H     RECORD OUTGOING LOAD
      SAVEVALUE PH1,0,H               RESET THE SAVEVALUE
      ADVANCE 180,60                  TIME NEEDED TO CLEAR THE DOCK
      ASSIGN  1,FN(GONE),PL           HOW LONG IS THE TRIP?
```

```
       TEST E  PH12,1,BLK7          IS THIS SECOND TIME THROUGH?
       ASSIGN  1,(PL1*.7),PL        REDUCE THE TIME
BLK7   TABULATE LOCTM               PUT THE TIME IN A TABLE
       SAVEVALUE 47+,1,H            SET UP A COUNTER
       MSAVEVALUE 2,XH47,&COLCT,C1,MX     RECORD THE START TIME
       MSAVEVALUE 5,XH47,&COLCT,PL1,MX    RECORD THE TRIP TIME
       ADVANCE PL1                  TIME THE TRUCK IS GONE
       SAVEVALUE 54+,1,H            SET UP A COUNTER
       MSAVEVALUE 4,XH54,&COLC2,C1,MX     RECORD THE RETURN TIME
       ASSIGN  3,PH1,H              REASSIGN THE OUTGOING BAY
       ASSIGN  1,FN(IBLOC),H        ASSIGN THE INCOMING BAY
       SEIZE  PH1                   TAKE UP THE DOCK SPACE
       SAVEVALUE FN(SIGNL),1,H      SET UP A SIGNAL FLAG
       SAVEVALUE PH1,FN(LOCCT),H    PICK UP LOAD COUNT
       SAVEVALUE 55+,1,H            SET UP A COUNTER
       MSAVEVALUE 5,XH55,&COLCT,XH(PH1),H  RECORD OUTGOING LOAD
       ADVANCE 300,120              TIME TO POSITION VEHICLE
       TEST E  XH47,4,BLK6          IS THIS THE LAST ONE?
       SAVEVALUE 47,0,H             RESET THE COUNTER
BLK6   TEST E  XH54,4,BLK5          IS THIS THE LAST ONE IN?
       SAVEVALUE 54,0,H             RESET THE COUNTER
       SAVEVALUE 55,0,H             RESET THE COUNTER
BLK5   TEST E  PH12,0,BLK3          IS THERE A CHECK DIGIT?
       ASSIGN  12,1,H               SET UP AN IDENTIFIER
       TRANSFER ,RED5               SEND TO HOLD UNTIL EMPTY
BLK3   ASSIGN  12,0,H               ZERO OUT THE FLAG
       TRANSFER ,RED5               SEND TO HOLD UNTIL EMPTY
*****************************************************************************
*   YARD TRACTOR OPERATION FOR THE MODEL
*****************************************************************************
       GENERATE ,,,1,,6PH           SET UP A MASTER TRANSACTION
       SPLIT  12,BLU11              SET UP FOR 12 TRAILERS IN THE POOL
YEL5   TEST E  BV6,1,YEL2           ARE THERE SLOTS OPEN FOR TRAILERS?
       SELECT NU 1,15,24,,,YEL2     PICK THE SLOT TO BE FILLED
       UNLINK  POOL,YEL3,1          TAKE A TRAILER FROM THE POOL
       SEIZE  34                    TAKE POSSESSION OF YARD TRACTOR
       ADVANCE 600,240              TIME TO HITCH UP AND MOVE
       ADVANCE 300,120              TIME TO POSITION TRAILER
       RELEASE 34                   FREE UP THE YARD TRACTOR
```

```
      ADVANCE 180,30            TIME TO OPEN UP THE TRAILER
      SPLIT 1,YEL4              SEND IN A CLONE
      ADVANCE 1                 HOLD FOR ONE SECOND
      TRANSFER ,YEL5            GO CHECK FOR MORE OPEN BAYS
YEL4 SEIZE  PH1                 TAKE UP POSITION IN BAY
      LINK   LOAD,1PH           KEEP TRACK OF TRUCKS AT DOCK
YEL2 LOGIC S RMOVE             CLOSE THE GATE FOR THE YARD TRACTOR
      GATE LR RMOVE             WAIT FOR THE GATE TO OPEN
      TRANSFER ,YEL5            GO BACK TO REMOVE THE NEXT TRAILER
YEL3 TERMINATE                 DUMP THE TRANSACTION
******************************************************************************
*  CONTROL STATEMENTS FOR THE MODEL
******************************************************************************
      START  1
      CLEAR
      START  1
      CLEAR
      START  1
      CLEAR
      START  1
      CLEAR
      START  1
      CLEAR
      START  1
      END
```

4

Modeling
Inventory Control

The study of inventory management, while not prevalent through the 1970s and part of the 1980s, has increased over the past decade. The study and virtual acceptance of just-in-time (JIT) policies, rather than just-in-case, has increased both the awareness and emphasis on maintenance and procurement procedures in the mainstream of many operations. However, despite this increased awareness, a large number of industries have not adopted the philosophy of just-in-time and still rely on standard lot-sizing inventory procedures. Many of these decisions are made on the basis of logistical constraints, which limit the practicality of just-in-time. For these industries the reliance on well-grounded mathematical models has provided necessary insight into the determination of optimal procurement strategies. Unfortunately, many of the assumptions underlying these mathematical models have been, or have become, unrealistic. In attempting to increase realism, models have been developed which are intractable mathematically. In these cases heuristic, or approximate, solutions are usually obtained. In either case, whether it be solving a nonrepresentative model or using heuristic solutions to a more representative one, the solutions provided do not necessarily prescribe an optimal solution with extremely high precision.

Costs related to the management of inventory can often represent the difference between financial success and failure for many operations.

Consider, for example, an organization that markets a product using a high volume, low markup tactic. Assume that the gross profit on sales is $2 per unit and that approximately sixteen thousand units are sold over the duration of one month. This leads to a monthly gross profit of $32,000. Now consider that related costs for retailing this product account for 80 percent of the gross profit on sales, not including the wholesale cost. This would leave approximately $6,400, before taxes, to show for the effort expended in acquiring and selling this product. Assume that inventory costs vary anywhere between $2,000 and $12,000 monthly, depending on whether inventory is effectively managed or not. If inventory is effectively managed, these costs can lead to a reasonable return, if not, they may lead to potentially disastrous financial consequences.

While the hypothetical example just discussed is drawn from the area of retail merchandising, it also applies to the domain of operations management. This understanding is critical, for it is often the case that both in the classroom and on the job it is forgotten that operations management has an impact on many of an organization's functions, such as sales and marketing, while not being limited to the more traditional studies of production and scheduling.

The example also illustrates a situation in which simulation can be effectively employed as a decision support tool. The use of simulation in cases such as these illustrates not only how likely it is that an organization will show gains or losses, but also helps evaluate various strategies regarding the procurement of product, and determine, for all intents and purposes, which strategy has the highest likelihood of yielding maximum gains.

To begin, consider those elements that constitute an inventory management problem. Organizations survive through the effective distribution of products (service industries have analogous components). The distribution of products involves the procurement and storage of products waiting to be sold. The determination of an effective procurement and storage strategy is the ultimate goal of an inventory management problem. Sufficient inventory must be maintained in order to meet demand with reasonable certainty, otherwise frequent stockouts may occur. These, in turn, may lead to customer dissatisfaction, and perhaps a lost sale. On the other hand, acquiring too much product may lead to other undesirable costs, such as obsolescence and deterioration, not to mention capital costs associated with the physical inventory itself. In effect, management must determine a strategy whereby adequate levels of stock are maintained, without being excessive.

While inventory problems have been studied extensively through the use of mathematical models, many of the underlying assumptions are limiting insofar as the model is basically not applicable. For example, consider the demand for product. After reasonable efforts are made to obtain or forecast this demand over a specified planning horizon, say monthly, an ordinary assumption is that demand is distributed uniformly over the month. Furthermore, it is assumed that demand does not fluctuate day to day, but remains static over the month. Both of these assumptions are highly unreasonable in most markets, because (1) demand ordinarily fluctuates daily (with the exception of prescheduled orders), and (2) demand is not necessarily distributed uniformly over the planning horizon. While uniform demand may be reasonable in some circumstances involving staple goods, most products demonstrate some type of seasonality in their demand patterns. Consequently, while the assumptions employed regarding demand in a standard inventory model increase the likelihood of being able to derive the optimal solution, the unrealistic nature of the assumptions underlying the model limits its applicability.

This chapter shows how the reality of changes in consumer demand from day to day has a tremendous impact on inventory costs, rendering the results of a standard theoretical model virtually useless. The material also shows how simulation, can be used effectively to locate the optimal solution for instances that otherwise require extensive mathematics to solve, if at all solvable.

INVENTORY MANAGEMENT STRATEGIES

Two prevalent types of inventory problems involve circumstances in which (1) product to be sold is obtained and resold as is or (2) raw materials are obtained, production of a product takes place, and sales then occur. The model in this chapter examines the first instance. The objective of the model is to determine an optimal strategy, that is, one that minimizes inventory-related costs. Excess inventories incur certain costs, while inadequate inventories incur other related costs.

Excess levels of inventory are undesirable for many reasons, even if obsolescence and deterioration do not apply. Costs incurred through the storage of inventory are commonly called holding costs. These costs represent whatever the business must pay for keeping more units in stock than are sold by the end of the day. One major factor in the assessment of this cost involves both the interest and opportunity cost of tying up capital in stock that is maintained, but not immediately needed, on the shelves. Other factors involve physical maintenance costs, such as, rental, utilities, insurance, and security, which may involve either personnel or a service company. Holding costs are usually expressed as a dollar amount per unit required to store one unit of product on the shelf for the duration of one year. Overall total holding costs are then found by multiplying this dollar amount by the average amount of inventory the organization maintains over the year.

An alternate strategy to holding excess inventory, involves understocking an item and accepting backorders, although some or all instances of stock-outs may also result in lost sales (although the model used here assumes that all stockouts are backordered). The costs incurred in those instances are commonly referred to as stockout costs. These costs represent whatever the business must pay because customer demand over a number of days has exceeded the inventory available to sell. They ordinarily include factors such as discounts rendered to customers to account for their inconvenience, procuring the unit from outside vendors at higher cost, or associated good-will costs. Classical mathematical inventory models sometimes do not consider stockout costs for the following reason: replenishment of inventory is timed so that its arrival occurs exactly when inventory is depleted. This is plausible under the assumption that demand is known with certainty over the planning horizon. While this represents an early view of the just-in-time philosophy, it is based on an unreasonable demand assumption. Regardless, the simulation in this chapter incorporates this cost, and appropriates a dollar value to it as follows: The average cost of being stocked out per unit multiplied by the number of units stocked out on a given day, summed across all days in the planning horizon.

A third cost pertinent to the study of inventory involves the costs incurred in placing and receiving orders. These costs—salaries for reorder clerks, shipping costs, and costs of receiving and unloading orders—are summed over the planning horizon (typically one year) and divided by the number of orders placed during the planning horizon.

In actuality, an order cost that varies may be traced to each order. This may be important in instances where a majority of the order cost is fixed, such as where the majority of the cost is associated with salaries and physical maintenance within the ordering department. In this case, placing fewer orders over the planning horizon will not decrease total order costs as much as if a majority of the ordering costs were variable. While true in reality, most standard theoretical models assume a constant average cost per order (regardless of order size) thus either neglecting the fixed portion of the ordering cost, or appropriating it on a per-order basis (neither of which is truly representative). While this may not be ideal, we will accept this notion of a constant per-order holding cost to comply with the theoretical model whose results will be compared to those generated by the simulation.

In reviewing the above costs, it becomes intuitively obvious that holding costs and stockout costs are both affected differently by the ordering strategy employed. If higher quantities are ordered over a fixed period of time, holding costs will ordinarily increase, while the probability, and hence the cost, associated with stockouts will decrease. The same relationship exists, only in reverse, if the order quantity is reduced. This effect is countered by varying the length of the period over which orders are placed. Ordering small quantities frequently can effectively diminish stockout costs ordinarily incurred when placing large orders infrequently. Hence, an optimal inventory strategy involves not only the determination of the order size, but the timing of the order as well. This leads to another pertinent relationship: As order frequency increases, annual ordering costs will increase while annual holding costs will drop. When smaller quantities are ordered more frequently, the average amount of inventory on hand decreases over the planning horizon.

In analyzing an inventory problem these tradeoffs must be studied, from which a best strategy emerges. Ordering massive quantities of inventory very infrequently will serve to minimize the number of dissatisfied customers, while creating excessive holding costs for the organization, as well as other problems, such as, obsolescence and deterioration. Similarly, these holding costs can be avoided by ordering only after customers are present, and by accepting backorders. Unfortunately, these customers most probably will not remain customers for long. Hedging your bets by placing orders every day results in increased ordering costs, not to mention confusion.

The Classical Model

Classical analysis has been brilliant as far as it goes. Under certain assumptions the ideal order quantity, appropriately named EOQ (economic order quantity), can be determined to minimize total inventory-related costs. In brief, the assumptions for the so-called standard EOQ classical model are

1. stockouts are prohibited;

2. demand is known with certainty and is constant over time;

3. the time required between placing and receiving an order, known as lead time, is known and constant;

4. the cost of the product is fixed (e.g., no quantity discounts);

5. adequate capacity and capital exist to implement the suggested strategy; and

6. the suggested strategy does not affect other products the organization handles.

In practice, it is found that these assumptions are so restrictive that the classical model is limited in its application. Hence the need for simulation is increased. While classical approaches must utilize heuristic-based methods for handling related problems in which some or all of the aforementioned assumptions are relaxed, simulation provides a viable alternative which can yield optimal solutions in the sense that a high degree of statistical confidence obtains because the suggested solution is in fact within a certain tolerance of the optimal solution.

Together with the order quantity, the trigger point for placing an order is also determined through classical analysis. This trigger point is commonly represented as an inventory level. When inventory is depleted to this level, an order for the EOQ is placed. The trigger point is commonly set at zero under conditions of no lead time. This is simply determined by noting that an order can be placed immediately upon depleting your inventory and becomes available at that time. However, when lead time exists, it becomes necessary to place an order before depleting inventory so that the order arrives at precisely when inventory is depleted.

The trigger point, called the reorder point, or ROP, is found by simply determining the amount of demand generated over the lead time, as shown in Figure 4.1.

The determination of the optimal order quantity involves the utilization of classical optimization techniques. While the mathematics is omitted for the purposes of clarity, the results are shown in Figure 4.2. Relaxation in some of the assumptions of this classical inventory model can lead to results which are disastrous if the model is applied. The impact of these relaxations can only be shown via simulation. Simulation can be utilized to generate a reasonable solution to the inventory

Figure 4.1
Classical Formula for Determining the Reorder Point

ROP	=	RL/N where
R	=	annual demand in units
L	=	lead time expressed in time unit
N	=	the number of time units in a year

management problem and to yield a far superior result, in terms of cost, than the classical model.

The Assumptions for Simulation

The simulation abides by the last three assumptions discussed earlier, but relaxes the first three, that is, it models a more realistic environment for an inventory management problem, and explores the probable financial losses that an organization will incur if it follows the advice obtained from the classical EOQ model rather than from a good simulation model. The changes implemented are moderate, as drastic changes would make the classical model obviously inappropriate. The changes are simply the following:

1. Stockouts can occur. Under situations when demand is variable, it is impossible to prohibit stockouts with one hundred percent certainty unless the order quantity over a given period exceeds the maximum demand over that period. It is doubtful that a strategy of this type is optimal, due to the tremendous holding costs that would be incurred.
2. Demand will be allowed to vary. For example, one of the two demand scenarios posed will allow demand to vary between 450 and 650 units daily, with a modal demand of 500 units.
3. Lead time will be allowed to vary. It will be assumed that lead time is either one, two, or three days. Each value is equally likely.

Regarding demand, it is assumed that demand is governed by a triangular distribution. This implies that the mean demand is simply the average of the three demand estimates provided above: the minimum, the maximum, and the most likely. For the values shown above, this yields a mean demand of 533.33 units daily. This is certainly not a tremendous amount of variability,

Figure 4.2
Classical Formula for Determining the Economic Order Quantity

---

EOQ $= \sqrt{2KD/C}$ where

  K $=$ the ordering cost, per order

  D $=$ demand over the planning horizon (equal to one year)

  C $=$ the holding cost, expressed in dollars per unit per year

---

and one would not expect that the classical model (which would use the mean demand per day with certainty) would yield solutions that are suboptimal. Contrary to common belief, the classical model can lead to disastrous results and large losses, as well as yielding a solution not near the optimal solution.

Regarding lead time, as all values are equally likely, it is simply determined that the mean lead time is two days. If the holding cost is assigned the value of $1 per unit annually, and an order cost of $1,000 applies, the following theoretical solutions obtain:

$$ROP = {}^{(533.33)(365)(2)}/_{365} = 1,066.67 \text{ units of inventory}$$

$$EOQ = \sqrt{(2)(1,000)(533.33)(365)/_1} = 1,973.5 \text{ units per order}$$

To demonstrate how the degree of variability in demand has an impact on the cost of the proposed theoretical solution given above, a second alternative will be analyzed for demand. This scenario will be titled the "high variance" scenario (the former set of values may be referred to as "low variance") and will maintain the same modal daily demand of 500 units, as well as the same mean, equal to 533.33 units daily. The difference lies in range of demand, constrained to a minimum of 100 units per day and a maximum of 1,000 units per day.

Second alternatives for other parameters will be analyzed as well. For instance, the effect of increasing and decreasing inventory-related costs will be considered. For each of these costs, two values will be considered:

Holding costs $1/unit per year and $10/unit per year
Stockout costs $.5/unit per day and $5/unit per day backordered
Ordering costs $100/order and $1,000/order

This 2x2x2x2 design (2 alternatives for each factor: demand, holding cost, stockout cost, and order cost) yields sixteen models, or scenarios, to analyze. This allows great flexibility in understanding how poorly the classical model works under varying conditions for various demand and cost estimates. Regarding lead time, each of the sixteen scenarios will follow the assumption that lead time is equally distributed and assumes a value chosen from one, two, or three days. Note that since the mean demand under both demand distributions is the same, the theoretical ROP will be equal in all scenarios, and equal to the predetermined value of 1,066.67 units.

THE SIMULATION MODEL

Consider the actual construction of the simulation model. In modeling our inventory management problem, one needs to consider (1) what the simulation model needs to do (i.e., it's purpose), and (2) how it needs to be constructed in order to be representative of the system at hand and accomplish its purpose.

Briefly, the purpose is twofold: (1) locate the best order quantity and (2) show that the classical EOQ and ROP yield greater costs then the one obtained through simulation, due to the relaxation of some of the assumptions deemed unrealistic. To accomplish this, information must be tracked by the simulation.

To begin, inventory level must be maintained. This level is represented by a value that is depleted each day by a simulated customer demand. Occasionally this value will be increased as well by the fact that an order has been placed with a vendor, the lead time has passed, and the incoming order is received. While the actual time of receipt may be considered, it is assumed that incoming orders are received at the beginning of the day, prior to any demand being generated for that day. This assumption eliminates customers arriving and finding no inventory on hand and having their request backordered (as well as leaving dissatisfied). For each set of parameters analyzed (i.e., one choice for each of the alternative values for the demand distribution, holding cost, stockout cost, and order cost), the simulation must be run a certain number of days. This number of days will be equal to thirty. Thus one trial consists of thirty days.

For each thirty-day trial, the simulation must begin with an initial inventory level, which is equal to the target order quantity which is being evaluated. Thus it is assumed that the simulation begins on the morning of a day on which an order has just arrived. For each day, the model must determine (1) whether inventory has dropped to the target reorder point, and if so, then (2) place an order and generate a lead time.

Besides monitoring inventory levels, the model must use the information garnered above in addressing two cost-based issues: (1) what is the inventory (or backorder) at the end of the day? (This allows the assessment of holding, or backorder, costs.) and (2) has an order been placed with the vendor? If so, an order cost is incurred. The model must maintain a running total of these costs, and calculate the resulting total incurred at the end of the thirty-day trial.

Other activities, named "front end" and "back end" activities, must also be considered. Front end activities involve the design of the experiments the simulationist performs. These have been introduced briefly, regarding the sixteen scenarios to be analyzed, and the number of days in a trial, set at thirty. Along with this, the simulationist must determine, for statistical purposes, how many trials will be run for a particular scenario at the prespecified order quantity and reorder point values. In this simulation, each trial will be run thirty times. This will yield, for each EOQ and ROP trial pair, thirty sets of output regarding total costs. From these thirty values one may determine the mean cost that the suggested EOQ and ROP trial pair yields. The final front end activity involves specifying the number of times the target EOQ and ROP pairs will be changed, and re-evaluated. Essentially, the procedure is the following: After thirty trials of thirty-days duration apiece have been completed for a target set of values, the target EOQ and ROP are changed. At this point another set of thirty trials, each of thirty-days duration, is run for a new set of target values. The mean cost is then computed again. A performance criteria is established to compare the performance of the new target values to the old trial values (based on both the outputted costs and variance, discussed later), and if the performance of the new target values (as deemed by the performance criteria based upon the output of the simulation) is better, the new set is retained as the best solution, while the old target values are discarded and considered suboptimal. A new set of target values is then considered (each new set of target values defines an experiment), and this sequence of steps is repeated continuously until enough target values (experiments) have been considered. The number of experiments must be sufficient for the simulationist to believe that the optimal solution has been zoned, or located, within some specified level of tolerance of the optimal solutions. The number of experiments, or sets of target values (each consisting of a pair of values representing the target EOQ and ROP), will be set equal to five hundred. Consequently, for each of the sixteen scenarios considered, five hundred experiments will be considered, each consisting of thirty trails, with each trial simulated for thirty days. In summary, the following terms may be defined as follows:

- *Scenario:* a specified set of inputs for exogenous variables, or those not ordinarily controlled internally by management. Demand, as well as all cost parameters are usually considered exogenous. Each set of inputs for a simulation comprises one scenario.

- *Experiment:* for each scenario, an experiment evaluates a target set of decision values, which in our case represents target values for the order quantity and reorder point. These variables are those ordinarily controlled by management and are considered endogenous. Each experiment is run a specified number of times.

- *Trial:* every experiment is run for a specified number of trials. Each trial is run for a given duration, or period, and uses the same values for the endogenous variables.

- *Duration:* the number of days (or time period) each trial is run.

Once the specified number of experiments have been completed, the simulation team (user) may request that more experiments be considered. This is discussed later when the actual simulation is considered.

Back end activities involve the statistical evaluation performed on the output of the simulation. From this analysis, the simulationist may determine whether additional experiments should be considered, whether certain parameters and bounds should be changed, and whether the simulation should be stopped with the belief that the best solution has been found for a particular scenario.

User Interaction and Inputs

The model presented here is interactive as it allows the user to input many initial values and maintain a high degree of control over how the simulation proceeds. To begin, the user is called on through computer prompts to enter a number of basic values. These include minimum and maximum values for anticipated daily demand, as well as the most likely (or modal) value. The user also enters parameter values for the per unit holding cost, the per unit daily backorder cost, and the reorder cost per order. An example of these inputted values (from which simulation results will be generated) is shown in Table 4.1.

Note that the initial inputted values for each item (holding, backorder, and order costs, as well as demand) correspond to one of the alternative values chosen when designing the simulation. The program now goes on to calculate the classical solution to the inventory problem using these inputs. Based on that information, the user is now prompted for a follow-up set of values. These values include a search range for the decision variables, that is, the order quantity and the reorder point. The simulation will search for the best estimate of these values from within this range. The pair of values considered is changed in each experiment, and after the experiment is run for the specified number of trials, the results of the new experiment are compared to the previously saved best results and updated, if better. The user also enters additional front end information, such as the duration (number of days) per trial, the number of trials to be evaluated at the chosen EOQ and ROP values, and the number of experiments to be run. Note that the user does not specifically enter a unique target value for the decision variables. Rather, the model chooses initial target values randomly from within the interval specified by the user. An example of a prototype set of follow-up inputs is provided in Table 4.2.

It is important to recognize that the user has full control over the range of values for ROP and EOQ. If this range is poorly chosen, then one should not expect very good results. Consequently, it is common to choose these values around a benchmark, which is typically provided by the results from a classical model. While there is little confidence that the classical model provides good solutions (since it is based on limiting assumptions), it does at least provide an initial estimate, or starting point, to work from. Whether the initial range contains the classical solutions or not, the

Table 4.1
Summary of Initial User Inputs for a Model Scenario

Lowest Value for Demand	100.00
Most Likely Value for Demand	500.00
Highest Value for Demand	1,000.00
Annual Holding Cost per Unit	$1.00
Daily Stockout Cost per Unit	$5.00
Reorder Cost per Order	$1,000.00

Table 4.2
Summary of Follow-Up User Inputs for a Model Scenario

The Classical Value for EOQ	6,239
The Classical Value for ROP	1,066
Lower Search Limit for ROP	400
Upper Search Limit for ROP	1,500
Lower Search Limit for EOQ	3,000
Upper Search Limit for EOQ	9,000
Duration per Trial (Days)	30
Number of Trials per Experiment	30
Number of Experiments	500

simulation procedure used herein should eventually zero in on the optimal solution.

As discussed, the model first generates random values for both ROP and EOQ. Thirty trials, each thirty days in duration are then run. At the completion of each of these thirty runs, which incidentally can be completed extremely fast when coded in GPSS/H™ on a good PC, the three inventory costs are calculated, from which a total cost can be determined. After the thirty trials are completed, the mean of the thirty trial total costs is determined, and a 95 percent confidence interval is generated for the total inventory-related costs over a thirty-day horizon. The program then calculates the performance criteria, stores this result as the best solution generated at this point, notes that this solution was generated in experiment number one, and prints the solution (regarding cost) to the screen so that the user can see it.

At this point the program proceeds to experiment number two by generating another random pair of target values for ROP and EOQ from within the inputted range specified by the user in the follow-up input. After thirty trials, each of thirty-days duration, have been completed, another calculation is made as in the first experiment regarding total cost and performance criteria. If this value for the performance criteria is superior to the previously stored best value, this new cost together with the new ROP and EOQ target values replace the previously stored ones. The simulation then goes on to experiment number three, and so on. Whenever a superior solution is found, the simulation prints this information to the screen. This allows the user to track the neighborhood from within which reasonably good answers have been found.

When the specified number of experiments has been completed, the simulation prompts the user as to whether he would like to continue the simulation and generate more experiments, called an additional search, by changing the follow-up input values regarding feasible ranges on ROP and EOQ. If, for example, the user has noticed that a majority of low cost solutions (printed to screen as discussed earlier) all have ROP and EOQ values near the upper limit of their respective ranges, then it would be a good idea to perform additional experiments with new ranges specified. These new ranges could have higher lower and upper limits, which would allow the simulation to search for lower cost solution in areas previously not investigated. For example, the second search conducted may have the search range for ROP increased, with a new lower limit of 1,300 units to a higher limit of 2,000 units. Since most of the low cost solutions printed to screen from the first 500 experiments (these intermediate results are not shown) indicated that EOQ was between 6,000 and 8,200 units, the user might input a range of values for the second search extending from a low of 5,500 units to a high of 8,500 units. After these new 500 experiments are conducted, the simulation will again prompt the user regarding whether additional searches (experiments) should take place. For our purposes, a third search was also conducted. The output results for the experiments, printed to screen after the three searches had been completed, are shown in Table 4.3.

Consider the output shown in Table 4.3. The user has attempted three successive searches, each consisting of 500 experiments, to zero in on the optimal solution for this particular scenario, where the inputs are reprinted in the top portion of the table. As shown in Table 4.2, the user responded to the classical EOQ and ROP values for the first search (500 experiments) by setting the range for the decision variables to 400 and 1,500 (lower and upper limits) for ROP and 3,000 to 9,000 for EOQ. Upon concluding the first search within these ranges, the simulation yielded the best solution on experiment number 460, where the EOQ value was set at 8,189 units, and the ROP set at 1,494 units. The .95 confidence interval estimate of total inventory costs (based on the output of thirty successive trials each of thirty-days duration) indicates that costs were bound between $535 and $623.

A second search of 500 additional experiments was conducted, with the upper limits increased for both EOQ (ranging between a low of 5,500 units to a high of 8,500 units) and ROP (ranging between a low of 1,300 to a high of 2,000) as discussed earlier. The resulting confidence interval for total inventory costs shows a considerable improvement, with the best solution generated on experiment number 11. As seen from Table 4.3, the .95 interval estimate for costs has decreased considerably. The proposed solution now indicates that EOQ should be set at 6,083 units with ROP equal to 1,716 units. A third search, conducted in a similar fashion, yielded only marginal improvements. Nonetheless, an improvement was noted. At this point the experimental portion of the simulation was concluded, as the user has sufficient confidence that the optimal solution has been zoned within an allowable tolerance.

Finally, when the user terminates the experimental portion of the simulation, the model continues to run one set of thirty trials, each of thirty-days duration, using the classical results from the analytically based classical model. The .95 confidence interval estimate for total inventory costs is determined and printed to screen. As evidenced from the lower portion of Table 4.3, the simulated solutions yield far lower costs than those generated with the analytic model, as hypothesized at the beginning of this chapter.

Table 4.3
Screen Output for the Completion of One Selected Simulation Scenario

Estimate of Customer Demand in Units per Day	
Low	450 Units
Modal	500 Units
High	650 Units

Inventory Costs	
Annual Holding Cost per Unit	$1.00
Daily Stockout Cost per Unit	$5.00
Reorder Cost per Order	$1000.00

Results of Experiments: 95% Confidence Interval, Total Inventory Costs

Search	Low	High	EOQ	ROP	Experiment
1	$535	$623	8,189	1,494	460
2	$478	$487	6,083	1,716	11
3	$463	$472	5,943	1,616	366

Classical Solutions

$1,521	$2,455	6,239	1,066	

Two final notes should be made before proceeding. First, while it might seem as if the comparison of total costs is sufficient to determine whether a particular experiment yields a result superior to a prior one, this is ordinarily not the case. To increase stability, the performance criterion for a particular experiment sometimes includes the impact of the output's variability. For purposes of this simulation, the performance criteria used for the comparison of each experiment was the sum of total costs (summed over the thirty trials for the experiment) plus the standard deviation of these thirty results. This allows for variation as well as long-run average costs to impact the decision as to which solution is preferred.

Second, as experimental results are generated, it is important for the user to look at the sequence of successively improved results as they print to screen. As they are generated, the user should decide if the model appears to be zeroing in on a narrow range within which the optimal solution is contained, or if the solutions seem to be exhibiting high variability and fluctuation, which would indicate that the search area for both EOQ and ROP might be reconsidered. Where the user has set the upper limit for ROP too low, for example, the best answers will all cluster near the upper limit. Common sense dictates at this point that another set of experiments should be pursued with a higher upper limit. Similar cases can be imagined by the reader.

Simulation Results

In order to deem the simulation complete, one set of input values is ordinarily far from sufficient. As one of the general purposes of a simulation model is to consider how changes in inputs have an impact on optimal solutions and increase or decrease the disparities found between the classical and simulated solutions, different scenarios should be conducted. One such scenario, with multiple searches and numerous experiments, has been discussed in detail. Note that alternate inputs for demand, as well as holding, stockout, and ordering costs were described earlier. A procedure similar to the one discussed in the prior section may be conducted for all combinations of the alternative input values, yielding sixteen separate scenarios, each containing one of the alternative values for the following: low variance (450 to 650 units) versus high variance (100 to 1,000 units) demand; low ($1.00 per unit per year) versus high ($10.00 per unit per year) holding costs; low ($.50 per unit per day) versus high ($5.00) stockout, or backorder, costs; and low ($100 per order) versus high

($1,000) reorder costs. The final results for the sixteen scenarios are shown below in Tables 4.4 and 4.5. Note that for each scenario, the optimal .95 interval estimate for total cost is shown for both the simulation and the classical solutions. From Tables 4.4 and 4.5 it is readily apparent that the simulated solutions yield lower costs for all scenarios when compared to the classical results. The result is due to the fact that while classical models are useful in their own right, a slight distortion from the assumptions upon which the classical model is based can lead to solutions that are far from optimal. It is also apparent from the results, however, that the accuracy of the classical model and the simulation vary according to the scenario under

Table 4.4
Simulation Output for Eight High Variance Scenarios

Scenario (Model Theory)		Costs Holding, Stockout, Reorder	.95 Interval Costs ($)		EOQ	ROP
H1	M	L. L, L	494	515	6,150	1,727
	T		648	796	6,239	1,066
H2	M	L, L, H	776	811	17,659	129
	T		930	969	19,731	1,066
H3	M	L, H, L	510	527	6,283	1,944
	T		2,350	3,985	6,239	1,066
H4	M	L, H, H	795	841	18,000	284
	T		930	969	19,731	1,066
H5	M	H, L, L	1,796	1,883	2,429	1,546
	T		2,068	2,412	1,973	1,066
H6	M	H, L, H	4,553	4,809	5,937	1,063
	T		4,725	4,834	6,239	1,066
H7	M	H, H, L	2,069	2,148	2,238	1,996
	T		8,127	12,333	1,973	1,066
H8	M	H, H, H	5,026	5,193	6,209	1,864
	T		6,563	8,127	6,239	1,066

Note: H and L designate high and low values respectively for the appropriate cost. M and T designate results based on the model and the theory, respectively.

study. That is, in some cases the simulation varies cost results that are closer to the classical model than in others. For example, there exist six scenarios when the simulation's cost benefits are extreme: L3, L7, L8, H3, H7, and H8. While this observation is worthy in itself, a good simulationist should attempt to attribute such disparities to some element, or group of elements, in the problem. Pursuing this further, note that all six scenarios correspond to those for which stockout costs are highest (two other cases with high stockout costs also exist, and are pursued subsequently). The classical model ignores stockout costs, as we have noted. This is because under the assumption that both demand and lead time are known with

Table 4.5
Simulation Output for Eight Low Variance Scenarios

Scenario (Model Theory)		Costs Holding, Stockout, Reorder	.95 Interval Costs ($)		EOQ	ROP
L1	M	L. L, L	455	466	5,850	1,566
	T		565	652	6,239	1,066
L2	M	L, L, H	664	675	16,320	342
	T		939	948	19,731	1,066
L3	M	L, H, L	463	472	5,943	1,616
	T		1,521	2,455	6,239	1,066
L4	M	L, H, H	675	683	16,502	431
	T		939	948	19,731	1,066
L5	M	H, L, L	1,637	1,684	2,177	1,398
	T		1,978	2,118	1,973	1,066
L6	M	H, L, H	4,372	4,415	5,696	1,066
	T		4,686	4,745	6,239	1,066
L7	M	H, H, L	1,757	1,819	2,314	1,609
	T		7,204	8,985	1,973	1,066
L8	M	H, H, H	4,576	4,678	5,861	1,576
	T		5,663	6,527	6,239	1,066

Note: H and L designate high and low values respectively for the appropriate cost. M and T designate results based on the model and the theory, respectively.

certainty, it can always be the case that goods on order can arrive at precisely the time when inventory is depleted. In consideration of this, the following conclusion can be reached: If stockout costs are high, the impact of this cost is exacerbated (as the classical model is not affected by stockouts) and creates high disparities between the solution suggested by the classical model and the simulation. Consequently, a relaxation in the stockout assumption renders the classical model virtually useless in these cases. In some of these six instances the inventory costs yielded by the classical model are nearly three times those generated through the use of the simulated solutions.

In the other two high stockout cost scenarios, L4 and H4, the classical advice is not as disastrous. The reason for this lies in the fact that for these cases the holding costs are very low while the reorder costs are very high. This allows the classical model to suggest very high EOQ levels, with infrequent orders being placed. These high levels of inventory tend to soften the impact of the stockout costs under the conditions of variable demand and lead time, as the frequency of stockouts is diminished due to the high order quantities and infrequent number of orders. Note, however, that it is the effect of the high holding cost, rather than the robustness of the classical model, which permits costs for the simulated and classical solutions to be reasonably close.

Other observations can be made as well. For instance, where customer demand varies more seriously under conditions of greater variation, the inventory system must compensate for the additional uncertainty in demand, thus inventory costs rise. Also, as each individual inventory cost is varied between its low and high values, total inventory costs increase as well. More interesting, perhaps, is the fact that while variability in demand creates far superior solutions when comparing the simulated results to those of the classical model, the total costs for high variance demand did not create tremendous disparities from the same scenarios under the conditions of low variance demand. Results such as these are for management to review prior to making specific recommendations regarding policy. Other such comparisons can be envisioned by the reader.

In general, it is reasonable to believe that the results generated by the simulation are nearly optimal throughout the sixteen scenarios. Consider that the results generated are bound within a 95 percent confidence interval, and that each of these intervals is based on 500 experiments, each of which consists of thirty trials running thirty days apiece, not to mention that for each scenario multiple searches were conducted.

Overall, it appears that the simulation model makes much more sense contrasted with the classical model based on questionable assumptions which do not necessarily reflect the attributes of the system being studied. What may be surprising is the extent of the disparity, in the instance under study here, created by the relaxation of lead time and demand, even though the degree of relaxation for these assumptions is relatively small. In practice, supplier lead times are often spoken of in terms of weeks, with relatively high levels of variance, whereas our model has limited lead time between one and three days.

In summation, the impact of simulation upon the determination of optimal management policy decisions is significant. The model illustrated in this chapter points out the weaknesses which classical models pose when the model's assumptions are excessively restricted. Even in cases where the violation of some assumptions appears comparatively small, simulation as a modeling tool becomes essential in avoiding potential catastrophic financial outcomes and in generating meaningful and potentially profitable solutions to the types of problems faced by management on a daily basis.

We pursue the development of inventory policies in Chapters 5 and 6, where the concept of just-in-time is explored.

Appendix 4.1
Simulation Code

```
*INV9318.GPS
   SIMULATE
* DEFINITIONS
   REAL    &HOLD1,&BACK,&ORDER1
   INTEGER &LOW(20),&UP(20),&EOQZ(20),&ROPZ(20),&TRY(20)
   INTEGER &DAYS,&TRIALS,&I,&ROP,&EOQ,&BEGIN,&J,&LOOK,&K
   INTEGER &TRI1,&TRI2,&TRI3,&EOQ1,&EOQ2,&ROP1,&ROP2,&GAME1
DEMAND FVARIABLE &TRI1
*DEMAND FVARIABLE RVTRI(1,&TRI1,&TRI2,&TRI3)
EXVAL FVARIABLE (&TRI1+&TRI2+&TRI3)/3
EOQX  FVARIABLE SQRT((2*&ORDER1*V(EXVAL)*365)/&HOLD1)
EOQ3  FVARIABLE &EOQ1+(FN(RAND1)*(&EOQ2-&EOQ1))
ROP3  FVARIABLE &ROP1+(FN(RAND1)*(&ROP2-&ROP1))
RAND1 FUNCTION  RN2,C2
0,0/1,1
   PUTPIC
0 Enter lowest expected # of units daily demand
   GETLLIST  &TRI1
   PUTPIC
0 Enter average expected # of units daily demand
   GETLLIST  &TRI2
   PUTPIC
0 Enter highest expected # of units daily demand
   GETLLIST  &TRI3
   PUTPIC
0 Enter holding cost per unit per year
   GETLIST  &HOLD1
   PUTPIC
0 Enter stockout cost per unit per day
   GETLIST  &BACK
   PUTPIC
0 Enter reorder cost
   GETLIST  &ORDER1
NUTRY LET  &K=&K+1
   PUTPIC  (V(EOQX))
0 The theoretical Economic Order Quantity is ****
```

```
    PUTPIC  (V(EXVAL)*2)
0 The theoretical Reorder Point is ****
    PUTPIC
0 Enter lowest experimental value for EOQ
    GETLIST  &EOQ1
    PUTPIC
0 Enter highest experimental value for EOQ
    GETLIST  &EOQ2
    PUTPIC
0 Enter lowest experimental value for ROP
    GETLIST  &ROP1
    PUTPIC
0 Enter highest experimental value for ROP
    GETLIST  &ROP2
HCOST FVARIABLE (X(HOLD)*&HOLD1)/365      $5 PER UNIT PER YEAR HOLDING
SCOST FVARIABLE X(GONE)*&BACK ($2.50)     10% OF PRICE PER DAY PER UNIT
                                          STOCKOUT
RCOST FVARIABLE X(REORDER)*&ORDER1        $100 PER REORDER
TCOST FVARIABLE V(HCOST)+V(SCOST)+V(RCOST)          TOTAL INVENTORY
                                                    COST

VALU1 FVARIABLE TB1+V(STDERR)
1   MATRIX  MX,1,30
2   MATRIX  MX,1,7                        STORE EXPERIMENT IMPROVEMENTS
3   MATRIX  MX,1,2                        STORE BEST RESULTS
1   TABLE   MX1(1,P1),1,1,10              MUST GIVE TABLE DEFINITION
STDERR FVARIABLE TD1/SQRT(&TRIALS)        STANDARD ERROR
LL  FVARIABLE TB1-1.96*V(STDERR)         LOWER LIMIT, 95% CONF. INTERVAL
UL  FVARIABLE TB1+1.96*V(STDERR)         UPPER LIMIT, 95% CONF. INTERVAL
* Segment 1
    GENERATE  1,,,,1                      DAILY DEMAND—TIME UNIT = DAY
    SAVEVALUE STOCK-,V(DEMAND)            DRAW FROM INVENTORY
    TEST LE  X(STOCK),0,OKAY              DETERMINE DAILY OUTCOME
    SAVEVALUE GONE-,X(STOCK)              MINUS NEGATIVE = CUMULATE
                                          STOCKOUT
    TERMINATE
OKAY SAVEVALUE HOLD+,X(STOCK)            CUMULATE TOTAL HOLDING
    TERMINATE
* Segment 2—reorder
    GENERATE  ,,,1,2                      REORDER PROCESS
```

```
AGAIN TEST LE  X(STOCK),&ROP          REORDER POINT
ORDER SAVEVALUE STOCK+,&EOQ           REPLENISH
     TRANSFER ,AGAIN                  NEXT TEST
* Timer
     GENERATE  &DAYS                  NUMBER OF DAYS IN EXPERIMENT
     SAVEVALUE REORDER,N(ORDER)       RECORD NUMBER OF REORDERS
     MSAVEVALUE 1,1,&I,V(TCOST)       SAVE TOTAL COST THIS TRIAL
     TEST E  &I,&TRIALS,EASY2         TIME TO RECORD VALUES?
     ASSIGN  1,&TRIALS                PREPARE FOR LOOP
NEXT1 TABULATE  1                     RECORD TOTAL COST FOR TRIAL = P1
     LOOP  1,NEXT1                    PERFORM UNTIL P1 = 0
     TEST L  V(VALU1),MX3(1,1),EASY1  RECORD NEW IMPROVEMENT?
     MSAVEVALUE 2,1,3,V(LL)           RECORD LL
     MSAVEVALUE 2,1,4,V(UL)           RECORD UL
     MSAVEVALUE 2,1,5,&EOQ            RECORD EOQ
     MSAVEVALUE 2,1,6,&ROP            RECORD ROP
     MSAVEVALUE 2,1,7,&J              RECORD TRIAL #
     MSAVEVALUE 3,1,1,V(VALU1)        RECORD NEW IMPROVEMENT
     BPUTPIC  (&J,&EOQ,&ROP,V(LL),V(UL))
   trial *** eoq ***** rop *** low ***** up *****
EASY1 TEST E  &J@(&LOOK/1),0,EASY2
     BPUTPIC  (&J)
       ***
EASY2 TERMINATE 1
* Control Statements
OUT1 FILEDEF  'B:INV9317.OUT'
     INITIAL  MX3(1,1),1000000        INITIAL VALUE VERY LARGE
     PUTPIC
0 Enter number of trials for experiment
     GETLIST &TRIALS
     PUTPIC
0 Enter number of days for trial
     GETLIST &DAYS
     PUTPIC
0 Enter number of experiments
     GETLIST &LOOK
     DO   &J=1,&LOOK
     RMULT  12345
     CLEAR  MX2,MX3
```

```
LET    &EOQ=V(EOQ3)
LET    &ROP=V(ROP3)
DO     &I=1,&TRIALS
INITIAL  X(STOCK),&EOQ
START  1
CLEAR   MX1,MX2,MX3
LET    &LOW(&K)=MX2(1,3)
LET    &UP(&K)=MX2(1,4)
LET    &EOQZ(&K)=MX2(1,5)
LET    &ROPZ(&K)=MX2(1,6)
LET    &TRY(&K)=MX2(1,7)
ENDDO
ENDDO
DO     &I=1,&K
PUTPIC  (&I,&LOW(&I),&UP(&I),&EOQZ(&I),&ROPZ(&I),&TRY(&I))
* LL ***** UL ***** EOQ ***** ROP ***** TRIAL ****
ENDDO
END
```

5

Modeling Just-in-Time:
The Push-Pull Concept

The philosophy of just-in-time (JIT) has been incorporated into the daily operations of virtually all industries in the 1990s. Despite the start-up costs associated with the development and implementation of this philosophy, most manufacturing industry leaders recognize that the potential future returns generated through the implementation of a just-in-time system are well worth the initial investment. In order to understand whether this philosophy will benefit any particular organization, management must utilize an evaluative tool to determine whether the initial investment needed to bring about this change in philosophy will be justified by improvement in their system's performance.

One such evaluative tool is simulation. Simulation allows the user to understand how a system behaves. It also allows the user to witness the effects of potential changes in the structure of the system. In this sense it serves as both a solution procedure and a decision support tool. Understanding how a system behaves, as well as understanding its limitations, or capacities, are all closely related. For example, simulation permits the study of how a system behaves with regard to a potential bottleneck at a critical station. This, in turn, allows the user to evaluate whether the expected increase in system performance realized through an investment of $50,000 in an additional piece of machinery at this station is justified.

The just-in-time philosophy can be examined through simulation with an example of a fairly simple system. This system is shown in Figure 5.1. There are seven stations at which workers perform either a machining or an assembly task in assembling and modifying parts that go into a finished piece of machinery. Stations 1, 2, and 3 receive supplies which are machined and then forwarded to station 6, where the machined components are made into one subassembly. Station 4 machines parts in a similar way, which are then sent to station 5, where a second subassembly is manufactured. Stations 5, 6, and 7 all assemble parts from previous stations and perform additional machining tasks on the product. It is assumed that stations 1 through 4 receive a continuously uninterrupted flow of supplies, which is common in manufacturing processes, barring emergency interruptions. Stations 5 and 6 do not require additional materials, aside from those received from their preceding stations. Station 7 assembles the two subassemblies received from stations 5 and 6, sending a finished unit to the warehouse or retail outlet. For purposes of simplicity, it is assumed that all stations have the same mean service time. Relaxing this assumption is a straightforward extension of the model.

In order to understand the benefits of the just-in-time philosophy, the system will be modeled as both a "push" system and a "pull" system, each under two considerations: concern for quality and no concern for quality. Consequently, four models will be evaluated.

Push systems are characterized by large amounts of work in process (WIP) inventory. These systems are sometimes referred to as just-in-case systems. The strategy involves creating excess inventories to the point of actually pushing the product forward through the system. Workers ordinarily work as quickly as possible, and reserve supplies are kept on hand to compensate for defective work which cannot be passed on to the next station. Work is conducted at any given station so long as all necessary subassemblies and materials are available.

In contrast, pull systems make sense only in a just-in-time context (although they can be implemented without reaping their potential benefits in systems not employing just-in-time philosophy. This is illustrated in forthcoming simulations). Workers begin working (processing a unit) only when the succeeding station has pulled the prior unit forward (usually through a demand kanban or some alternate means of notification), and then only at such a rate that the target goal of zero defects is achieved. Workers are usually trained to incorporate zero defect philosophy into their daily work routine, and ordinarily work at a slower rate when

Figure 5.1
Manufacturing Cell Layout

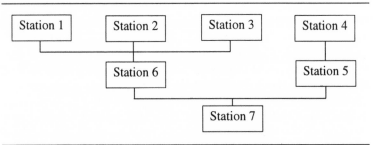

compared to a system which pushes product through the system. Even if materials and all necessary parts are available for work at a given station, the station remains idle until there is a demand for work. As mentioned, this demand is created by the following station in the production process pulling the most recently completed part for processing. Furthermore, in the ideal case, the entire assembly line stops when defects occur and only starts up again when reworking the defective unit is completed. Consequently, there are no discards for scrap. There are a variety of manufacturing strategies possible with respect to the degree of perfection expected in the product. The current model uses a simplifying convention that all units of the product are able to be corrected where defects in the process occur.

The simulations are presented in pairs. The first pair of simulations examines both push (model 1) and pull (model 2) systems under the assumption that product quality is not of concern to the people who work in and manage the system. Inspection is done at some later time, perhaps elsewhere within the company or even deferred until it reaches the consumer. The push system is expected to have greater output than the pull system, since the essence of push systems is to literally push as many units out as possible. Keep in mind that the pull system modeled here (model 2) does not truly represent a just-in-time system due to the lack of concern with product quality.

In the second pair of simulations the producer bears the responsibility for product quality. As before, the push system (model 3) produces WIP inventory as quickly as possible to offset possible idle time incurred when a previous station has failed to produce a good unit and must repeat its work (defective units are scrapped). In contrast, the pull system (model 4) represents a just-in-time system. It is assumed that retraining has occurred, consequently the mean service time at each station is 20 percent slower, but work is performed more consistently leading to a smaller variance in service time. Perhaps more importantly, the defect rate will be decreased from 10 percent (the assumed rate for each of the first three simulations) to .10 percent of production. The results are interesting even for these restrictive cases; the resulting differences between performance measures for the models would be exacerbated if the system's complexity were increased.

For the first three simulations, service time will be uniformly distributed over an interval of 6 to 14 minutes, yielding a mean service time of 10 minutes with a standard deviation of 2.31 minutes. The variability in service time is significant: On average, an observed service time will vary by 2.31 minutes from the mean time of 10 minutes. The uniformity of service time provides assurance that any service time over the feasible range is equally likely. Note that this is in contrast to many of the common queuing analyses in which service times are assumed to be exponential in order to increase the mathematical tractability of analysis. Also, these service times exhibit no tendency to cluster about the mean, as they would if the normal distribution or some other mound-shaped distribution were utilized. For the fourth simulation, however, which is a pull system with product quality concerns, service times are still uniformly distributed but with an increased mean and decreased variance. The mean service time is increased by 20 percent to 12 minutes, while the range of service times is bounded between 11.9 to 12.1 minutes (from which the standard deviation may be determined to be equal to .06 minutes). This reflects the effects of retraining, where workers perform in rhythm and coordination with both preceding and succeeding stations, according to carefully prescribed motions.

For all four models, the simulated work day will be of 480 minutes duration. A typical procedure utilized for simulations of this nature might incorporate thirty separate one-day simulations in order to generate a representative random sample of results. This also allows the central limit theorem and the normal distribution to be invoked in obtaining approximations for statistical measures and confidence bounds. For purposes of clarity in this demonstration, however, only ten days will be simulated for each case. When simulating each day, the model will actually be run for two days. The first day is run in order to allow the system to reach equilibrium, or steady state: At the completion of the first day the model's statistical values are reset at zero after which they are recompiled for the second day. Results for the second day are retained. Performing the simulation in this manner frees the model from initial condition effects witnessed at the beginning of an operating day (by running one complete day prior to collecting statistics the initial condition at the beginning of the second day is randomized and the system is already in equilibrium).

For the simulations performed, the following attributes represent the type of information which might be recorded:

- the number of defect free units of output per day
- the average number of defect free units produced over the total simulation runs
- the idle time percentage for the workers over a typical day
- the total number of units either being scrapped or reworked
- the level of WIP inventory

Although the simulations presented here reflect a simple seven station production process, the effect of the implementation of a just-in-time system can be extended to a more complex one containing many more dependencies between stations. Despite the simplicity of the system being studied, dependency within stations still exists to a limited extent. For example, station 6 is dependent for its supply of work on stations 1, 2, and 3. If these stations fail to provide work in a timely manner station 6 is forced into temporary idleness. This can occur due to errors and/or slow work at stations 1, 2, or 3, or forced idleness at these stations due to problems at earlier stations on which they depend (the simple assembly process shown in Figure 5.1 does not include predecessors for stations 1, 2, and 3.). This forced idle time is one of the supporting arguments for proponents of the push system in which case WIP inventory can be utilized to compensate for slowdowns and forced idle time.

The extreme case of dependency occurs in the standard assembly line process, in which all stations are linked sequentially. The fact that the sample production system analyzed here illustrates parallel channels of production allows for some degree of "forgiveness" regarding potential slowdowns due to forced idle time.

In general, resulting problems at one or more locations in the system have a magnified effect on delay and inefficiency for larger systems. On the other hand, more complex systems may also be characterized by a greater amount of work being performed in parallel stages, which increases the flexibility of the system. The overall impact on performance of these two contrasting perspectives is unclear. What is clear is that problems of scheduling, product mix, and the like are not necessarily amenable to analysis, even in cases where service times are deterministic, for any realistic application in which there are numerous stations and assembly nodes. This is why simulation is such a valuable and often used method of analysis for problems concerning real-world systems.

Summarizing briefly, the models presented here vary in two regards: the nature of the system (push or pull) and the concern with quality (within process or not within process). Models 1 and 3 are push systems. Each worker works continuously as long as necessary materials are present. Finished work continues to accrue as WIP inventory until it is demanded by the succeeding station. Model 1 assumes no concern for quality while model 3 incorporates concern within the production process itself. The simplifying assumption in the model is that the worker always discovers that a defective unit has been produced after the time has elapsed for the completion of the unit.

Models 2 and 4 are pull systems. Only the worker at station 7 is authorized to work whenever necessary materials and subassemblies are available. Workers at all other stations may not work until notification is received from the succeeding station that a new unit is required. For example, work at station 6 is not initiated until the most recently completed unit at this station is taken by station 7. The notification to begin work is the model's way of simulating the demand kanban found within systems of this nature. For example, when stations 5 and 6 have completed one defect free subassembly each, they are stored for station 7. Stations 5 and 6 remain idle until station 7 pulls these two subassemblies from their storage area. Ideally, station 7 will pull these two units as soon as they are completed, hence balancing the flow of work through the system. Greater flow balancing takes place when the work is distributed evenly among work stations, or cells. (This is incorporated into the simulations here by assuming that the mean service time and distribution are identical across all stations. Ordinarily perfect line balancing of this sort would be the exception, not the rule.) Forced idle time at station 6 can also occur if, pending the signal from station 7, parts from stations 1, 2 and 3 have not yet been completed, thus, work cannot be initiated until the supply kanban is also present. If this occurs, station 6 is unable to initiate work until all three preceding stations have completed their work.

For a push system, this supply kanban is not a problem, since workers at all stations are continually having work pushed at them from the preceding stations. They, in turn, push work to their succeeding station. For a pull system, it may be the case that since work at the preceding station does not begin until its last unit is pulled, the next unit may not be ready for work to begin at the succeeding station when it is required. This additional delay is expected to occur for any system where there is anything less than absolute deterministic mechanical repetitiveness. Probabilistic service times increase this effect, especially in the presence of high variance and unbalanced workloads. For purposes of the simulations, it is assumed that each station has one unit to process when the simulation is initiated, and no initial inventory exists in the system.

Proceeding with the simulations, the first simulation comparisons will be made between models 1 and 2. Recall that product quality is not monitored within the production-assembly process for these models. Presumably units are inspected later, either by the producer or the consumer. Also, the push-pull aspect of the system has no relevance to product quality, as the mandated retraining period has not been conducted, and service times are governed by the same distribution with no check for quality in both cases. Consequently, workers perform at their quickest pace in both simulations with the same level of accuracy (with service time uniformly distributed between 6 and 14 minutes and a defect rate of 10 percent). The primary interest in this comparison is to observe the rate of output for the production-assembly process (i.e., the number of units that have passed through station 7) and the percentage of time during the day when the workers as a group were gainfully occupied as opposed to being idle. Defective units are not monitored in this pair of simulations, since, for either process, one would expect that 10 percent of all completed units are defective, and the results regarding defective units are withheld until discovered at some downstream point in the system or by the consumer at a later date. The results of the ten simulations for models 1 and 2 are shown in Tables 5.1 and 5.2, respectively.

It is clear from the results that when production quality is not considered in the production-assembly process, the push system, which has been traditional for many manufacturing firms in the United States, appears to provide greater output per dollar of invested capital. There also exists significant differential in worker utilization. This is primarily due to the fact that in a push system workers continue to work whether or not there is immediate demand for their intermediate product. Consequently, if a

Table 5.1
Results of Ten Iterations for Model 1
(push system with no inspection for product quality)

Model Run	Units Produced	Model Run	Units Produced
1	48	6	46
2	45	7	47
3	46	8	46
4	47	9	47
5	47	10	46
Average units produced		46.50	
Average utilization of workers		99.39%	

worker takes an inordinate amount of time to complete a unit, the succeeding station is not forced idle, since a stockpile of inventory usually exists (just-in-case). Since idle time throughout the system is correspondingly reduced, it is no surprise that the corresponding output increases significantly for the push system relative to the pull system.

In contrast, considering that there exists no concern for product quality in the production-assembly process one may speculate (1) why there exists so much idle time in model 2? and (2) why should waiting for notification from a succeeding station create such idle time disparity between models?

Table 5.2
Results of Ten Iterations for Model 2
(pull system with no inspection for product quality)

Model Run	Units Produced	Model Run	Units Produced
1	38	6	39
2	37	7	37
3	36	8	38
4	38	9	37
5	37	10	38
Average units produced		37.50	
Average utilization of workers		78.51%	

One possible explanation involves the imperative that workers should work as quickly as possible (for both models) resulting in the prespecified high variance in performance time for any given unit. In turn, this disrupts any degree of line balancing in the pull system which may have been present, thus increasing idle time significantly. Also, where there exists dependency between stations, with no stockpiling of inventory, the failure to match demand with production will be frequent, also resulting in increased levels of idle time.

Given the results from these simulations, it might seem difficult to understand why a pull system is desirable if product quality and associated costs of neglecting it in new competitive markets proliferated by global entrants had not become so significant. The critical tie-in here is the point, developed so well by the Japanese with the aid of statistician W. Edward Deming of the United States, that quality assurance in a product is achieved only if the process is monitored continually. For now, in summary, these notions can be simplified by assuming that (1) the bottom line cost to the company of marketing defective products is the potential elimination of the firm from the market itself and (2) even if it were cost-effective to produce first and inspect later, experience has reiterated emphatically that there exists a high degree of correlation between the amount of success a product has in a highly competitive market and the emphasis on quality in the production process itself.

Consider now simulations 3 and 4, which differ significantly from simulations 1 and 2 with regard to one critical factor: quality. For these cases no defective units are passed through the final assembly phase of the production process. The workers in the production-assembly process are now responsible for any errors which take place, and when a defect is discovered the unit is either scrapped (in the push system) or reworked (in the pull system). In the push system (model 3) workers continue to work as fast as possible. As the simulation comparison shows, despite the continual work and stockpiling at all stations, this will not compensate for the idle time created when a station does not receive a unit from its feeder station due to defective work as long as there exists (1) some degree of continued dependency between stations, (2) high variance in processing time, and (3) a high rate of defective units. As noted earlier, the nature of push systems tends to yield higher variance and defective rates than just-in-time systems.

Since quality is a concern here, and the service time distributions vary between the two cases, the simulation output will include information regarding defective work as well as work in process (WIP) inventory. The results generated from ten runs of the push system (model 3) are presented in Table 5.3. Note the low idle time (6.34 percent), indicating that workers are still very busy. Politically this may have some positive utility associated with it. The sole reasons for the utilization dropping below 100' percent are (1) variance in the service time and (2) scrapping of defective units. This creates a small degree of forced idle time when a station finds that its preceding stations do not have their components completed on time, and no WIP inventory exists. Unfortunately, quantity does not necessarily imply quality. Noting that simulations 1 and 3 are identical with the exception that defective units are now discarded, observe how the overall mean output per run has dropped dramatically (from 46.5 to 34.1 units). Of equal concern are the associated costs for the scrap from the defective units, amounting to approximately three units per run, and the large WIP inventory, close to three stockpiled units for each of the six feeder stations.

When the same production run is made using a JIT pull philosophy including quality considerations, significant benefits are achieved. Recall that the retrained worker in a JIT system works slower with higher precision and a lower variance on service time, at the expense of increasing the mean service time. This additional time is taken so that self-correction

Table 5.3
Results of Ten Iterations for Model 3
(push system with inspection for product quality)

Model Run	Units Produced	Model Run	Units Produced
1	38	6	33
2	40	7	32
3	35	8	29
4	37	9	30
5	34	10	33
Average units produced		34.10	
Average utilization of workers		93.66%	
Average units scrap		30.70	
Average WIP inventory		15.94	

and mastery of the process is attained. The pull system attempts to achieve a symphony of synchronized line-balanced work, where all stations are in rhythm. This principle is so important that when a defect is discovered the entire process temporarily shuts down until the correction is made, the unit is reworked, and the completed defect-free unit is sent forward. Numerous improvements in the way of sophistication or added realism could be made in this model, with respect to the detailed nature of the reworking process. What is done in this model, by way of simplification to achieve the point with a minimum of detail, is merely to represent the reworking of a unit as occurring with the same service time distribution used for processing a unit in general. Moreover, some defects are bound to exist within a manufacturing assembly process due to such things as material defects. Again, this has been left out, for the sake of a single-minded focus on the just-in-time strategy versus its absence. The shutting down principle discussed above is utilized in model 4 (the just-in-time system), for which the simulated results are shown in Table 5.4

Comparing models 3 and 4, the pull system (model 4) achieves, per run, higher average output (39.9 to 34.1), lower idle time (0.84 percent idle versus 6.34 percent), lower defective units (0.1 versus 30.7) and lower WIP inventory in the system (.03 units versus 15.94 units). These results are aggregated over the ten runs, by virtue of the model storing the

Table 5.4
Results of Ten Iterations for Model 4
(pull system with inspection for product quality)

Model Run	Units Produced	Model Run	Units Produced
1	40	6	40
2	40	7	39
3	40	8	40
4	40	9	40
5	40	10	40

Average units produced	39.90
Average utilization of workers	99.16%
Average units scrap	0.10
Average WIP inventory	0.03

outcome after each run and averaging at the end of the simulation. Consequently, a higher level of output is achieved in conjunction with lower material costs (due to no scrap) and lower inventory carrying costs.

In addition to illustrating the benefits of the pull system when quality is inherent in the process, it is equally important to note that whether a push or pull system is used, quality has a tremendous impact. Note that the output in model 3 is significantly lower than that of model 1 due to the high percentage of defects discovered in the production-assembly process. Conversely, the low percentage of defects is not primarily what causes the dramatic improvement in idle time, as well as the modest increase in output, between models 2 and 4. Although the mean processing time per station is 20 percent slower in model 4, the decrease in variance coupled with higher synchronization between stations plays a significant role in decreasing the overall idle time. This more than compensates for the slower mean process time, and as a result, output is higher. In general, the only idle time witnessed in this system accrues when the whole system shuts down during a rework period. Implications with respect to dramatically reduced costs for rework and WIP inventory are obvious.

The richness of using simulation as a methodology for decision support is readily seen in some additional observations which can be drawn from these fairly simple models. For example, if thirty iterations (as opposed to ten) are used for each experimental case, with the same random number stream inputted for each, a frequency distribution of model outcomes can be generated to measure the sensitivity of the parameters of interest to changes in the defect rates. That is, to say, the model is run for a simulated thirty days at each incremental defect rate, and comparative confidence intervals are therefore available. For these cases, the mean service time and variance are the same as models 3 and 4, while the defect rate is changed incrementally. One might anticipate that significant improvement in system performance may not be attainable in the push system, where workers are constantly pushing work through as fast as possible, at the expense of coordination. On the other hand, when increasing the defect rate in the pull system where just-in-time quality assurance has been attained, one might assume that a similar type of deterioration will not evolve.

To examine this issue, first consider the pull system. The defect rate is initialized at .0001, then subsequently changed to the following values: .001, .002, .003, .004, and .005. Results regarding the sensitivity of the system's performance to these changes are illustrated in Figures 5.2

through 5.7. Note from the figures that a change in the defect rate of one additional defect per thousand units (the first change from .0001 to .001 is slightly less than the desired incremental change of one per thousand) results in a negligible decline in average daily output, peaking at about four-tenths of a unit less per day. This is not a very significant decrease in production, although it is caused by what must seem a relatively negligible change in the defect rate. In other words, the day-to-day variation in system output increases substantially as the defect rate is experimentally increased, because of the wider range of probability that there will or will not be lost time through starving the stations while they wait for the defective unit to be replaced with a good one. What is more noteworthy is the deterioration in constancy of output as we move away from the zero-defects rate by increasing the defect rate.

Figures 5.8–5.13 illustrate respective results for the push system. The defect rate is initialized at .1, and incrementally decreased by .005 to a minimum value of .075. As the defect rate is reduced (incrementally by one half of one percent, or one less defective unit per two hundred produced) the average daily output increases, generally between one-half and one and one-half completed units per day on average. It is noteworthy that there is no significant pattern of change in the variance in the number of units produced per day over the thirty simulations, as the experimental value for the defect rate changes. In other words, the push system is comparatively less sensitive to different levels of defect rate, as far as this produces an effect of degree of variance from day to day in total output. Results for these figures are shown in tabulated form in Table 5.5.

The table demonstrates that with hypothetical changes in the defect rates for the push system (improvements in the defect rate) or the pull system (deterioration in the defect rate), costly inefficiencies with respect to scrap/rework and WIP inventory continue to be large in the push system and small in the pull system. For example, consider first that even if the defect rate in the push system is cut by .025 percent (one less defect per forty units produced) from .1 percent to .075 percent, the increase in worker utilization is still small (93.6 percent to 95.16 percent) compared to the pull system, where a larger increase in worker utilization results (96.4 percent to 99.4 percent) from changing the defect rate by a lesser amount, namely, .0039 percent. Consequently, worker utilization sensitivity is much greater for the pull system, with significant gains realized by decreasing the defect rate. However, note that regardless of the defect rate for the pull system, the utilization is still very high. Although one might be tempted to assume that the push system might also attain similar high utilization values if the defect rate were lowered to the range considered for the JIT pull model, keep in mind that this low level of defects is unattainable for the push system in which workers work as quickly as possible with shorter mean service times but higher variance. Second, examine the amount of scrap yielded from the two processes. The mean decrease in scrap units per .005 decrease in the defect rate for the push system is approximately 1.74 units, while the change over the entire defect rate range for the pull system (also .005) is 1.233. Consequently, *greater* benefits are achieved by decreasing the defect rate for the push system, although high levels of cost inefficiency still exist in terms of the actual absolute level of scrap produced by pushing product through the system opposed to pulling the work through. Third, note that decreasing the defect rate in the push system actually increases the WIP inventory in the system, increasing otherwise avoidable inventory holding costs, while WIP inventory levels decrease for lower levels of defects in the pull system. These three points support the contention that cost efficiencies are attained through the implementation of a JIT production-assembly philosophy, and that even for modest decreases in the defect rate for the push system, truly significant gains are unlikely to be achieved.

So what help do these simulation models provide to a manager who is prominent in the decision-making process of a firm considering the implementation of a just-in-time system? It has been the presumption in this chapter that the choice is really between developing just-in-time or eventually being driven from the market. As shown numerically by the results in this chapter, higher levels of productivity and output can be achieved by just-in-time, as well as lower inventory and scrap costs. In addition, the higher level of accuracy and lower variation in one's work leads to intangible benefits such as greater pride and awareness of one's competence and efficiency. Consequently, whether or not competition is the sole dictator in advancing the just-in-time philosophy, these benefits help guide the interested manager in making sound decisions based not only on cost mandates, but good sense as well.

Chapter 6 pursues the discussion of the just-in-time philosophy by illustrating how simulation can assist policymakers in understanding the tradeoffs between cost and quality.

Figure 5.2
Sensitivity of the Pull System to Changes in Defect Rate at .0001 over 30 Iterations

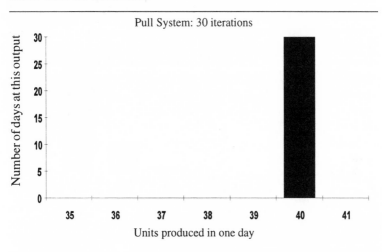

Figure 5.3
Sensitivity of the Pull System to Changes in Defect Rate at .001 over 30 Iterations

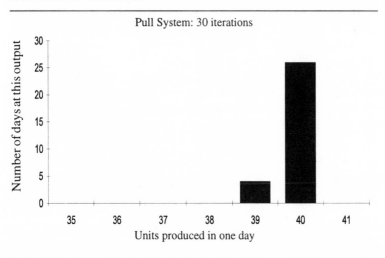

Figure 5.4
**Sensitivity of the Pull System to Changes in Defect Rate at
.002 over 30 Iterations**

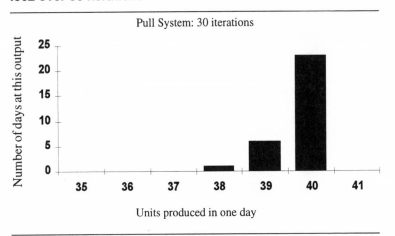

Figure 5.5
**Sensitivity of the Pull System to Changes in Defect Rate at
.003 over 30 Iterations**

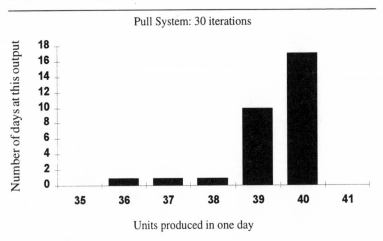

Figure 5.6
Sensitivity of the Pull System to Changes in Defect Rate at
.004 over 30 Iterations

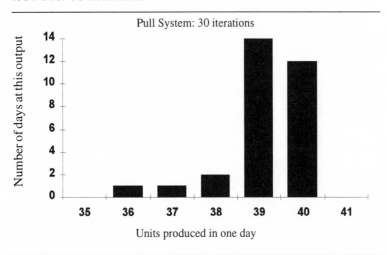

Figure 5.7
Sensitivity of the Pull System to Changes in Defect Rate at
.005 over 30 Iterations

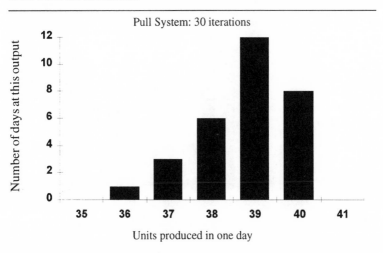

Figure 5.8
**Sensitivity of the Push System to Changes in Defect Rate at
.10 over 30 Iterations**

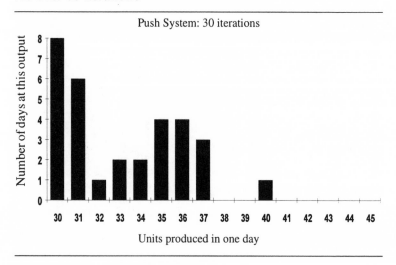

Figure 5.9
**Sensitivity of the Push System to Changes in Defect Rate at
.095 over 30 Iterations**

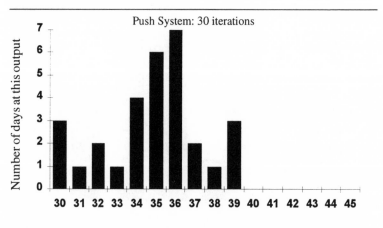

Figure 5.10
Sensitivity of the Push System to Changes in Defect Rate at .09 over 30 Iterations

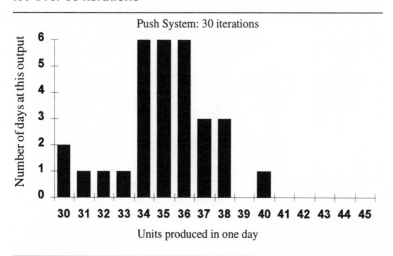

Figure 5.11
Sensitivity of the Push System to Changes in Defect Rate at .085 over 30 Iterations

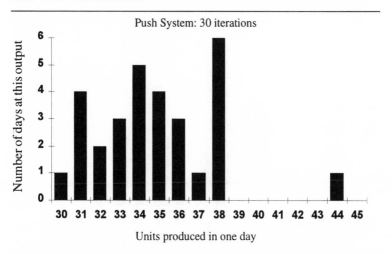

Figure 5.12
**Sensitivity of the Push System to Changes in Defect Rate at
.08 over 30 Iterations**

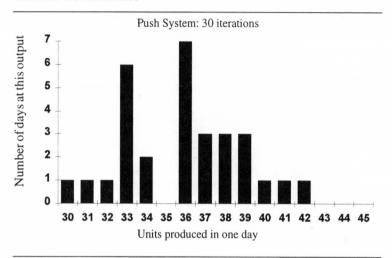

Figure 5.13
**Sensitivity of the Push System to Changes in Defect Rate at
.075 over 30 Iterations**

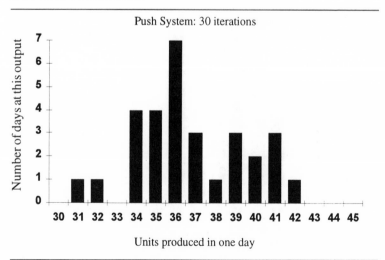

Table 5.5
Six Scenarios (average for thirty days of operation)

Percent Defects	Units Completed	Worker Utilization	Units Scrapped	WIP Inventory
A. Just-in-Time System				
.0001	40.00	99.43	0.00	0.028
.0010	39.87	99.08	0.13	0.032
.0020	39.73	98.75	0.27	0.038
.0030	39.37	97.87	0.63	0.538
.0040	38.77	96.40	1.23	0.083
B. Push System				
.100	32.93	93.66	31.93	13.23
.095	34.70	94.41	30.47	13.27
.090	34.97	94.17	28.40	12.38
.085	35.60	94.79	27.10	15.10
.080	35.87	94.84	25.27	14.92
.075	36.73	95.16	23.23	14.79

Appendix 5.1
Description of Block Code and Control Statements in the Model

The following description only touches on some major features of the models used in this chapter, to offer the reader a general feel for the simulation strategy employed. As in all cases for material in this book, readers are encouraged to contact the authors for further details.

Also, as in all cases for material in this book, we assume a general understanding of GPSS/H™ for those readers who want to follow the details in the appendices in a technical manner. A ready example is that of the use of the ADVANCE block. This can be explained, of course, but then there will be fifty to one hundred more such explanations for other GPSS/H™ entities, which would be prohibitive in terms of space. For the nontechnical reader, a general understanding of these explanations on a common sense level should be quite sufficient and quite accessible. The reader should reference Appendix 5.2 while reading the material below.

The push system model is easier to describe than the pull system model, because in the push system model we do not have to worry about synchronizing the workers at the several stations. Therefore the push system model is discussed first. The GPSS/H™ model shown here is model 3 as in the chapter, that is, this is the model of the push system where product quality does matter and inspected units which are found to be defective are scrapped.

This model needs to be looked at in two parts: first, the GPSS/H™ block code, representing the activity of the workers in the system, then, the control statements of the model, which govern execution of the experiments done with the model.

The push system model uses the GPSS/H™ entity of a multiple server, or the STORAGE, to represent work in process inventory at six of the seven work stations. The STORAGE is most often used in models to represent several workers or machines which can then process a number of jobs simultaneously at one work station, office, computer lab, and so on. The moving entity in GPSS/H™ models is the TRANSACTION, often abbreviated as XACT. In a GPSS/H™ model, when a STORAGE has been defined and an XACT approaches an ENTER block referencing that STORAGE, the XACT will be permitted or denied entry into that block depending on whether or not the number of XACTs already using that STORAGE is below the defined capacity of the STORAGE.

If the XACT does enter a STORAGE, GPSS/H™ records the current contents of the STORAGE as increased by one. Whenever an XACT goes through a LEAVE block referencing a STORAGE, GPSS/H™ records the contents of the STORAGE as decreased by one. So this logic is ordinarily used to model customers or jobs trying to get into a service process, finally succeeding, being processed, and leaving.

In this push system model, the STORAGE is used in the reverse way from its usual use. In our approach the STORAGE represents work in process inventory, at stations one through six. We want an XACT representing a worker, seeking a unit to do some work on, to be able to enter the STORAGE only when there is at least one unit of work available. Using the ENTER block, that means that the model must have the STORAGE at less then full capacity when there is a unit of work in process inventory available, so the XACT can successfully enter. So, the lower the current contents of the STORAGE, the more work in process inventory units it has (this is the reverse logic). This may seem a bit tricky, but it makes for an efficient model, as shown.

Since the push system can pile up several units of work in process inventory at one or more stations, we need to define a large enough work in process inventory capacity, so the six STORAGEs are defined with a capacity of thirty each. This representation is not needed for the final station, which simply sends its finished work to shipping or to the next location in the factory. Then the first block activity in the model in Segment 1 is that of priming the model by representing entry into all six of the STORAGES of the equivalent of twenty-nine XACTS. In this way each STORAGE will permit the entry of just one XACT until another XACT executes a LEAVE block for that STORAGE, since its initial current contents is equal to twenty-nine (for this model that means that it has one unit of work in process inventory, and the capacity to receive twenty-nine more—it is clearly a reversal of the usual logic in employing a STORAGE). Whenever a worker represented by an XACT completes a unit of work and passes it along to the next station, the XACT leaves the STORAGE for that station, in effect making room for the XACT which needs a unit of work to enter.

This logic eliminates the need to have XACTs perform a test every time they try to take a unit for work. The STORAGE will automatically deny entry unless that unit of work is on hand.

To reduce the amount of code needed for this model, a large amount of indirect addressing has been used. While seven separate code segments could have been written, one for each station, parameters are instead attached to each XACT and used throughout to identify both the work station and the source station for each worker XACT. The tradeoff is a much shorter model but a more abstract one.

This abstract logic pays off especially when faced with the task of showing how a worker at a given station needs anywhere from one to three parts or subunits available before he or she can proceed to the next task. The two lines of code at the label SEG2 accomplish this. The station number of the worker is stored in parameter one. The number of subunits needed at that worker's station is stored in parameter 2. The number(s) of the one or more source stations for this worker is (are) stored in a GPSS/H™ MATRIX which is then referenced in the line of code at SEG2. The XACT will negotiate this block for the number of times necessary for its particular work station.

The worker represented at station six will have to enter three separate STORAGEs before being able to proceed to the assembly and processing task. This logic eliminates a number of elaborate look-ups and tests before the next worker task can proceed. In the current model, XACTs for stations one through four are sent, by the TRANSFER block right after the label NEXT1, directly to work on their next task, since their supply of work is theoretically infinite. Designing the model so that every XACT can be sent to a checkpoint, if necessary, comes in handy for model 4 (the pull system with product quality), since there every worker XACT must check for either a demand or a supply kanban and some must check for both.

The last major feature of the block code is an easy one. To represent inspection for defective units, we have a TEST block. We generate a random number. If this value is greater than the value we have entered for the average defect rate, the XACT passes through the TEST block representing a successfully completed unit of work. What is important is that the XACT then goes on to negotiate the LEAVE block which increases the work in process inventory needed by another worker. However, on average, for that percentage of tasks completed at stations which matches the defect rate we have entered, the simulated unit of work will be rejected as defective. This is represented by the event of the XACT branching to the block labeled JUNK, skipping over the LEAVE block and contributing to the count on total number of defective units, which we can get by asking GPSS/H to print out the total number of XACT entries at JUNK.

The control logic of the model, which enables us to perform a series of experiments in a single computer run, is divided equally between the third segment of block code, labeled Timer, and the control statements themselves. The purposes of this control logic are two: (1) to have GPSS/H™ run a series of controlled experiments, where nothing changes except the defect rate, and (2) to both store and statistically analyze the data representing what happens in the model under each specific defect rate.

The control logic for setting up a number of controlled experiments is in the first part of the control statements. The person running the model selects the number of experiments desired, the defect rate for each experiment, and the number of model iterations for each experiment. Suppose that the person wants five experiments of thirty model iterations each. The control loops will run the model for thirty simulated times, each of which are statistically independent of the other twenty-nine runs. But they will repeat these identical thirty model runs under each of the five experimental conditions. In this way the user compares simulation results with nothing changed except the one experimental variable.

The control logic for generating and analyzing the model output has six steps, beginning in the block code and concluding in the control statements. For five experiments with thirty iterations each, there would be one hundred fifty carefully controlled runs of the model, each representing one day's production. Five experiments are carried out, testing the simulated system for sensitivity to improvements or deteriorations. Statistically sound results are achieved through repeating the experiment for thirty independent observations.

The first step in generating the desired output observations is incorporating into the model the identity of seven workers in the form of seven GPSS/H™ FACILITYs. The corresponding STORAGE entities for each station cannot be used, since they have variable content as work in process inventory locations. The FACILITY is a single server entity, like the actual individual worker. Therefore, it is ideal for generating a measure of worker utilization, and, in turn, the seven workers are each represented as a FACILITY in the model (even though this is not needed for model correctness) to generate an output measure of worker utilization.

In step two, for each of the thirty runs in an experiment, the model records a running total of system performance, such as worker utilization and work in process inventory. In step three, at the thirtieth, that is the last, run of the experiment, the model writes the thirty-run average of worker utilization, and so on, to a MATRIX. It is important that between each of these thirty runs, GPSS/H™ executes a CLEAR control statement, erasing what happened, for example, on day seventeen, so that the model can start over again in simulating day eighteen. However, the MATRIX can be and is exempted from this CLEAR order, and other value storage devices are used which are automatically exempt, that is, AMPERVARIABLES (which are identified by the fact that they begin with an ampersand).

In the fourth step, on the very last of the one hundred fifty runs, for each experiment, the model reads the thirty values stored in the MATRIX for number of good units produced in each of the thirty simulated days, and writes these thirty values into a GPSS/H™ statistical TABLE. This allows us to complete a sensitivity analysis of the simulated system with a minimum of labor.

The fifth step is made necessary by the fact that the GPSS/H™ TABLE is one of the few GPSS/H™ entities which cannot be protected from a CLEAR control statement. Therefore, in the control statements, for each of the one hundred fifty runs, a nested IF statement is examined. For one hundred forty-nine runs, the model results are erased with the CLEAR control statement, and an option is used to avoid printing the customary GPSS/H™ listing file to disk space, since the volume of output would be large and wasteful. On the very last run, the listing file is printed which includes the statistical distributions recorded by a TABLE for each experiment. While the TABLE output has not been used for more complex analysis, it should be noted that it would print out the standard deviation of the data, as well as the mean.

The final step of the control strategy for model output is simply the formatting of output results of thirty-run averages for each experiment, showing unit output, worker utilization, units scrapped or reworked, and work in process inventory levels. The rather free-form GPSS/H™ PUTPIC statement is used throughout for this, printing results to a second output file which is readily retrieved.

Model 4, the pull system model with responsibility for product quality, is basically the same as model 3. There are just a few important differences in the GPSS/H code which make this a model of a pull system.

First, the STORAGEs at stations one through six each have a capacity equal only to one unit of work. This is consistent with the work strategy of minimal work in process inventory.

Second, there is the additional constraint in the control logic that the simulated workers do not just push out as many units as they can, but rather they do not begin another unit of work until two conditions are attained. They must of course have a unit to work on, but they must also receive a demand kanban, which means that the unit they have sent on to the station they supply is now in use.

An effective way to model this condition in GPSS/H™ is to place the XACTs representing workers on a USER CHAIN after the simulated completion of each unit of work. This is never done for the worker at station 7, since this worker pulls the rest of the system of work forward. For the other six worker XACTS, a two step logic relating to a USER CHAIN is followed. Every time they complete a unit of work, they LINK onto a USER CHAIN, which puts them in suspension of activity within the model until they are UNLINKed from the chain.

The second step in this logic occurs every time any XACT (including the worker at station 7) establishes the supply kanban(s) condition. Having negotiated all the required ENTER repetitions which represent gathering the needed parts for work, this worker XACT has obviously used up the parts made available for his or her station. Therefore, the worker XACT sends one or more demand kanbans by executing the UNLINK block. Worker XACTs are UNLINKED from the chain and sent to the appropriate place in the model to undertake the next task. If the system is well synchronized the simulated time spent on the USER CHAIN will be infinitesimal and frequently zero. Substantial indirect addressing is used here, so that each station's worker calls for exactly the correct combination of additional parts to be made.

Finally, the additional difference in code which gives us the model of the pull system occurs with regard to inspection of product quality. In model 3 when a defective unit was found, the worker XACT represented the loss of value and efficiency involved in scrapping of the unit by leaping over the LEAVE block and going back to work on the next unit. In model 4, when a defective unit is found, the worker XACT stops the entire line for this division by executing a FUNAVAIL block. Here the representation of the seven workers each as a FACILITY turns out to be of still more use for us. Once the FUNAVAIL block is executed for the entire range of facilities, from one through seven, each XACT using up time in an ADVANCE block while it has captured its FACILITY will be suspended until the worker XACT who is responsible for the defect completes its own ADVANCE to restore the unit to proper quality. The signal to go back to work is represented through the FAVAIL block.

Appendix 5.2
Simulation Code

The following is the GPSS/H™ code for the twin models presented in this chapter. Model 1 corresponds to the push system with concern for quality, while model 2 corresponds to the pull (JIT) system with concern for quality.

Model 1

```
*BK14M.GPS
* Push system for complex assembly
* STORAGE empty = part IS there to work on, therefore worker CAN enter.
* workers enter STORAGE for previous station(s), execute LEAVE for their own.
   SIMULATE
* definitions
   INTEGER  &I,&RUNS,&GAME1,&XP,&J
   REAL    &ETIME,&TOT,&UTIL,&P,&JUNK1,&INV1,&PVAL(10)
   LET    &ETIME=480
1  MATRIX  X,7,3                      TRACK ASSEMBLY ROUTES
   INITIAL  MX1(5,1),4/MX1(6,1),1/MX1(6,2),2/MX1(6,3),3
   INITIAL  MX1(7,1),5/MX1(7,2),6
2  MATRIX  X,30,10                    STORE OUTPUT RESULTS
1  MATRIX  ML,10,4                    STORE PERFORMANCE AVGS.
   STORAGE  S1-S7,30                  6 STATIONS BEFORE END
WHERE FUNCTION  P1,D2
4,GO4IT/5,SEG2
MANY FUNCTION  P1,D3                  NUMBER OF PARTS TO ASSEMBLE
5,1/6,3/7,2
RAND2 FUNCTION  RN4,C2
0,1111111/1,9999999
RM1  VARIABLE  FN(RAND2)             SET RMULT
TOTR  FVARIABLE  FR1+FR2+FR3+FR4+FR5+FR6+FR7
JOB1  FUNCTION  RN1,C2               PROCESS UNIT
0,6/1,14
RAND1 FUNCTION  RN3,C2
0,0/1,1                              FOR PROBABILITY DEFECT
WIP1 FVARIABLE  180-SA1-SA2-SA3-SA4-SA5-SA6
* segment 1—prime mover
   GENERATE  ,,,1
```

```
       SPLIT  6,NEXT2,1
NEXT2 ENTER  P1,29                     REPRESENTS ONLY 1 AVAIL PART
       TERMINATE
* segment 2—workers
       GENERATE ,,,1                   SEED XACT
       SPLIT  6,NEXT1,1                7 WORKERS
NEXT1 ASSIGN  2,FN(MANY)               ASSIGN # OF PARTS
       TRANSFER ,FN(WHERE)             REQUIRE OTHER PARTS OR NOT
SEG2  ENTER  MX1(P1,P2)                GET NEEDED PART
       LOOP  2,SEG2                    MAY NEED MULTIPLE PARTS
GO4IT SEIZE  P1                        UTILIZATION OF WORKER
       ADVANCE 10,4                    ASSEMBLE, MODIFY PRODUCT
       RELEASE P1                      WORKER IDLE (TIME =0)
       ASSIGN  2,FN(MANY)              RESTORE LOOPED PARAMETER
       TEST G  FN(RAND1),&P,JUNK       IF DEFECT, SCRAP AND MAKE ANOTHER
       TEST L  P1,7,DONE               FINAL STATION?
       LEAVE  P1                       DEPOSIT PART FOR NEXT STN
       TRANSFER ,FN(WHERE)             REQUIRE OTHER PARTS OR NOT
DONE  TRANSFER ,SEG2                   BLOCK COUNT = OUTPUT
JUNK  TRANSFER ,FN(WHERE)              REQUIRE OTHER PARTS OR NOT
* segment 3—timer
       GENERATE &ETIME,,,1
       BRESET                          WARMUP
       ADVANCE &ETIME                  PRODUCTION RUN
       BLET  &TOT=&TOT+N(DONE)         RUNNING TOTAL OUTPUT
       BLET  &UTIL=&UTIL+V(TOTR)       RUNNING TOTAL UTILIZATION
       BLET  &JUNK1=&JUNK1+N(JUNK)     RUNNING TOTAL REWORK
       BLET  &INV1=&INV1+V(WIP1)       RUNNING TOTAL WIP INVENTORY
       MSAVEVALUE 2,&I,&J,N(DONE)      STORE ITERATION OUTPUT
       TEST E  &I,&RUNS,EXIT
       MSAVEVALUE 1,&J,1,&TOT/&RUNS,ML STORE AVG OUTPUT
       MSAVEVALUE 1,&J,2,&UTIL/(70*&RUNS),ML   STORE AVG UTILIZATION
       MSAVEVALUE 1,&J,3,&JUNK1/&RUNS,ML        STORE AVG REWORK
       MSAVEVALUE 1,&J,4,&INV1/&RUNS,ML         STORE AVG WIP
EXIT  TERMINATE 1
* control
OUT1  FILEDEF  'B:BK14M.OUT'
       PUTPIC
0 Enter # of experiments
```

```
   GETLIST &XP
   DO    &I=1,&XP
   PUTPIC  (&I)
0 Enter a probability value for defects in exper *
   GETLIST &PVAL(&I)
   ENDDO
   PUTPIC
0 Enter # of iterations for each experiment
   GETLIST &RUNS
   DO    &J=1,&XP
   LET   &P=&PVAL(&J)
   RMULT ,,,1234567
   DO    &I=1,&RUNS
   RMULT V(RM1),V(RM1),V(RM1)
   CLEAR MX1,MX2,ML1
   START 1,NP
   ENDDO
   LET   &TOT=0
   LET   &UTIL=0
   LET   &JUNK1=0
   LET   &INV1=0
   ENDDO
   PUTPIC  FILE=OUT1,LINES=3,_
(&PVAL(1),&PVAL(2),&PVAL(3),&PVAL(4),&PVAL(5))
EXPER:  1   2   3   4   5
p(defect) **.**** **.**** **.**** **.**** **.****
Iter/output:
   DO    &I=1,&RUNS
   PUTPIC  FILE=OUT1,(&I,MX2(&I,1),MX2(&I,2),MX2(&I,3),_
MX2(&I,4),MX2(&I,5))
   **   **   **   **   **   **
   ENDDO
   PUTPIC  FILE=OUT1
ROWS: 1=AVG OUTPUT 2=AVG UTILIZ 3=AVG REWORK 4=AVG WIP INVENTORY
   DO    &I=1,4
   PUTPIC  FILE=OUT1,(ML1(1,&I),ML1(2,&I),ML1(3,&I),ML1(4,&I),_
ML1(5,&I))
    **.**** **.**** **.**** **.**** **.****
   ENDDO
```

END_

Model 2

```
*BK14L.GPS
* JIT system for complex assembly
* STORAGE empty = part IS there to work on, therefore worker CAN enter.
* workers enter STORAGE for previous station(s), execute LEAVE for their own.
*   REALLOCATE COM,10000
    SIMULATE
* definitions
    INTEGER  &I,&RUNS,&GAME1,&XP,&J
    REAL    &ETIME,&TOT,&UTIL,&P,&JUNK1,&INV1,&PVAL(10)
    LET   &ETIME=480
    STORAGE S1-S7,1                     7 STATIONS
WHERE FUNCTION P1,D2
4,GO4IT/5,SEG2
MANY FUNCTION P1,D3                     NUMBER OF PARTS TO ASSEMBLE
5,1/6,3/7,2
STN FUNCTION P1,D2                      INITIAL ASSIGN TO WORK OR WAIT
6,WAIT1/7,SEG2
1   MATRIX X,7,3                        TRACK ASSEMBLY ROUTES
2   MATRIX X,30,10                      STORE OUTPUT RESULTS
1   MATRIX ML,10,4                      STORE PERFORMANCE AVGS.
    INITIAL  MX1(5,1),4/MX1(6,1),1/MX1(6,2),2/MX1(6,3),3
    INITIAL  MX1(7,1),5/MX1(7,2),6
1   BVARIABLE P1'G'X(LO)*P1'L'X(HI)     FIND RIGHT PARTS
JOB1 FUNCTION RN1,C2                    PROCESS UNIT
0,11.9/1,12.1
JOB2 FUNCTION RN2,C2                    PROCESS UNIT
0,11.9/1,12.1
LO   FUNCTION P1,D4                     FIND RIGHT PARTS
4,7/5,3/6,0/7,4
HI   FUNCTION P1,D3                     FIND RIGHT PARTS
5,5/6,4/7,7
TOTR FVARIABLE FR1+FR2+FR3+FR4+FR5+FR6+FR7
RAND1 FUNCTION RN3,C2
0,0/1,1                                 FOR PROBABILITY DEFECT
RAND2 FUNCTION RN4,C2
```

```
0,1111111/1,9999999
RM1 VARIABLE FN(RAND2)              SET RMULT
WIP1 FVARIABLE 6-SA1-SA2-SA3-SA4-SA5-SA6
* segment 1—workers
     GENERATE  ,,,1                 SEED XACT
     SPLIT  6,NEXT1,1               7 WORKERS
NEXT1 ASSIGN  2,FN(MANY)           ASSIGN # OF PARTS
     TRANSFER ,FN(STN)             WORK OR WAIT
SEG2 ENTER  MX1(P1,P2)             GET NEEDED PART
     LOOP  2,SEG2                  MAY NEED MULTIPLE PARTS
     SAVEVALUE LO,FN(LO)           SET LOWER LIMIT OF SEARCH
     SAVEVALUE HI,FN(HI)           SET UPPER LIMIT OF SEARCH
     UNLINK  WORKERS,STOP1,ALL,BV1  SEND DEMAND KANBAN(S)
GO4IT SEIZE  P1                    UTILIZATION OF WORKER
     ADVANCE FN(JOB1) ·            ASSEMBLE, MODIFY PRODUCT
     RELEASE P1                    WORKER IDLE (TIME =0)
     ASSIGN  2,FN(MANY)            RESTORE LOOPED PARAMETER
     TEST L  FN(RAND1),&P,OK1      IF DEFECT, STOP LINE AND FIX
JUNK FUNAVAIL 1-7                  STOP LINE
     ADVANCE FN(JOB2)              ASSEMBLE, MODIFY PRODUCT
     FAVAIL  1-7                   RESTART LINE
OK1 TEST L  P1,7,DONE             FINAL STATION?
     LEAVE  P1                     SUPPLY KANBAN
WAIT1 LINK  WORKERS,FIFO   1-6     WAIT UNTIL NEEDED
* segment 2—misc.
STOP1 TRANSFER ,FN(WHERE)          NEED/DON'T NEED PREVIOUS STATION
DONE TRANSFER ,SEG2                BLOCK COUNT = OUTPUT
* segment 3—timer
     GENERATE &ETIME,,,1
     BRESET                        WARMUP
     ADVANCE &ETIME                PRODUCTION RUN
     BLET  &TOT=&TOT+N(DONE)       RUNNING TOTAL OUTPUT
     BLET  &UTIL=&UTIL+V(TOTR)     RUNNING TOTAL UTILIZATION
     BLET  &JUNK1=&JUNK1+N(JUNK)   RUNNING TOTAL REWORK
     BLET  &INV1=&INV1+V(WIP1)     RUNNING TOTAL WIP INVENTORY
     MSAVEVALUE 2,&I,&J,N(DONE)    STORE ITERATION OUTPUT
     TEST E  &I,&RUNS,EXIT
     MSAVEVALUE 1,&J,1,&TOT/&RUNS,ML  STORE AVG OUTPUT
     MSAVEVALUE 1,&J,2,&UTIL/(70*&RUNS),ML    STORE AVG UTILIZATION
```

```
  MSAVEVALUE 1,&J,3,&JUNK1/&RUNS,ML      STORE AVG REWORK
  MSAVEVALUE 1,&J,4,&INV1/&RUNS,ML       STORE AVG WIP
EXIT  TERMINATE 1
* control
OUT1  FILEDEF  'B:BK14L.OUT'
  PUTPIC
0 Enter # of experiments
  GETLIST  &XP
  DO    &I=1,&XP
  PUTPIC  (&I)
0 Enter a probability value for defects in exper *
  GETLIST  &PVAL(&I)
  ENDDO
  PUTPIC
0 Enter # of iterations for each experiment
  GETLIST  &RUNS
  DO    &J=1,&XP
  LET    &P=&PVAL(&J)
  RMULT  ,,,1234567
  DO    &I=1,&RUNS
  RMULT  V(RM1),V(RM1),V(RM1)
  CLEAR  MX1,MX2,ML1
  START  1,NP
  ENDDO
  LET    &TOT=0
  LET    &UTIL=0
  LET    &JUNK1=0
  LET    &INV1=0
  ENDDO
  PUTPIC  FILE=OUT1,LINES=3,_
(&PVAL(1),&PVAL(2),&PVAL(3),&PVAL(4),&PVAL(5))
 EXPER:  1   2   3   4   5
 p(defect) **.****  **.****  **.****  **.****  **.****
Iter/output:
  DO    &I=1,&RUNS
  PUTPIC  FILE=OUT1,(&I,MX2(&I,1),MX2(&I,2),MX2(&I,3),_
MX2(&I,4),MX2(&I,5))
   **   **   **   **   **   **
  ENDDO
```

```
    PUTPIC   FILE=OUT1
ROWS: 1=AVG OUTPUT 2=AVG UTILIZ 3=AVG REWORK 4=AVG WIP INVENTORY
    DO    &I=1,4
    PUTPIC   FILE=OUT1,(ML1(1,&I),ML1(2,&I),ML1(3,&I),ML1(4,&I),_
ML1(5,&I))
      **.**** **.**** **.**** **.**** **.****
    ENDDO
    END
```

6

Modeling Just-in-Time: The Quality Effect

The process involved in improving manufacturing productivity may be presented under many different headings, such as zero defects, total quality management (TQM), just-in-time (JIT), or the "search for excellence" as espoused by Tom Peters. Although the more recently advocated name just-in-time is used here, bear in mind the words of William Shakespeare, "What's in a name? that which we call a rose / By any other name would smell as sweet" (*Romeo and Juliet*, Act II, ii). Regardless of the name used, the emphasis remains the same: achieve high quality at low cost. Of course, the question of whether these can be achieved simultaneously is an open one of great interest to many organizations.

Although many firms adopt a JIT philosophy, this alone is not sufficient for the philosophy to be operational; however, acceptance is necessary condition for its eventual implementation. As discussed in Chapter 5, the JIT philosophy seeks the elimination of all work in process inventory and the minimization of defective units. Within the process of attaining these goals there must be a careful analysis of all phases of the manufacturing process, coupled with a willingness to experiment with new and somewhat untested approaches in producing a finished good.

THE MANUFACTURING ENVIRONMENT

In providing a product to consumers, it is desirable to ensure that the product is defect free. If the product is under warranty, it is imperative that the failure rate of the unit be kept to a minimum. This, in turn, minimizes the expected recompense to the customer in the form of a replacement unit or a direct cash payout. Keep in mind that although the JIT philosophy adheres to the zero-defect goal, there still exists the small chance that defective items can pass through the system. Adherence to strict quality regulations in the workplace, which will have the effect of increasing the expected percentage of defect-free products as they complete the manufacturing process, is one way to achieve this minimum. Quality regulations of this sort require both the introduction of defect-free inputs, such as raw materials and component parts, as well as a highly efficient assembly process which produces defect-free final products.

By adopting this type of environment, the firm will increase the probability of achieving its goal of satisfying consumer needs, while improving its chances of gaining a repeat customer. Side benefits may accrue as well, that is, the firm may realize (1) a reduction or elimination of defective items, (2) a reduction in the manufacturing cycle time, or (3) an increase in productivity and the efficiency of individual work cells. As shown in Chapter 5, increased productivity as well as higher levels of output are attainable through the implementation of a JIT philosophy. This chapter illustrates, via simulation, the extent to which these benefits may be achieved in a JIT system through the reduction of product defects.

A manufacturing model is considered which utilizes eight work stations in the construction of a hypothetical widget. Five of the stations require the input of a raw material or a component part. The remaining stations serve as assembly stations at which no new parts or materials are introduced. The actual flow diagram for individual stations and successors is provided in Figure 6.1.

The system is designed as a pull system, as opposed to a push system. As discussed in Chapter 5, pull systems are control-based systems which signal the requirements for production only as they are needed; push systems are more planning-based, incorporating safety stock and the production of parts based on anticipated needs. Upon completion of its assigned task, each station inspects the item produced for defects. Consequently, defects, whether material defects or defects in workmanship, are not detected until the work station has completed its assigned tasks on the unit being produced.

Figure 6.1
The Just-in-Time System

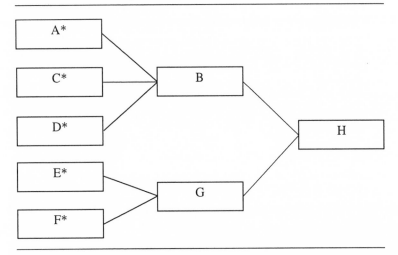

* Denotes the introduction of a raw material or a semifinished item into the flow process.

Defective items are discarded, while nondefective items are declared ready for the next work station. Discarding defective items is an alternative to reworking them and represents the approach taken in this chapter. The worker at a station then remains idle until the most recently completed item is taken by the following station at which time work on the next item is begun. Consequently, work is pulled through the system.

To incorporate the spirit of uncertainty into the problem, it is assumed that the service time at each station is probabilistic, as opposed to deterministic. For example, many queuing models assume that service times are exponential, and thus, memoryless. However, service times in actual workplaces tend to be nonexponential. This points out one strength of simulation models: Various service time distributions can be analyzed which would be otherwise mathematically intractable. For the example at hand, the cumulative distribution function (CDF) for service time at each station, given in Figure 6.2 will be employed. It is further assumed that each station has the same CDF regarding service times. The nonlinearity of the CDF implies that service times are not uniform, as in Chapter 5. Rather, the density function for this distribution would be mound shaped, with some service times more likely than others.

Figure 6.2
Cumulative Distribution Function for Service Time

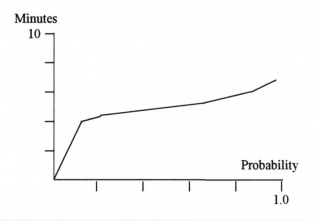

For those stations where raw materials or component parts are introduced, there are material/component part costs to be considered. These costs are provided in Table 6.1. In addition, the cost for labor is $12/hour (across all stations), and overhead costs equal 200 percent of total labor costs.

The Simulation Model

The simulation model will study the benefits attained when using a JIT system through the reduction of (1) the defect rate for raw materials, called the material defect rate, as well as (2) the defect rate at individual work stations, which will be called the station defect rate. The model is coded in GPSS/H™. It is assumed that a minimum production requirement (MPR) of 5,000 defect-free widgets is imposed. As mentioned, defective components are discarded with no scrap value, however, all costs are captured and accrued for defective as well as nondefective components. The range for both material and station defect rates will be from 0 to 6 percent. The simulation will attempt to clarify the effect that changes in these error rates have on run time and manufacturing costs accrued in meeting the MPR of 5,000 defect-free units. For each error rate simulated, ten runs will be made to help smooth out transient effects and the average of the ten runs will be used in the analysis.

Table 6.1
Material/Component Part Costs

Station	Cost/Unit ($)
A	.60
C	3.00
D	1.20
E	1.80
F	1.30

Simulation Results

Utilizing a forty-hour work week, and an MPR of 5,000 defect-free widgets, consider first the expected required production run (in units) at various error rates. Both material and station defect rates are initially set to their maximum value of 6 percent. The material defect rate is first dropped incrementally until it reaches its minimum of 0 percent, while holding the station defect rate constant at six percent. At this point the station defect rate is then incrementally dropped until it reaches its minimum of zero percent. Decreasing the error rate in this fashion, .005 percent at a time, will be referred to as the sequential error rate reduction. The defect rates will also be dropped in the opposite order, allowing one to understand how the order impacts various items of interest. One would assume that the minimum expected production run and error rate will show high degrees of correlation and simultaneously increase or decrease. This effect is encountered, as shown in Figures 6.3 and 6.4. Note that the label for the horizontal axis indicates the order in which the defect rates are dropped. From Figure 6.3, a 12 percent defect rate yields a run time required to meet the 5,000 defect-free MPR of approximately 19.6 weeks. As the material defect rate approaches 0 percent, the run time decreases to approximately 14 weeks, or a reduction of 6.25 weeks. From Figure 6.3 also note that the run time benefits accrued through the reduction of the material defect rate in raw materials is not nearly as dramatic as that found by reducing the station defect rate in Figure 6.4. This effect would be intensified if the number of stations in the system increased relative to the number of stations that input a raw material, simply because when the station defect rate is dropped, it is dropped at each station, and the greater the number of total stations relative to those stations with raw material inputs, the greater the ratio of stations witnessing improvement relative to the whole. Figure 6.4 illustrates similar results for the case where the station defect is dropped to 0 percent first, followed by the material defect rate. Note that a more significant drop in time is realized when the station defect rate is reduced regardless of the order in which the defects rates are dropped.

One would also expect that as the defect rate decreases, the number of defective units produced by a given station should also decrease. Figures 6.5–6.8 illustrate this effect by reducing the material/station defect rates for two different work stations. Figures 6.5 and 6.6 focus on station A which incorporates a raw material, while Figures 6.7 and 6.8 focus on station H, which is simply an assembly station. At station A we observe the effect of both the reduction of the defect rate in the raw material and the reduction of the defect rate at the individual station in Figures 6.5 and 6.6. The error rate drops from a maximum of 12 percent to the minimum of 0 percent, 0.5 percent at a time, with material cost dropped first in Figure 6.5, and second in Figure 6.6. Note that at the maximum total error rate of 12 percent, 770 defective units are produced at station A. Consequently, a total of 5,770 units must be produced to meet the MPR requirement. As the overall defect rate is reduced to 0 percent, the number of defects approaches 0, not surprisingly. However, if the defect rate equals .2 percent, .1 percent for both material and station defect rates, the expected number of defects is still 10 units, necessitating a production run of 5,010 units, or 13 percent less than the run size required to meet the production run requirement at the 12 percent defect rate. Contrast these results to those for station H, shown in Figures 6.7and 6.8. This station is an assembly station which does not introduce a raw material or component part. Note from Figure 6.7 that the reduction in defective units does not vary greatly over the range where the raw material defect rate is dropped from an overall error rate of 12 percent to 6 percent, a result which intuition would suggest. As the station defect rate is subsequently decreased, the number of defective items begins to drop more rapidly. Consequently, assembly stations are not sensitive to changes in the material defect rate, but more sensitive to decreases in the station defect rate, a result which intuition would suggest. A similar analysis for the case where the station defect rate is dropped first may be made using Figure 6.8.

Figures 6.9–6.12 illustrate station utilization, measured per thousand time units that the station is busy as a function of the defect rate. Recall

Figure 6.3
Production Time, Station A (variable material defect rate)

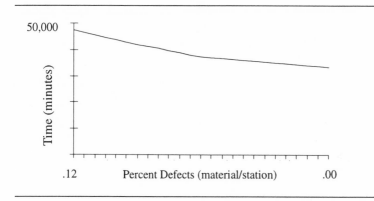

Figure 6.4
Production Time, Station A (variable station defect rate)

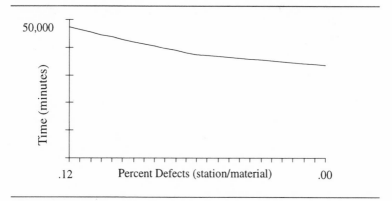

Figure 6.5
Defective Units, Station A (variable material defect rate)

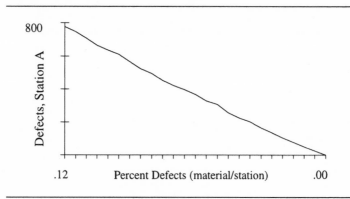

Figure 6.6
Defective Units, Station A (variable station defect rate)

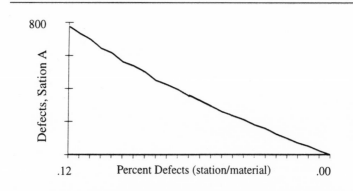

Figure 6.7
Defective Units, Station H (variable material defect rate)

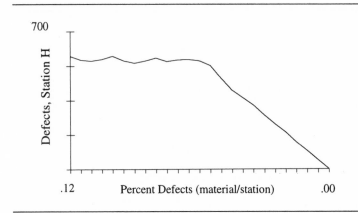

Figure 6.8
Defective Units, Station H (variable station defect rate)

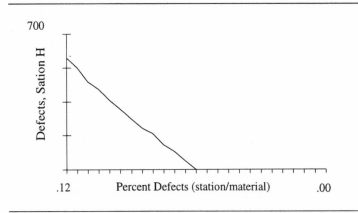

Figure 6.9
Utilization, Station A (variable material defect rate)

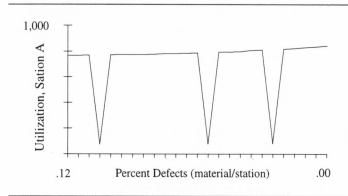

Figure 6.10
Utilization, Station A (variable station defect rate)

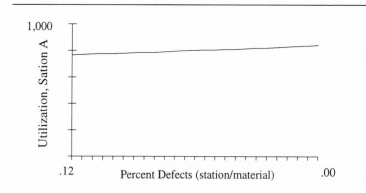

Figure 6.11
Utilization, Station H (variable material defect rate)

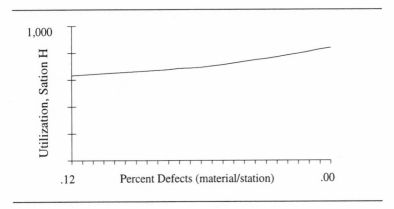

Figure 6.12
Utilization, Station H (variable station defect rate)

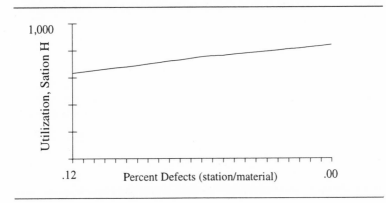

that a work station is only busy when the previously completed unit has been removed by the succeeding station. Defect rates are dropped sequentially. The analysis in Figure 6.9 is applied to station A, a raw material inputting station, since assembly-only stations are not impacted greatly through reduction in the material defect rate. Note that the increase in utilization is modest while the raw material defect rate is decreased, and more dramatic when the production error rate is decreased. The remaining Figures—6.10, 6.11, 6.12—illustrate other results for stations A and H incurred through the decrease in material and station defect rates. In general, why does utilization increase when the defect rate decreases? To understand this, note that as the defect rates decrease, the work stations increase the percentage of defect-free units produced on the first try, consequently decreasing the variability in the time required for a station to complete a defect-free unit. This, in turn, leads to a significant decrease in line-balancing effects, which have a tremendous impact on efficiency and utilization. Hence, station utilization increases as the station defect rate decreases. This result would be more pronounced for a work station which serves as an assembly-only station, such as station H. In this case, station utilization would be expected to be relatively flat as the raw material defect rate decreases, with a sharp increase in utilization as the work station defect rate decreases. Note that even at the minimum overall defect rate utilization is still below 85 percent. This may be due to the nature of the manufacturing system, where bottlenecks occur due to the variability in service times. This has the effect of decreasing the degree of line balancing across stations, suppressing the utilization of stations not located at the bottleneck.

Next the impact of defect rates on cost is considered. In Figures 6.13 and 6.14 costs attributed to defective items are plotted as a function of the defect rates, which are again decreased sequentially, material defect rate in Figure 6.13 and station defect rate in Figure 6.14. Note from Figure 6.13 that the cost decrease, or savings, is most pronounced when the work station defect rate is reduced. This will always be the case since station defects include both the cost of material as well as labor costs. More important to the analysis is the effect of defect rates on total costs. Total costs for the MPR of 5,000 defect-free units are plotted as a function of the overall defect rate in Figures 6.15 and 6.16. Intuitively, decreasing defect rates should have the desirable features of (1) decreasing material costs and (2) increasing utilization, which decreases expected production times and, consequently, decreases labor costs, as well as overhead costs.

Figure 6.13
Cost of Defective Units (variable material defect rate)

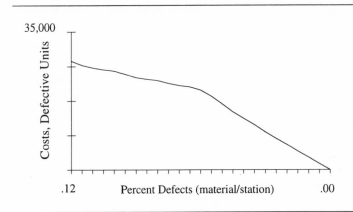

Figure 6.14
Cost of Defective Units (variable station defect rate)

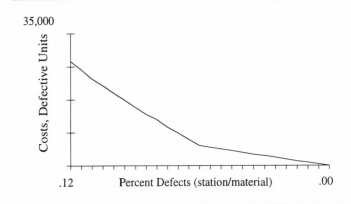

Figure 6.15
Total Cost for 5,000 Units (variable material defect rate)

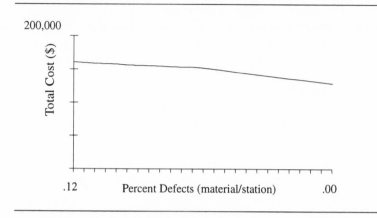

Figure 6.16
Total Cost for 5,000 Units (variable station defect rate)

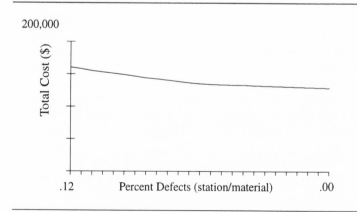

Conclusion: total costs should drop. The simulation results verify this hypothesis. Using Figure 6.15, the cost savings percentage between the maximum error rate of 12 percent and the zero-defect rate is approximately 19.7 percent, with costs ranging from a high of $160,176 to a low of $128,620. Consequently, while it was shown in Chapter 5 that significant benefits accrue regarding output levels and utilization through the implementation of a JIT system, it has been shown here that the impact of defect rates on costs within a JIT system is also significant. In order to successfully implement a JIT system, the goal of zero defects is critical in the reduction of costs. Figure 6.16 illustrates the effect of decreasing the defect rate on cost when the station defect rate is decreased first.

Additional Simulation Results

Simulation can be used to analyze a variety of "what-if" situations. For example, consider maintaining the station defect rate at 0.5 per cent while varying the material defect rate at those stations introducing raw materials from 6 percent to 0 percent, where the rate is changed uniformly across all stations using raw material. The service time distribution is maintained regardless of defect rate. However, assume that material costs are inversely related to the material defect rate, reflecting the standard assumption that higher quality materials carry higher costs. The specific cost/quality tradeoffs used in the simulation are presented in Table 6.2. The percentage cost increases apply to the base costs given earlier in Table 6.1 Simulating, the resulting run time needed to meet the MPR for varying material defect rates is illustrated in Figure 6.17. As expected, Figure 6.17 illustrates how the required production time for 5,000 defect-free widgets appears to drop uniformly as the material defect rate decreases. Savings of 1.48 weeks are realized when the material defect rate varies between its upper and lower extreme. Whether this savings is sufficient to warrant the additional expenditure for higher quality materials is a policy question which is now addressed.

To assess the viability of obtaining these higher quality raw materials involves determining the overall change in costs due to decreasing the material defect rate. When material costs were held constant, it was shown that total costs drop. When the new increasing material costs are considered one sees from Figure 6.18 that overall costs attributable to defective units decline as the material defect rate is decreased. Costs range from a high of $10,361 at the maximum material defect rate to a low of $3,321 at the

Table 6.2
Cost/Quality Tradeoffs

Percentage Material Defect	Percentage Cost Increase
6.0	0
5.5	5
5.0	10
4.5	15
4.0	20
3.5	25
3.0	30
2.5	35
2.0	40
1.5	45
1.0	50
0.5	55

minimum material defect rate. A similar effect is realized when considering dropping the station defect rate while fixing the material defect rate at .06. This is illustrated in Figure 6.19. Despite the fact that a cost savings is achieved in defective unit costs, Figure 6.20 shows that a decrease in material percent defects actually increases the per unit cost in production.

Regarding total costs, Figure 6.21 illustrates that total costs increase when the material defect rate decreases. In other words, labor and overhead costs increase as the material defect rate drops. Note that it is possible that the total cost of materials may also drop, since less materials will be needed to reach the MPR when lower defect rates are encountered. This result could be reversed depending on the relationship and the magnitudes of material, labor, and overhead costs. Needless to say, even if total costs increase as the material defect rate declines, these additional costs could still be offset due to the decrease in future payouts for warranty claims. Recall that although it is assumed that no defective units exist in the system, unless work stations are 100 percent reliable in their quality inspection, there exists a small, but significant probability that some defective units will reach the consumer. Clearly, as the defect rates drop, the associated probability and percentage of defective units reaching the

Figure 6.17
Time to Produce 5,000 Units (variable material defect rate)

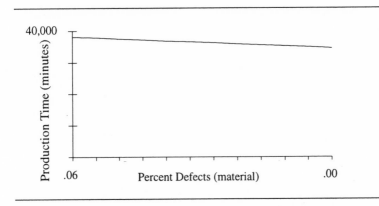

Figure 6.18
Total Cost of Defective Units (variable material defect rate)

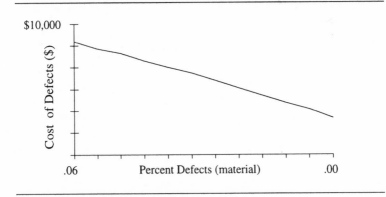

Figure 6.19
Total Cost of Defective Units (variable station defect rate)

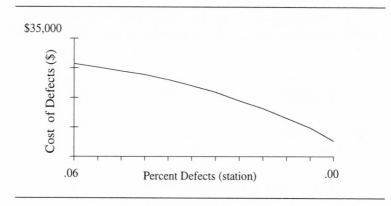

Figure 6.20
Per Unit Cost of Production (variable material cost)

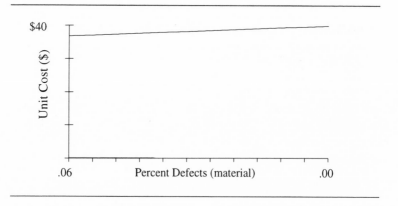

Figure 6.21
Total Cost to Produce 5,000 Units

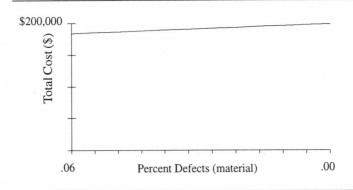

consumer also drop. Finally, in Table 6.3, note the relatively small change in utilization for various work stations as the material defect rate declines. This is consistent with the results shown in Table 5.5 in Chapter 5.

Consider now a second illustrative example in which the material defect rate is held constant at 0.5 percent while the station defect rate at the work stations is varied uniformly across all stations. Assume that as the station defect rate decreases the corresponding mean completion time at the work station increases, which is typical of JIT systems, while the variance for service time decreases. This would be attributable to the worker taking more time to perform his or her tasks with greater precision. Specifically, for the simulation at hand, consider the tradeoffs as described in Table 6.4.

The expected consequences of this change are twofold. First, one would expect that the mean completion time per unit would increase as the station defect rate decreases. This, in turn, increases the expected time to manufacture the MPR of 5,000 defect-free units, and is verified through simulation, as illustrated in Figure 6.22. Note that although results from Chapter 5 illustrated that decreasing the defect rate increased output, that result was obtained without changing the service time distribution. For this case, each decrease in the defect rate increases the mean service time. More specifically, the total increase in the expected production time for 5,000 units ranges from 43,442 to 67,220 minutes as the defect rate is dropped over the applicable range. Regarding costs, one would anticipate that the defective-units cost will decrease as the station defect rate decreases. Simulation results support this contention and are shown in Figure 6.23.

Table 6.3
Utilization of Work Stations versus Percent Material Defect Rate

Station	Percent Material Defects										
	0.060	0.055	0.050	0.045	0.040	0.035	0.030	0.025	0.020	0.015
A	0.796	0.797	0.795	0.798	0.800	0.803	0.805	0.809	0.811	0.817
B	0.800	0.800	0.796	0.798	0.801	0.804	0.805	0.809	0.813	0.815
C	0.798	0.798	0.795	0.800	0.800	0.803	0.806	0.808	0.810	0.815
D	0.751	0.751	0.752	0.758	0.764	0.771	0.778	0.785	0.791	0.799
E	0.799	0.799	0.797	0.797	0.802	0.802	0.808	0.810	0.812	0.814
F	0.799	0.799	0.797	0.797	0.802	0.804	0.806	0.809	0.813	0.815
G	0.749	0.749	0.752	0.756	0.764	0.771	0.778	0.784	0.791	0.798
H	0.746	0.746	0.748	0.754	0.761	0.764	0.773	0.780	0.786	0.795

Table 6.4
Defect Rate/Completion Time Information

Station Defect Rate	Range for Completion Time at Work Station
6.0	[1.0, 8.0]
5.5	[2.0, 8.5]
5.0	[3.0, 9.0]
4.5	[4.0, 9.5]
4.0	[5.0, 10.0]
3.5	[6.0, 10.5]
3.0	[7.0, 11.0]
2.5	[8.0, 11.5]
2.0	[9.0, 12.0]
1.5	[10.0, 12.5]
1.0	[11.0, 13.0]
0.5	[11.5, 13.0]

As in the prior analysis, where the production rate was constant and the material costs were changed, the overall cost per unit has increased, attributable to the increased labor and overhead costs associated with the greater mean service time, as shown in Figure 6.24. Consequently, the reduction in the station defect rate at the work stations may not be justifiable. Note from Figure 6.24 that the per unit cost has nearly doubled as the defect rate drops to the value of 0.5 percent. Although higher precision, in terms of lower variance, may decrease the total labor time required to reach the MPR of 5,000 units, this savings may or may not be offset by the increased labor costs incurred through the increase in service time per unit to ensure higher precision. Again, the extent of this cost increase/decrease is a function of the magnitude of and the relationship between the hourly costs and the increased service time for various degrees of precision. In addition, the effect on demand and profits has not been examined. One would need to consider these issues in determining the level of quality (in terms of production and material defect rates) which is optimal.

Figure 6.22
Time to Produce 5,000 Units

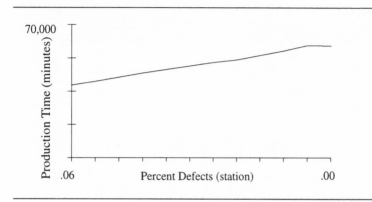

Figure 6.23
Total Cost of Defective Units

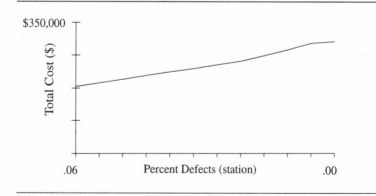

Figure 6.24
Per Unit Cost of Production

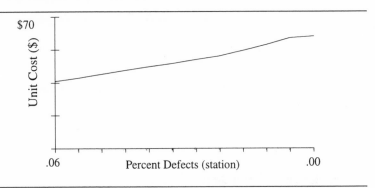

FINAL COMMENTS

The reduction of defects in both raw materials/component parts and production has a dramatic impact on the overall costs associated with the manufacture of a particular product. The effect is easily observed through simulation.

The illustrations provided only touch upon the multitude of alternatives which can be investigated through simulation. The value of scrap, the impact of allowing a part to be reworked, the input of market conditions and demand forecasts all represent avenues of investigation which can be pursued. In general, simulation is limited only by the imagination and the blocks to creativity of the user himself. Models can be established which are highly interactive and provide immediate feedback to the user. Sensitivity analysis, and the pursuit of "what-if" scenarios can be examined with minimal redesign, increasing the attractiveness of the simulating environment. Further, more mathematically intractable models can be investigated.

Despite the fact that many of the conclusions drawn from simulations cannot be verified mathematically with absolute certainty, increases in technology allow for a tremendous volume of runs to be performed, resulting in high levels of confidence in those cases where repetitive runs lead to reinforcing results regarding hypotheses. Hence, simulation should be considered as a viable and potentially invaluable tool in the design and evaluation for any manufacturing process which cannot be solved through standard analytic techniques.

Appendix 6.1
Defect Differences and Total Cost Determination

Consecutive differences of the number of defects for Station A for the initial sequential decreasing of the defect rates:

31, 38, 43, 28, 26, 44, 45, 28, 42, 32, 24, 30, 39, 20, 50, 32, 24, 37, 27, 32, 26, 28, 26, 26

Consecutive differences of the number of defects for Station A for the reverse sequential decreasing of the defect rates:

44, 37, 54, 29, 53, 24, 35, 52, 25, 31, 40, 28, 31, 34, 27, 23, 31, 20, 34, 26, 28, 20, 27, 24

Calculation for Total Cost

First recall that the average time to produce a part at each station was 5.57 minutes.

$$TC = \left\{ \frac{(5.57)(12)(3)}{60}.8 + [7.9 + 7.9\%] \right\} 5{,}000 + \text{defect cost}$$

The total cost equation is similar for the second experiment but the term is omitted and the 5.57 is changed at each successive step (5.57, 6.03, 6.55, 7.07, 7.60, 8.12, 8.70, 9.27, 10.05, 10.92, 11.90, 12.30).

Appendix 6.2
Simulation Code

```
SIMULATE
   UNLIST
   NOXREF
   REALLOCATE COM,550000
******************************************************************************
*  SOME HOUSE KEEPING INFORMATION FOR FUNCTIONS AND VARIABLES
******************************************************************************
MACHA FUNCTION  RN1,C4              ;PROCESSING TIME MACHINE A
0,11.5/.3,12/.6,12.5/1.0,13
MACHC FUNCTION  RN1,C4              ;PROCESSING TIME MACHINE C
0,11.5/.3,12/.6,12.5/1.0,13
MACHD FUNCTION  RN1,C4              ;PROCESSING TIME MACHINE D
0,11.5/.3,12/.6,12.5/1.0,13
MACHB FUNCTION  RN1,C4              ;PROCESSING TIME MACHINE B
0,11.5/.3,12/.6,12.5/1.0,13
MACHE FUNCTION  RN1,C4              ;PROCESSING TIME MACHINE E
0,11.5/.3,12/.6,12.5/1.0,13
MACHF FUNCTION  RN1,C4              ;PROCESSING TIME MACHINE F
0,11.5/.3,12/.6,12.5/1.0,13
MACHG FUNCTION  RN1,C4              ;PROCESSING TIME MACHINE G
0,11.5/.3,12/.6,12.5/1.0,13
MACHH FUNCTION  RN1,C4              ;PROCESSING TIME MACHINE H
0,11.5/.3,12/.6,12.5/1.0,13
MACHA FVARIABLE (((FT(MACHA)*1200)/60)*3)+60 +(60*.55))
MACHC FVARIABLE (((FT(MACHC)*1200)/60)*3)+300 +(300*.55))
MACHD FVARIABLE (((FT(MACHD)*1200)/60)*3)+120 +(120*.55))
MACAB FVARIABLE (((FT(MACHB)*1200)/60)*3)
MACHB FVARIABLE V(MACAB)+V(MACHA)+V(MACHC)+V(MACHD)
MACHE FVARIABLE (((FT(MACHE)*1200)/60)*3)+180 +(180*.55))
MACHF FVARIABLE (((FT(MACHF)*1200)/60)*3)+130 +(130*.55))
MACAG FVARIABLE (((FT(MACHG)*1200)/60)*3)
MACHG FVARIABLE V(MACAG)+V(MACHE)+V(MACHF)
MACAH FVARIABLE (((FT(MACHH)*1200)/60)*3)
MACHH FVARIABLE V(MACAH)+V(MACHB)+V(MACHG)
PCTDA FVARIABLE 10000*N(DUMP1)/FC(MACHA)
PCTDC FVARIABLE 10000*N(DUMP2)/FC(MACHC)
```

```
PCTDD  FVARIABLE  10000*N(DUMP3)/FC(MACHD)
PCTDB  FVARIABLE  10000*N(DUMP4)/FC(MACHB)
PCTDE  FVARIABLE  10000*N(DUMP5)/FC(MACHE)
PCTDF  FVARIABLE  10000*N(DUMP6)/FC(MACHF)
PCTDG  FVARIABLE  10000*N(DUMP7)/FC(MACHG)
PCTDH  FVARIABLE  10000*N(DUMP8)/FC(MACHH)
1      MATRIX  X,9,6
*******************************************************************************
* INITIALIATION OF THE MACHINES
*******************************************************************************
       GENERATE  ,,,1              ;CREATES A MASTER TRANSACTION
       ASSIGN  1,1                 ;SETS UP PARAMETER FOR SPLIT
       SPLIT  P1,RED1              ;SENDS RAW MATERIAL TO MACH A
       SPLIT  P1,RED2              ;SENDS RAW MATERIAL TO MACH C
       SPLIT  P1,RED3              ;SENDS RAW MATERIAL TO MACH D
       SPLIT  P1,RED4              ;SENDS RAW MATERIAL TO MACH E
       SPLIT  P1,RED5              ;SENDS RAW MATERIAL TO MACH F
       TERMINATE                   ;DUMPS THE TRANSACTION
*******************************************************************************
* MAIN PORTION OF THE JUST-IN-TIME MODEL        *
* ALL MACHINES HAVE DEFECTS AT AN 0.005 LEVEL AND MATERIAL WILL
* BE REDUCED FROM 0.06 TO 0.005 BY 0.005 PERCENT AT A TIME
* (THEN MATERIAL WILL BE 0.005 AND THE MACHINE WILL BE REDUCED
* FROM 0.06 TO 0.005 IN INCREMENTS OF 0.005 WHILE THE TIME TO
* PRODUCE THE PRODUCT IS NARROWED AND INCREASED.)
*******************************************************************************
RED1   QUEUE  WAITA               ;GETS IN LINE FOR MACHINE A
       GATE LR  AMACH             ;SET UP GATE FOR IDLE
       SEIZE  MACHA               ;MACHINE IS AVAILABLE FOR USE
       DEPART  WAITA              ;GETS OUT OF THE WAITING LINE
       ADVANCE  FN$MACHA          ;TIME TO DO THE WORK
       RELEASE  MACHA             ;MACHINE IS AVAILABLE
       TEST NE  Q$WAITA,0,GRN1    ;ARE THERE 2 LEFT IN BIN?
GRN3   TRANSFER  .01,,DUMP1       ;REMOVE BAD MATERIAL
       TEST NE  CH$MACH1,1,BLU1   ;HAVE 30 BEEN COLLECTED?
BLU2   LINK  MACH1,FIFO           ;HOLD TILL PALLET IS FILLED
BLU1   LOGIC S  AMACH             ;CLOSE IDLE GATE
       GATE LR  MACHA             ;OPEN GATE FOR UNITS TO B
       UNLINK  MACH1,WHT1,ALL     ;SENDS PIECES TO MACHINE B
```

```
        LOGIC S  MACHA            ;CLOSE THE GATE FOR NEXT TRIP
        LOGIC R  AMACH            ;OPEN THE IDEL GATE
        TRANSFER  ,BLU2           ;SENDS PART TO NEXT PALLET
GRN1 SPLIT  1,RED1               ;SEND IN THIRTY MORE ITEMS
        TRANSFER  ,GRN3           ;SEND BACK TO THE MAIN FLOW
RED2 QUEUE  WAITC                ;GETS IN LINE FOR MACHINE C
        GATE LR  CMACH            ;SET UP GATE FOR IDLE
        SEIZE  MACHC              ;MACHINE IS AVAILABLE FOR USE
        DEPART  WAITC             ;GETS OUT OF THE WAITING LINE
        ADVANCE  FN$MACHC         ;TIME TO DO THE WORK
        RELEASE  MACHC            ;MACHINE IS AVAILABLE
        TEST NE  Q$WAITC,0,GRN4   ;ARE THERE 2 LEFT IN BIN?
GRN6 TRANSFER  .01,,DUMP2        ;REMOVE BAD MATERIAL
        TEST NE  CH$MACH2,1,BLU3  ;HAVE 30 BEEN COLLECTED?
BLU4 LINK   MACH2,FIFO           ;HOLD TILL PALLET IS FILLED
BLU3 LOGIC S  CMACH              ;CLOSE IDLE GATE
        GATE LR  MACHC            ;OPEN GATE FOR UNITS TO B
        UNLINK   MACH2,WHT2,ALL   ;SENDS PIECES TO MACHINE B
        LOGIC S  MACHC            ;CLOSE THE GATE FOR NEXT TRIP
        LOGIC R  CMACH            ;OPEN THE IDEL GATE
        TRANSFER  ,BLU4           ;SENDS PART TO NEXT PALLET
GRN4 SPLIT  1,RED2               ;SEND IN THIRTY MORE ITEMS
        TRANSFER  ,GRN6           ;SEND BACK TO THE MAIN FLOW
RED3 QUEUE  WAITD                GETS IN LINE FOR MACHINE C
        GATE LR  DMACH            ;SET UP GATE FOR IDLE
        SEIZE  MACHD              ;MACHINE IS AVAILABLE FOR USE
        DEPART  WAITD             GETS OUT OF THE WAITING LINE
        ADVANCE  FN$MACHD         TIME TO DO THE WORK
        RELEASE  MACHD            MACHINE IS AVAILABLE
        TEST NE  Q$WAITD,0,GRN7   ARE THERE 2 LEFT IN BIN?
GRN9 TRANSFER  .01,,DUMP3        REMOVE BAD MATERIAL
        TEST NE  CH$MACH3,1,BLU5  HAVE 30 BEEN COLLECTED?
BLU6 LINK   MACH3,FIFO           HOLD TILL PALLET IS FILLED
BLU5 LOGIC S  DMACH              CLOSE IDLE GATE
        GATE LR  MACHD            ;OPEN GATE FOR UNITS TO B
        UNLINK   MACH3,WHT3,ALL   ;SENDS PIECES TO MACHINE B
        LOGIC S  MACHD            ;CLOSE THE GATE FOR NEXT TRIP
        LOGIC R  DMACH            ;OPEN THE IDEL GATE
        TRANSFER  ,BLU6           ;SENDS PART TO NEXT PALLET
```

```
GRN7  SPLIT  1,RED3              ;SEND IN THIRTY MORE ITEMS
      TRANSFER  ,GRN9            ;SEND BACK TO THE MAIN FLOW
WHT1  QUEUE  SUBA               ;GET IN LINE FOR ASSEMBLY
ADONE MATCH  CDONE              ;IS PART C DONE?
      DEPART  SUBA              ;GET OUT OF THE LINE
      TRANSFER  ,PUR1           ;SEND TO ASSEMBLY
WHT2  QUEUE  SUBC               ;GET IN LINE FOR ASSEMBLY
CDONE MATCH  ADONE              ;IS PART C DONE?
      DEPART  SUBC              ;GET OUT OF THE LINE
PUR1  ASSEMBLE  2              ;COMBINES THE TWO PARTS
ACDNE MATCH  DDONE              ;IS PART D DONE?
      TRANSFER  ,PUR2           ;SEND TO ASSEMBLY
WHT3  QUEUE  SUBD               GET IN LINE FOR ASSEMBLY
DDONE MATCH  ACDNE              ;ARE PARTS A AND C DONE?
      DEPART  SUBD              ;GET OUT OF LINE
PUR2  ASSEMBLE  2              ;COMBINES THE THREE PARTS
      QUEUE  WAITB              ;GETS IN LINE FOR MACHINE C
      GATE LR  BMACH            ;SETS UP IDLE GATE
      SEIZE  MACHB              ;MACHINE IS AVAILABLE FOR USE
      DEPART  WAITB             ;GETS OUT OF THE WAITING LINE
      ADVANCE  FN$MACHB         ;TIME TO DO THE WORK
      RELEASE  MACHB            ;MACHINE IS AVAILABLE
      TEST NE  Q(WAITB),0,ONX1  ;ARE PARTS NEEDED?
ONX2  TRANSFER  .005,,DUMP4     ;REMOVE BAD MATERIAL
      TEST NE  CH$MACH4,1,BLU7  ;HAVE 30 BEEN COLLECTED?
BLU8  LINK  MACH4,FIFO          ;HOLD TIL PALLET IS FILLED
BLU7  LOGIC S  BMACH            ;CLOSE THE IDLE GATE
      GATE LR  MACHB            ;IS THE SUPPLY GATE OPEN?
      UNLINK  MACH4,WHT6,ALL     ;SENDS PIECES TO MACHINE G
      LOGIC S  MACHB            ;CLOSE THE SUPPLY GATE
      LOGIC R  BMACH            OPEN THE IDLE GATE
      TRANSFER  ,BLU8           ;SENDS PART TO NEXT PALLET
ONX1  LOGIC R  MACHA            ;OPEN GATE FOR MACHINE A PARTS
      LOGIC R  MACHC            ;OPEN GATE FOR MACHINE C PARTS
      LOGIC R  MACHD            ;OPEN GATE FOR MACHINE D PARTS
      TRANSFER  ,ONX2           ;SEND BACK TO COMPLETE PROCESS
WHT6  QUEUE  SUBB               ;GET IN LINE FOR PART G
BDONE MATCH  GDONE              IS PART G READY?
      DEPART  SUBB              ;GET OUT OF THE LINE
```

```
        TRANSFER  ,PUR4              ;TRANSFER TO MESH WITH PART G
RED4 QUEUE  WAITE                    ;GETS IN LINE FOR MACHINE E
     GATE LR  EMACH                  ;SET UP AN IDLE GATE
     SEIZE  MACHE                    ;MACHINE IS AVAILABLE FOR USE
     DEPART  WAITE                   ;GETS OUT OF THE WAITING LINE
     ADVANCE FN$MACHE                ;TIME TO DO THE WORK
     RELEASE  MACHE                  ;MACHINE IS AVAILABLE
     TEST NE  Q$WAITE,0,GRN13        ;ARE THERE 2 LEFT IN BIN?
GRN15 TRANSFER  .01,,DUMP5           ;REMOVE BAD MATERIAL
     TEST NE  CH$MACH5,1,BLU13       ;HAVE 30 BEEN COLLECTED?
BLU14 LINK   MACH5,FIFO              ;HOLD TILL PALLET IS FILLED
BLU13 LOGIC S  EMACH                 ;CLOSE IDLE GATE
     GATE LR  MACHE                  ;OPEN GATE FOR UNITS TO B
     UNLINK   MACH5,WHT7,ALL         ;SENDS PIECES TO MACHINE G
     LOGIC S  MACHE                  ;CLOSE THE GATE FOR NEXT TRIP
     LOGIC R  EMACH                  ;OPEN THE IDEL GATE
     TRANSFER  ,BLU14                ;SENDS PART TO NEXT PALLET
GRN13 SPLIT   1,RED4                 ;SEND IN THIRTY MORE ITEMS
     TRANSFER  ,GRN15                ;SEND BACK TO THE MAIN FLOW
RED5 QUEUE  WAITF                    ;GETS IN LINE FOR MACHINE F
     GATE LR  FMACH                  ;SET UP AN IDLE GATE
     SEIZE  MACHF                    ;MACHINE IS AVAILABLE FOR USE
     DEPART  WAITF                   ;GETS OUT OF THE WAITING LINE
     ADVANCE FN$MACHF                ;TIME TO DO THE WORK
     RELEASE  MACHF                  ;MACHINE IS AVAILABLE
     TEST NE  Q$WAITF,0,GRN16        ;ARE THERE 2 LEFT IN BIN?
GRN18 TRANSFER  .01,,DUMP6           ;REMOVE BAD MATERIAL
     TEST NE  CH$MACH6,1,BLU15       ;HAVE 30 BEEN COLLECTED?
BLU16 LINK   MACH6,FIFO              ;HOLD TILL PALLET IS FILLED
BLU15 LOGIC S  FMACH                 ;CLOSE IDLE GATE
     GATE LR  MACHF                  ;OPEN GATE FOR UNITS TO B
     UNLINK   MACH6,WHT8,ALL         ;SENDS PIECES TO MACHINE G
     LOGIC S  MACHF                  ;CLOSE THE GATE FOR NEXT TRIP
     LOGIC R  FMACH                  ;OPEN THE IDEL GATE
     TRANSFER  ,BLU16                ;SENDS PART TO NEXT PALLET
GRN16 SPLIT   1,RED5                 ;SEND IN THIRTY MORE ITEMS
     TRANSFER  ,GRN18                ;SEND BACK TO THE MAIN FLOW
WHT7 QUEUE  SUBE                     ;GET IN LINE FOR ASSEMBLY
EDONE MATCH  FDONE                   ;IS PART C DONE?
```

```
        DEPART   SUBE              ;GET OUT OF THE LINE
        TRANSFER  ,PUR3            ;SEND TO ASSEMBLY
WHT8  QUEUE  SUBF                  ;GET IN LINE FOR ASSEMBLY
FDONE MATCH  EDONE                 ;IS PART C DONE?
        DEPART  SUBF               ;GET OUT OF THE LINE
PUR3  ASSEMBLE  2                  ;COMBINES THE TWO PARTS
        QUEUE  WAITG               ;GETS IN LINE FOR MACHINE C
        GATE LR  GMACH             ;SETS UP IDLE GATE
        SEIZE  MACHG               ;MACHINE IS AVAILABLE FOR USE
        DEPART  WAITG              ;GETS OUT OF THE WAITING LINE
        ADVANCE  FN$MACHG          ;TIME TO DO THE WORK
        RELEASE  MACHG             ;MACHINE IS AVAILABLE
        TEST NE  Q(WAITG),0,ONX3   ;ARE PARTS NEEDED?
ONX4  TRANSFER  .005,,DUMP7        ;REMOVE BAD MATERIAL
        TEST NE  CH$MACH7,1,BLU17  ;HAVE 30 BEEN COLLECTED?
BLU18 LINK   MACH7,FIFO           ;HOLD TIL PALLET IS FILLED
BLU17 LOGIC S  GMACH              ;CLOSE THE IDLE GATE
        GATE LR  MACHG             ;IS THE SUPPLY GATE OPEN?
        UNLINK   MACH7,WHT9,ALL    ;SENDS PIECES TO MACHINE G
        LOGIC S  MACHG             ;CLOSE THE SUPPLY GATE
        LOGIC R  GMACH             ;OPEN THE IDLE GATE
        TRANSFER  ,BLU18           ;SENDS PART TO NEXT PALLET
ONX3  LOGIC R  MACHE              ;OPEN GATE FOR MACHINE A PARTS
        LOGIC R  MACHF             ;OPEN GATE FOR MACHINE C PARTS
        TRANSFER  ,ONX4            ;SEND BACK TO COMPLETE PROCESS
WHT9  QUEUE  SUBG                  ;GET IN LINE FOR PART B
GDONE MATCH  BDONE                 ;IS PART D DONE?
        DEPART  SUBG               ;GET OUT OF LINE
PUR4  ASSEMBLE  2                  ;COMBINES PARTS B AND G
        QUEUE  WAITH               ;GETS IN LINE FOR MACHINE C
        GATE LR  HMACH             ;SETS UP IDLE GATE
        SEIZE  MACHH               ;MACHINE IS AVAILABLE FOR USE
        DEPART  WAITH              ;GETS OUT OF THE WAITING LINE
        ADVANCE  FN$MACHH          ;TIME TO DO THE WORK
        RELEASE  MACHH             ;MACHINE IS AVAILABLE
        TEST NE  Q(WAITH),0,ONX5   ;ARE PARTS NEEDED?
ONX6  TRANSFER  .005,,DUMP8        ;REMOVE BAD MATERIAL
        TEST NE  CH$MACH8,1,BLU19  ;HAVE 30 BEEN COLLECTED?
BLU20 LINK   MACH8,FIFO           ;HOLD TIL PALLET IS FILLED
```

```
BLU19 LOGIC S  HMACH              ;CLOSE THE IDLE GATE
      GATE LR  MACHH              ;IS THE SUPPLY GATE OPEN?
      UNLINK   MACH8,WHT10,ALL    ;SENDS PIECES TO MACHINE G
      LOGIC S  MACHH              ;CLOSE THE SUPPLY GATE
      LOGIC R  HMACH              ;OPEN THE IDLE GATE
      TRANSFER ,BLU20             ;SENDS PART TO NEXT PALLET
ONX5  LOGIC R  MACHG              ;OPEN GATE FOR MACHINE A PARTS
      LOGIC R  MACHB              ;OPEN GATE FOR MACHINE C PARTS
      TRANSFER ,ONX6              ;SEND BACK TO COMPLETE PROCESS
WHT10 LOGIC R  MACHH              ;OPEN THE GATE FOE MORE PARTS
      TEST E   N(WHT10),5000,WHT11 ;DUMP ALL BUT THE LAST ONE
      MSAVEVALUE 1,1,3,FR(MACHA),MX
      MSAVEVALUE 1,1,4,FC(MACHA),MX
      MSAVEVALUE 1,1,5,(FT(MACHA)*1000),MX
      MSAVEVALUE 1,1,6,V(PCTDA),MX
      MSAVEVALUE 1,9,3,C1,MX
      MSAVEVALUE 1,2,3,FR(MACHC),MX
      MSAVEVALUE 1,2,4,FC(MACHC),MX
      MSAVEVALUE 1,2,5,(FT(MACHC)*1000),MX
      MSAVEVALUE 1,2,6,V(PCTDC),MX
      MSAVEVALUE 1,3,3,FR(MACHD),MX
      MSAVEVALUE 1,3,4,FC(MACHD),MX
      MSAVEVALUE 1,3,5,(FT(MACHD)*1000),MX
      MSAVEVALUE 1,3,6,V(PCTDD),MX
      MSAVEVALUE 1,4,3,FR(MACHB),MX
      MSAVEVALUE 1,4,4,FC(MACHB),MX
      MSAVEVALUE 1,4,5,(FT(MACHB)*1000),MX
      MSAVEVALUE 1,4,6,V(PCTDB),MX
      MSAVEVALUE 1,5,3,FR(MACHE),MX
      MSAVEVALUE 1,5,4,FC(MACHE),MX
      MSAVEVALUE 1,5,5,(FT(MACHE)*1000),MX
      MSAVEVALUE 1,5,6,V(PCTDE),MX
      MSAVEVALUE 1,6,3,FR(MACHF),MX
      MSAVEVALUE 1,6,4,FC(MACHF),MX
      MSAVEVALUE 1,6,5,(FT(MACHF)*1000),MX
      MSAVEVALUE 1,6,6,V(PCTDF),MX
      MSAVEVALUE 1,7,3,FR(MACHG),MX
      MSAVEVALUE 1,7,4,FC(MACHG),MX
      MSAVEVALUE 1,7,5,(FT(MACHG)*1000),MX
```

```
         MSAVEVALUE  1,7,6,V(PCTDG),MX
         MSAVEVALUE  1,8,3,FR(MACHH),MX
         MSAVEVALUE  1,8,4,FC(MACHH),MX
         MSAVEVALUE  1,8,5,(FT(MACHH)*1000),MX
         MSAVEVALUE  1,8,6,V(PCTDH),MX
         TERMINATE  1                       ;COUNT THE COMPLETED PARTS
WHT11  TERMINATE
DUMP1  ASSIGN   1,V(MACHA),H               ;PICKS UP COST OF DEFECT AT A
         MSAVEVALUE  1+,1,1,PH1,MX          :RECORDS COST OF DEFECT
         MSAVEVALUE  1+,1,2,1,MX            :ADDS TO TOTAL DEFECT COUNT
         MSAVEVALUE  1+,9,1,PH1,MX          :ADDS TO TOTAL DEFECT COST
         TERMINATE                          ;DUMP FROM MACHINE A
DUMP2  ASSIGN   1,V(MACHC),H               ;PICKS UP COST OF DEFECT AT C
         MSAVEVALUE  1+,2,1,PH1,MX          :RECORDS COST OF DEFECT
         MSAVEVALUE  1+,2,2,1,MX            :ADDS TO TOTAL DEFECT COUNT
         MSAVEVALUE  1+,9,1,PH1,MX          :ADDS TO TOTAL DEFECT COST
         TERMINATE                          ;DUMP FROM MACHINE C
DUMP3  ASSIGN   1,V(MACHD),H               ;PICKS UP COST OF DEFECT AT D
         MSAVEVALUE  1+,3,1,PH1,MX          :RECORDS COST OF DEFECT
         MSAVEVALUE  1+,3,2,1,MX            :ADDS TO TOTAL DEFECT COUNT
         MSAVEVALUE  1+,9,1,PH1,MX          :ADDS TO TOTAL DEFECT COST
         TERMINATE                          ;DUMP FROM MACHINE D
DUMP4  ASSIGN   1,V(MACHB),H               ;PICKS UP COST OF DEFECT AT B
         MSAVEVALUE  1+,4,1,PH1,MX          :RECORDS COST OF DEFECT
         MSAVEVALUE  1+,4,2,1,MX            :ADDS TO TOTAL DEFECT COUNT
         MSAVEVALUE  1+,9,1,PH1,MX          :ADDS TO TOTAL DEFECT COST
         TERMINATE                          ;DUMP FROM MACHINE B
DUMP5  ASSIGN   1,V(MACHE),H               ;PICKS UP COST OF DEFECT AT E
         MSAVEVALUE  1+,5,1,PH1,MX          :RECORDS COST OF DEFECT
         MSAVEVALUE  1+,5,2,1,MX            :ADDS TO TOTAL DEFECT COUNT
         MSAVEVALUE  1+,9,1,PH1,MX          :ADDS TO TOTAL DEFECT COST
         TERMINATE                          ;DUMP FROM MACHINE B
DUMP6  ASSIGN   1,V(MACHF),H               ;PICKS UP COST OF DEFECT AT F
         MSAVEVALUE  1+,6,1,PH1,MX          :RECORDS COST OF DEFECT
         MSAVEVALUE  1+,6,2,1,MX            :ADDS TO TOTAL DEFECT COUNT
         MSAVEVALUE  1+,9,1,PH1,MX          :ADDS TO TOTAL DEFECT COST
         TERMINATE                          ;DUMP FROM MACHINE B
DUMP7  ASSIGN   1,V(MACHG),H               ;PICKS UP COST OF DEFECT AT G
         MSAVEVALUE  1+,7,1,PH1,MX          :RECORDS COST OF DEFECT
```

```
      MSAVEVALUE  1+,7,2,1,MX        :ADDS TO TOTAL DEFECT COUNT
      MSAVEVALUE  1+,9,1,PH1,MX      :ADDS TO TOTAL DEFECT COST
      TERMINATE                      ;DUMP FROM MACHINE B
DUMP8 ASSIGN   1,V(MACHH),H          ;PICKS UP COST OF DEFECT AT H
      MSAVEVALUE  1+,8,1,PH1,MX      :RECORDS COST OF DEFECT
      MSAVEVALUE  1+,8,2,1,MX        :ADDS TO TOTAL DEFECT COUNT
      MSAVEVALUE  1+,9,1,PH1,MX      :ADDS TO TOTAL DEFECT COST
      TERMINATE                      ;DUMP FROM MACHINE B
      START  1
      END
```

7

Modeling
Jobshop Operations

The concept of scheduling generally has to do with any production or service process in which tasks are assigned to one of various workstations in accordance with a set of rules, in order to pursue the best that can be achieved in terms of efficient throughput and cost-effective use of resources. This concept distinguishes between continuous process or flow control systems, such as an assembly line, and intermittent process or order control systems where discrete jobs can be identified as they move through the system. Obviously, the second type of process is also the type which is frequently called a jobshop, and jobshop scheduling pertains to this domain of operations.

Jobshop operations are typically smaller in scale than continuous process operations. Probably in the vast majority of cases a jobshop scale and approach is chosen either because of the limits of the entrepreneur's resources or the specialization of the market, with a tendency toward requests for highly customized products on short notice and a customer's willingness to pay for the implied higher costs per unit (service processes should be managed in the same effective manner).

This chapter confines itself to a manufacturing operation, albeit on a very general level. The principles of simulation explored here can easily be extended to other domains of jobshop operation.

JOBSHOP SCHEDULING

Large Japanese manufacturing concerns, famous for just-in-time control systems that certainly fall totally in the continuous process category, nonetheless typically outsource a great deal of their parts production to small suppliers of the jobshop variety. The larger manufacturing concern shows little care that the supplier works in a jobshop environment, just so long as the supplied part is a total quality product and supplied when the manufacturer needs it (and not before that). In this just-in-time overall environment the smaller supplier must absorb whatever costs are involved if the product must be produced early and temporarily held in order to avoid being late with deliveries. Effective jobshop scheduling techniques can reduce these costs for the jobshop supplier, whether the customer is a large manufacturer or an individual.

One state-of-the-art environment in which jobshop scheduling is highly relevant is the management of the virtual organization. Through the powerful and user friendly channels of today's data communications technology, including the Internet and the World Wide Web, as well as dedicated and strictly proprietary networks, a growing volume of business is being conducted without the traditional grouping of persons in the same office buildings, factories, warehouses, and loading docks. Marketing, supplies, secretarial support, and information processing are among the many services now being both managed and provided by third-party providers. Innovative businesses can already attract hundreds of thousands of potential customers over the Internet and World Wide Web, and at least one university in the United States is operating primarily in an electronic environment.

Jobshop scheduling will be highly relevant to many of these cutting edge, evolving ways of doing business. At least for the next few years, with very small overhead investments for such businesses, it may be very profitable to market a special order approach; it is easy to visualize the use of a jobshop type of scheduling to manage operatives performing delivery, stocking, and service at a number of remote customer sites.

Moreover, just as there are still approximately eighty-five billion lines of COBOL code in use in industry, for a computer language that has been "done and gone" for about ten years, so there are many jobshop production processes based on high customization requirements, relatively small order size, specialization of product, and, sometimes, especially high-quality requirements when there is no continuous flow process in place to produce these. In summary, there is enough applicability of this scheduling technique, even in today's high-technology world, to make this topic one of ongoing interest for years to come.

As jobshop scheduling is a topic of ongoing importance in operations management, our subsequent concern is that of what special support is obtainable through simulation modeling in this area. A review of the traditional nonsimulation approach to decision support of jobshop scheduling will provide the proper background for consideration here.

Typically jobshop operations involve many workstations. Some problems of scheduling are of the machine assignment type, where it is necessary to find the method of assigning jobs of different types to a priority order based on the effect on system queuing as the jobs proceed to several different types of workstations in the system. Another form of work assignment method is used to load jobs at several work centers performing not the same but similar operations (machines can often be reconfigured to perform alternate tasks), such as the index method, or linear programming.

Priority Rules of Jobshop Scheduling

Another aspect of jobshop scheduling is that of priority rules for the sequencing of orders in the queue for one individual workstation. A number of such priority rules are in common use in industry. In this chapter four commonly used rules are tested: first in first out (FIFO), process in order of due date (EDD, earliest due date), process in order of amount of slack between time due and required operating time (LS, least slack), and process the shortest task first (SPT, shortest processing time).

The first rule, FIFO, is self-evident. It has the merit of requiring no analysis. If testing, perhaps by simulation, shows that FIFO is on average as good as any other method for the characteristic distribution of processing times and due dates for your shop, then there is good reason to use it as your rule. On the other hand, there is no intuitive reason why FIFO should be a good processing rule, since it ignores all measurable considerations of efficiency, such as reducing average queue time by doing shorter jobs first.

The other three rules all have in common the logic of seeking the job with the smallest value remaining in the queue. The process in order of due date rule (EDD) is based on the intuition that a job which is due soon should be done soon, to avoid lateness. However, no consideration is given to the differences between required operations times or their possible effect on the queue.

The process the shortest task first rule (SPT), is both a rule in widespread use in queuing discipline in general, and the obverse of EDD. Here due dates are ignored with operation times forming the criterion for processing order. It is widely found that the queue discipline of shortest tasks first reduces average time of jobs in the overall queue. However, it may not make for efficient processing control in other respects, particularly where concerned with the due date for individual jobs.

The process in order of amount of slack between time due and required operating time rule (LS), combines considerations of EDD and SPT. The slack for a job is the result of the time remaining until it is due, minus the time required to process the job. The less slack, the earlier the job in the queue. The intuition is that the smaller the safety margin, the earlier the job should be processed to avoid being late. This is probably the rule which corresponds most closely to common sense. However, operations management is always ready to discover that, depending on the nature of the phenomena in question, common sense is not always correct. As mentioned, these four priority rules will be used in modeling explorations in this chapter.

Three frequently used criteria for selecting a particular priority rule as preferable are: flow time, lateness, and tardiness. Flow time is time in the system. It is simply calculated as the sum of the respective exit or finish times of each job, averaged over the number of jobs (provided that arrivals are static, that is, all jobs are available at time zero when the shop begins operations). Lateness is the average amount of time between the completion time for a job and its due date, where early completions are allowed to enter the sum as negative values. This assumes that early completion has some value which offsets late completion. Tardiness is a stricter measure. Early completions are simply not late, so that they figure as zero in their effect on the sum.

Flow time is valuable as a measure of results, in that it provides average time in the shop, a cost to both the customer and the jobshop unless the jobshop absorbs all of this cost. Tardiness is clearly a measure of the degree to which you can match your performance with your commitments. Contrasting tardiness with lateness may show that there is some way to restructure the contracting process and/or overall batching of jobs to take advantage of the fact that some jobs get done early. Alternately, the difference between lateness and tardiness, may indicate some positive marketing advantage, where customers value the early arrival of the orders.

Deterministic Analysis

It is worth noting a second time that our assumption in this treatment is that where a supplier must meet just-in-time requirements of a customer, and jobshop conditions inevitably result in some degree of "lateness," the supplier must provide some sort of time buffer whereby resources and accepted orders are matched with use of a safety margin. If the conditions are those of a traditional jobshop, implying considerable variance between target due dates and completion times, then just-in-case will have to be the focus for the supplier, so that "late" is really on time from the customer's point of view, and "on time" is really early. Again, market conditions and other competitive advantages must justify this for the supplier.

Tables 7.1 and 7.2 illustrate the way in which a simple program in virtually any third or fourth generation language environment will perform the requisite analysis in order to support jobshop scheduling with some of the standard priority rules. Two different sets of data are provided (results in these are in minutes). The reason for this lies in the fact that when the assumption of deterministic operating times is relaxed in the latter portion of this chapter, and stochastic operating times prevail, deterministic results will not always lead to the more optimistic measures of effectiveness.

Note that standard results apply. For instance, SPT is known to minimize the mean flow time at a single station under conditions of deterministic operating times. An examination of 7.1 indicates that the minimum mean flow time of 7.48 minutes is, in fact, achieved by this priority rule. The same result applies for 7.2, where the minimum mean flow time is 9.53 minutes. Also note that minimum late times and tardy times are also generally determined from the SPT rule. The one exception is the mean tardy time in the first example shown in data set 1, where the minimum mean tardy time of 1.95 minutes is determined by incorporating the EDD rule. These results are not coincidental, as SPT is known to be an efficient priority rule. While one may expect EDD to yield superior results in terms of lateness/tardiness based on the fact that it is driven by due dates, the minimum mean late/tardy time is not necessarily generated by this rule, as just exemplified. However, it may

Table 7.1
Deterministic Scheduling Problems, Measures of Effectiveness, Data Set 1

Due Time	Process Time	Slack Time	Complete Time	Flow Time	Late Time	Tardy Time
A. First in First Out (FIFO)						
7.22	2.21	5.01	2.21	2.21	-5.01	0.00
3.91	3.08	0.83	5.29	5.29	1.38	1.38
9.89	5.41	4.48	10.70	10.70	0.81	0.81
6.34	2.56	3.78	13.26	13.26	6.92	6.92
2.88	1.82	1.06	15.08	15.08	12.20	12.20
			Means:	9.31	3.26	4.26
B. Earliest Due Date (EDD)						
2.88	1.82	1.06	1.82	1.82	-1.06	0.00
3.91	3.08	0.83	4.90	4.90	0.99	0.99
6.34	2.56	3.78	7.46	7.46	1.12	1.12
7.22	2.21	5.01	9.67	9.67	2.45	2.45
9.89	5.41	4.48	15.08	15.08	5.19	5.19
			Means:	7.79	1.74	1.95
C. Least Slack (LS)						
3.91	3.08	0.83	3.08	3.08	-0.83	0.00
2.88	1.82	1.06	4.90	4.90	2.02	2.02
6.34	2.56	3.78	7.46	7.46	1.12	1.12
9.89	5.41	4.48	12.87	12.87	2.98	2.98
7.22	2.21	5.01	15.08	15.08	7.86	7.86
			Means:	8.68	2.63	2.80
D. Shortest Processing Time (SPT)						
2.88	1.82	1.06	1.82	1.82	-1.06	0.00
7.22	2.21	5.01	4.03	4.03	-3.19	0.00
6.34	2.56	3.78	6.59	6.59	0.25	0.25
3.91	3.08	0.83	9.67	9.67	5.76	5.76
9.89	5.41	5.41	15.08	15.08	5.19	5.19
			Means:	7.48	1.39	2.24

Table 7.2
Deterministic Scheduling Problems, Measures of Effectiveness, Data Set 2

Due Time	Process Time	Slack Time	Complete Time	Flow Time	Late Time	Tardy Time
A. First in First Out (FIFO)						
3.42	3.12	0.30	3.12	3.12	-0.30	0.00
4.47	4.02	0.45	7.14	7.14	2.67	2.67
7.63	7.62	0.01	14.76	14.76	7.13	7.13
2.08	1.68	0.40	16.44	16.44	14.36	14.36
9.63	3.71	5.92	20.15	20.15	10.52	10.52
			Means:	12.32	6.88	6.94
B. Earliest Due Date (EDD)						
2.08	1.68	0.40	1.68	1.68	-0.40	0.00
3.42	3.12	0.30	4.80	4.80	1.38	1.38
4.47	4.02	0.45	8.82	8.82	4.35	4.35
7.63	7.62	0.01	16.44	16.44	8.81	8.81
9.63	3.71	5.92	20.15	20.15	10.52	10.52
			Means:	10.38	4.93	5.01
C. Least Slack (LS)						
7.63	7.62	0.01	7.62	7.62	-0.01	0.00
3.42	3.12	0.30	10.74	10.74	7.32	7.32
2.08	1.68	0.40	12.42	12.42	10.34	10.34
4.47	4.02	0.45	16.44	16.44	11.97	11.97
9.63	3.71	5.92	20.15	20.15	10.52	10.52
			Means:	13.47	8.03	8.03
D. Shortest Processing Time (SPT)						
2.08	1.68	0.40	1.68	1.68	-0.40	0.00
3.42	3.12	0.30	4.80	4.80	1.38	1.38
9.63	3.71	5.92	8.51	8.51	-1.12	0.00
4.47	4.02	0.45	12.53	12.53	8.06	8.06
7.63	7.62	0.01	20.15	20.15	12.52	12.52
			Means:	9.53	4.09	4.39

be shown that EDD does indeed minimize the *maximum* late time. This result cannot be supported from the information provided in 7.1 and 7.2.

Use of these priority rules can be supported by something as basic as a spreadsheet file with built-in sorting macros. The calculations are done as already explained. To produce the results for the first three sections of 7.1, the spreadsheet need only sort, respectively, on the values for due date, process time, and slack.

This suggests as well the logic which a simulation model must follow to capture the basic logic of using priority rules, that is, even before introducing the stochastic element to the process. Among other things, the simulation model must run its program once for each priority rule tested, duplicating everything that has gone before except the scheduling order of the jobs, which will be sorted much as just illustrated in the spreadsheet context.

As is often the case with operations management at the machine level, so in jobshop scheduling for the individual workstation, there are no algorithms which provide a derived solution. Rather, there are some traditional prioritizing schemes and criteria by which to measure their results, and judgment is left in the final analysis to the scheduler. Therefore there is considerable room for simulation to offer assistance.

Further, as is the case with many rules of thumb as well as algorithms, the assumptions in jobshop scheduling tend to be that operating times are deterministic. The usual understanding is that the mathematical model, whether it is complex or simple, points us in the right direction and then individual judgment must come into play in applying the model's results.

Here also simulation may improve on the management situation by lifting the unrealistic assumption of deterministic operating times. The cost is the difficulty of deriving and using a simulation model. The benefit is improved accuracy, if the model is indeed effective.

THE SIMULATION MODEL

In examining the structure of the simulation model needed for this problem, consider both the basic structure of the jobshop single workstation prioritizing schedule, and the more specific requirements of a simulation model which will help note some important observations about the overall process. The actual simulation model and some commentary on its coding appear in Appendix 7.1 at the end of this chapter.

The jobshop single workstation and its operations are characterized in the model by the following assumptions:

1. only one job can be processed by the workstation at one time;
2. a batch of jobs is received by the workstation at the beginning of a time period;
3. product quality assurance is built into the operations time, and so is not modeled separately;
4. the management objective is to turn out high-quality completed jobs from the workstation with a minimum of variance between promised time and delivery and a minimum of time sitting in the system, through the best job queue discipline.

To model the basic structure of the jobshop single workstation prioritizing schedule, work within the four assumptions just indicated. The model needs to receive as basic input data the number of jobs to be sequenced, the due dates, and operating times for each of these jobs. Slack times are then calculated and also stored. Since a simulation language executes a program instead of displaying a two-dimensional spreadsheet for manually made entries, the model goes through a sequential calculation and averages a running sum for flow time, lateness, and tardiness, selecting the next represented job until all are done. Within this framework, the model needs to run the identical sequence four times, resorting the jobs to correspond to the four priority rules to be evaluated. With regard to output, the model must capture and temporarily store start and end times for each job, and then obtain the average for the entire batch of jobs.

All of this thus far is compatible with a preliminary execution of the simulation model in deterministic mode, to correspond to the way that the priority rules are typically used. This is a good preliminary validity test of the basic model structure, and a recommended procedure on the way to construction of a stochastic mode of the model.

Stochastic Analysis

The simulation process becomes more interesting when we assume that real-world operating times are not deterministic, and that the real variance in day-to-day operations often has an important impact on efficient and effective management of operations in a system. Therefore, consider the inclusion of stochastically generated data values for the processing time of a job. In the modeling approach used for this chapter, we assume that due dates are deterministic for a given time period of operation. However, operating times are distributed stochastically around the mean time that is traditionally expected, which is also to say around the deterministic value which would be used in the traditional application of the priority rule.

It is necessary to maintain repeated random number streams for each priority rule tested. Since we are looking to generate multiple runs of the model with an eye to statistical conclusions, the model's logic has an important nesting of control loops. First we receive the number of jobs, due dates, and deterministic operating times. Second, in the outer control loop, a random operating time is generated as distributed around the theoretical or deterministic operating time, for each of a number of runs, say in a sample of size. Third, in the inner control loop, the randomly generated operating time for each of the jobs in the queue is saved and repeated for each of the four priority rules being tested. Averages for each criteria for each of the thirty runs are saved, and 0.95 confidence intervals are generated at the very end of the model execution.

In addition to surveying the impact of stochastic processing times upon the effectiveness of the system, we can also use the simulation model to look for unbiased cases where the simulation process shows a result which is both more likely to match the real world (stochastic rather than deterministic) and is significantly different from the predictions of the deterministic model.

Results of the Simulation

The results that, while in no instance out of thirty randomly selected scenarios did the deterministic comparison of the priority rules indicate a preference for a rule which was different from that of the simulation model (the stochastic case), large differences in predicted system performance were observed, some as great as 25 percent. The implications of these results are considered later in the chapter.

When utilizing the model for comparative purposes, it is obviously important to have proportionality between due dates and operating times, since both are generated randomly. This is achieved by making the random value for the due date of a job the subsequent base on which to generate a matching but random value for the operating time. The mean operating time is allowed to range between 25 percent and 100 percent of the amount of time represented by the due date. This is, in a sense, a randomly generated "deterministic" time value, and during the thirty simulations of the processing of each job, a uniformly distributed value for each processing time is generated in the range between 75 percent and 125 percent of this "deterministic" time value. Results for the simulation of stochastic scheduling problems are illustrated in Tables 7.3 and 7.4.

For purposes of clarity, note that upper limits represent the upper 95 percent confidence limits, while the mean values are generated from the data stream of thirty operating times which are serviced. Two particular examples out of thirty randomly generated scenarios are selected here for examination. These have the same data values for due dates and operating times as those which were shown in the spreadsheet formats of two examples in Tables 7.1 and 7.2. (The reader may request the entire data set of thirty scenarios from any of the authors.)

The first example was selected because it shows a clear case of significant difference between performance results predicted by the deterministic approach versus those using simulation. By every criteria and every priority rule tested, the simulation predicts much higher time values. Suppose that instead of being randomly generated due dates and expected operating times, these ten values in this scenario represent a manager's expectations for a given batch of jobs. Then, relying on the simulation model, the manager would be much more cautious with respect to commitments than would be the case if the deterministic priority rules were used.

Note that the analysis provided in the figures shows both the mean and the upper limit of a 0.95 confidence interval. Recall that a 0.95 confidence interval means that there is a 95 percent probability that the actual mean derived from our sampling technique lies somewhere in the confidence interval. If the manager wants to maximize customer satisfaction in a highly competitive market, the upper limit of the confidence interval is probably a good safety measure to use.

The second data set example was chosen from several among the thirty random scenarios for the purposes of illustrating that situations do exist where the stochastic results predict a more optimistic set of outcomes than those given by the deterministic priority rules. It should be noted that the differences between the simulation model predictions and deterministic results are significant for several values.

To conclude our observations with respect to jobshop scheduling and simulation, simulation, by using realistic assumptions of stochastic vari-

Table 7.3
Simulation Results of Stochastic Scheduling Problems,
Comparison with Deterministic Results, Data Set 1

Measure	Deterministic Solution			Measure	Stochastic Solution		
	Flow	Late	Tardy		Flow	Late	Tardy
A. First in First Out (FIFO)							
Upper Limit	9.37	3.33	4.35	Upper Limit	9.83	3.78	4.77
Mean Result	9.31	3.26	4.26	Mean Result	9.60	3.55	4.56
Max. % Savings	5.61	15.89	11.92				
Mean % Savings	3.14	9.02	6.99				
B. Earliest Due Date (EDD)							
Upper Limit	7.80	1.75	1.97	Upper Limit	8.19	2.14	2.33
Mean Result	7.79	1.74	1.95	Mean Result	8.00	1.95	2.15
Max. % Savings	5.19	23.20	19.49				
Mean % Savings	2.68	12.00	10.26				
C. Least Slack (LS)							
Upper Limit	8.82	2.77	2.95	Upper Limit	9.39	3.35	3.50
Mean Result	8.68	2.63	2.80	Mean Result	9.11	3.06	3.23
Max. % Savings	8.20	27.26	25.18				
Mean % Savings	4.92	16.29	15.34				
D. Shortest Processing Time (SPT)							
Upper Limit	7.41	1.36	2.26	Upper Limit	7.79	1.74	2.54
Mean Result	7.44	1.39	2.24	Mean Result	7.60	1.55	2.40
Max. % Savings	4.73	25.11	13.39				
Mean % Savings	2.18	11.47	7.14				

Table 7.4
Simulation Results of Stochastic Scheduling Problems,
Comparison with Deterministic Results, Data Set 2

Measure	Deterministic Solution			Measure	Stochastic Solution		
	Flow	**Late**	**Tardy**		**Flow**	**Late**	**Tardy**
A. First in First Out (FIFO)							
Upper Limit	11.76	6.31	6.42	Upper Limit	12.47	7.03	7.11
Mean Result	12.32	6.88	6.94	Mean Result	12.12	6.67	6.77
Max. % Savings	1.68	3.03	2.47				
Mean % Savings					1.20	2.17	2.51
B. Earliest Due Date (EDD)							
Upper Limit	9.91	4.46	4.56	Upper Limit	10.44	4.99	5.08
Mean Result	10.38	4.93	5.01	Mean Result	10.18	4.73	4.82
Max. % Savings	1.96	4.20	3.83				
Mean % Savings					0.60	1.18	1.36
C. Least Slack (LS)							
Upper Limit	11.74	6.30	6.41	Upper Limit	13.14	7.70	7.78
Mean Result	13.47	8.03	8.03	Mean Result	12.44	7.00	7.10
Max. % Savings	7.67	12.83	11.64				
Mean % Savings					2.48	4.14	3.11
D. Shortest Processing Time (SPT)							
Upper Limit	9.09	3.64	4.06	Upper Limit	9.57	4.12	4.43
Mean Result	9.53	4.09	4.39	Mean Result	9.33	3.88	4.25
Max. % Savings	2.14	5.10	3.35				
Mean % Savings					0.38	0.76	0.87

ation, is not likely to give recommendations which differ from a deterministic application of traditional priority rules, where a single workstation is concerned. For example, note that for the SPT rule, the stochastically generated outcomes indicate that the mean flow time is minimized through the incorporation of this priority rule, which is known to be the case for deterministic operating times for systems functioning with a single workstation. As to the outcomes for multiple and/or differentiated stations, that may be another matter, subject to some investigation in the future. However, we believe that regarding time commitments in this arena of scheduling, simulation shows itself to be a highly reliable tool and worth the effort of development. A final cautionary note—the 0.95 confidence intervals used in this chapter are based on a sample size of $n = 30$. A larger sample size would presumably yield smaller upper limits than those reported here.

Appendix 7.1
Simulation Code

```
* BK13K.GPS
  SIMULATE
1   ML4(PH3,1),0,10,10
2   ML4(PH3,2),0,10,10
3   ML4(PH3,3),0,10,10
4   ML4(PH3,4),0,10,10
5   ML4(PH3,5),0,10,10
6   ML4(PH3,6),0,10,10
7   ML4(PH3,7),0,10,10
8   ML4(PH3,8),0,10,10
9   ML4(PH3,9),0,10,10
10  ML4(PH3,10),0,10,10
11  ML4(PH3,11),0,10,10
12  ML4(PH3,12),0,10,10
  REAL   &VAL1(10)
  INTEGER &K,&I,&J,&RUNS,&XP,&L
1 MATRIX ML,10,5               STORE DATA, CALCULATIONS
2 MATRIX ML,10,5               STORE AVERAGES
4 MATRIX ML,30,12              STORE FOR TABULATE
LATE FVARIABLE ML1(PH1,3)-ML1(PH1,1)
SLACK FVARIABLE ML1(PH1,1)-ML1(PH1,2)    DUE DATE LESS OP TIME
LL FVARIABLE TB(PH2)-V(STD)
UL FVARIABLE TB(PH2)+V(STD)
LOW FVARIABLE &VAL1(PH1)*.75.     75 OF ESTIMATED MEAN
RANGE FVARIABLE &VAL1(PH1)*.5     50% OF ESTIMATED MEAN
FLOW FVARIABLE V(LOW)+FN(RAND1)*V(RANGE)          STOCHASTIC
                                                  ESTIMATE
JTIME FVARIABLE FN(PART1)*ML1(&I,1)
STD FVARIABLE (TD(PH2)/SQRT(30))*1.96
WHERE VARIABLE (&J*3)-2+(PH2-3)
DUE FUNCTION RN1,C2
0,2/1,10
PART1 FUNCTION RN1,C2
0,.25/1,1
RAND1 FUNCTION RN2,C2
0,0/1,1
```

```
TARDY FUNCTION  V(LATE),E2
0,X(DUMMY)/.001,V(LATE)
WHICH FUNCTION  &J,D4                    CONTROL JOB SEQUENCE
1,RUN2/2,RUN3/3,RUN4/4,RUN5
* initialize
  PUTPIC
0 Enter # of expers
  GETLIST  &XP
  PUTPIC
0 Enter # of iterations
  GETLIST  &RUNS
  PUTPIC
0 Enter # of jobs, up to 10
  GETLIST  &K
* segment 1
  GENERATE  ,,,1,,5PL,3PH
  SPLIT  &K,NEXT1,1PH
  ADVANCE  1
  ASSIGN  1,4,PH                         4 STRATEGIES
AGAIN BLET  &J=&J+1
  UNLINK  JOBS,CALC1,ALL
  BUFFER
  MSAVEVALUE 2,&J,3,ML2(&J,3)/&K,ML  CALC AVG OPERATION TIME
  MSAVEVALUE 2,&J,4,ML2(&J,4)/&K,ML  CALC AVG DAYS LATE
  MSAVEVALUE 2,&J,5,ML2(&J,5)/&K,ML  CALC AVG DAYS TARDY
  ASSIGN  2,3,PH      3 STATISTICS
RITE1 MSAVEVALUE 4,&I,V(WHERE),ML2(&J,PH2),ML          STORE FOR LATER
  ASSIGN  2+,1,PH
  TEST G  PH2,5,RITE1
  SAVEVALUE FLOW,0,XL                    REINITIALIZE
  LOOP  1PH,AGAIN
  BLET  &J=0
  TEST E  &I,&RUNS,EXIT
  ASSIGN  2,12,PH                        12 COLUMNS IN MATRIX
DATA1 ASSIGN  3,&RUNS,PH                 30 ITERATIONS
DATA2 TABULATE PH2
  LOOP  3PH,DATA2
  MSAVEVALUE 4,1,PH2,V(LL),ML            STORE LOWER LIMIT
  MSAVEVALUE 4,2,PH2,V(UL),ML            STORE UPPER LIMIT
```

```
    LOOP   2PH,DATA1
EXIT  TERMINATE 1
*
NEXT1 ASSIGN  1-,1,PH                 CORRECT FOR JOB #
    PRIORITY  1
    ASSIGN  1,ML1(PH1,1),PL           STORE DUE DATE
    ASSIGN  2,&VAL1(PH1),PL           STORE OPERATION TIME
    ASSIGN  3,V(SLACK),PL             STORE SLACK
    MSAVEVALUE 1,PH1,2,V(FLOW),ML     STOCHASTIC ESTIMAT
    LINK   JOBS,FIFO
*
CALC1 SAVEVALUE FLOW+,ML1(PH1,2),XL         ADD OPERATION TIME
    MSAVEVALUE 1,PH1,3,XL(FLOW),ML    STORE TIME FOR JOB
    MSAVEVALUE 1,PH1,4,V(LATE),ML     STORE DAYS LATE FOR JOB
    MSAVEVALUE 1,PH1,5,FN(TARDY),ML   STORE DAYS TARDY FOR JOB
    MSAVEVALUE 2+,&J,3,ML1(PH1,3),ML  CUMULATE OPERATION TIME
    MSAVEVALUE 2+,&J,4,ML1(PH1,4),ML  CUMULATE DAYS LATE
    MSAVEVALUE 2+,&J,5,ML1(PH1,5),ML  CUMULATE DAYS TARDY
    TRANSFER ,FN(WHICH)               SUCCESSIVE STRATEGIES
RUN2 LINK   JOBS,1PL                  BY DUE DATE
RUN3 LINK   JOBS,3PL                  BY MIN SLACK
RUN4 LINK   JOBS,2PL                  SHORTEST TASK
RUN5 TERMINATE                        RANDOM
* control
OUT1 FILEDEF 'B:BK13K.OUT'
    DO    &L=1,&XP
    DO    &I=1,&K
    INITIAL  ML1(&I,1),FN(DUE)        RANDOMIZE DUE DATE
    LET   &VAL1(&I)=V(JTIME           RANDOMIZE OPER TIME & STORE
    INITIAL  ML1(&I,2),&VAL1(&I)      OPER TIME IN WORKING MATRIX
    ENDDO
    DO    &I=1,&RUNS
    START  1,NP
    CLEAR  ML1,ML4
    ENDDO
    PUTPIC  FILE=OUT1,LINES=13,_
(&L,ML1(1,1),&VAL1(1),ML1(2,1),&VAL1(2),ML1(3,1),_
&VAL1(3),ML1(4,1),&VAL1(4),ML1(5,1),&VAL1(5),_
ML4(1,1),ML4(2,1),ML4(1,2),ML4(2,2),ML4(1,3),ML4(2,3),_
```

```
ML4(1,4),ML4(2,4),ML4(1,5),ML4(2,5),ML4(1,6),ML4(2,6),_
ML4(1,7),ML4(2,7),ML4(1,8),ML4(2,8),ML4(1,9),ML4(2,9),_
ML4(1,10),ML4(2,10),ML4(1,11),ML4(2,11),ML4(1,12),ML4(2,12)
```

Exper **	Due Date	Operating Time
Job 1	**.**	**.**
Job 2	**.**	**.**
Job 3	**.**	**.**
Job 4	**.**	**.**
Job 5	**.**	**.**

	Flow	Late	Tardy
FIFO	**.** to **.**	**.** to **.****	**.** to **.**
Due Date	**.** to **.**	**.** to **.****	**.** to **.**
Min Slack	**.** to **.**	**.** to **.****	**.** to **.**
Shortest Task	**.** to **.**	**.** to **.****	**.** to **.**

```
CLEAR
ENDDO
END
```

The foundational modeling logic here, for GPSS/H™, depends on the use of the User Chain, accessed by the LINK and UNLINK blocks, and the SPLIT block to create a Transaction for each of the jobs. For the FIFO priority rule we take advantage of the default situation and just put the jobs on the User Chain as they are generated. Each Transaction has a parameter to be used for the 2nd, 3rd, and 4th priority rules, representing due date, slack, and operating time. At the end of each model run, the TRANSFER block uses a discrete valued Function to send model control to RUN2, RUN3, RUN4, RUN5 respectively, with RUN5 being a TERMINATE block. The other control destinations are LINK blocks, each of which sorts the job Transactions on the User Chain based on their parameter values for the corresponding priority rule in use. The split block numbers the Transactions in the parameter representing their job identity and enables the simulation to reference each job by row when simulated result values are stored in a Matrix for later use.

The use of the 12 entities is a little strategy which enables GPSS/H™ models to generate confidence intervals without linking to statistical software. The entity always generates not only a distribution of values for data gathered, but also a mean and standard deviation. Therefore we can get these values for our confidence intervals from the severals. The B,C,D operand values of 0 are default because we really don't care about generating an actual distribution.

8

Machine Configuration Simulation Supported by Neural Network Technology

Simulation is widely used to support planning, design, and management of industrial production processes. On the larger scale (Schreiber, 1991) alternate plant layouts can be tested prior to any actual design decisions. The operating details of individual machine stations are not likely to be represented in such models. Even middle-level modeling problems, such as changing the number of machines at a number of sequential stations in order to maximize use of resources and throughput, tend not to represent operating details of individual machines but rather only the moments of the distribution of processing times and the sequential flow of various job types.

At the other end of the continuum of size and refinement of detail, there may be important occasion to indeed model the predicted operating details of one or more individual machine stations in order to recalibrate machine settings in the midst of the production process. This will have special importance in the context of highly automated manufacturing cells.

The modeling problem examined in this chapter is on the level of operating details of an individual machine station. It involves simulating the probable results of alternate recalibrations of a machine's settings in order to achieve optimal control during the production process. The process would be briefly suspended, a simulation sequence run, and the predictive results used to achieve a recalibration for optimal results. Such a model may be an important part of a larger model of a production process. However, here the strategy and technique of simulation is applied to the model of an individual machine.

CHARACTERISTICS OF THE MODEL

The model of interest is one of an extrusion machine producing plastic parts, operated by a skilled machinist. For simplicity, this machine has just two settings. These are (1) speed at which parts are extruded, measured in parts per hour and (2) the pressure applied to the material in the extrusion process, measured in pounds per square inch. The difficult part of the machinist's job lies in the fact that since it is not cost-effective to control the density property of the material used in the process, a proper recalibration of the machine to compensate for change in a batch of material must be based on the results of a trial run of the machine, in terms of good units versus bad units produced in a given time period. The skilled machinist has learned the relation between, on the one hand, the number of good units, bad units, initial machine speed, and pressure, and, on the other, the recalibration needed.

For such a modeling problem the model properties are specified as follows:

1. An initial mean and standard deviation for number of parts per hour are specified, normally distributed. In representing a machine within tolerance limits, the standard deviation is small. In a real-world application these values, as well as the next several, would be read from the machine's performance.

2. An initial value of pounds per square inch of pressure is specified.

3. It is assumed that the number of machine jams, causing down time, are a negative exponential function of the mean time between produced units. They are therefore positively correlated with increased speed of extrusion.

4. Times to restore the machine to operation are assumed uniformly distributed and independent of machine operating speed and pressure.

5. The probability that each particular unit produced will be scrap is a function of a least squares equation. The independent variables are material density and the machine settings for pressure and speed. The dependent variable is a value between zero and one. The

occurrence of a given unit being scrap is simulated through a simple Bernouilli test, using the long-range probability value, p, generated by the least squares equation. Any random number greater than or equal to p represents a unit which must be discarded as scrap. In order to further represent the difficult, skilled task situation in which the machinist must operate, the independent variable representing material density is varied randomly by the simulation, but within a controlled range in order to prevent the dependent variable from becoming a negative value.

6. A constant value is established for the gross profit expected from the production of each good unit, representing price less material and production costs.

7. A constant value is established as the cost of producing a unit of scrap. No salvage value is assumed, so this is equal to the material and production costs.

8. A trial run of the model is obtained. The simulation provides results regarding the number of good and bad units, together with total dollars of gross profit from good units less scrap costs of bad units.

9. The simulationist conducts a series of experiments, modifying the values of machine speed and pressure, observing the relations between these changes and changes in gross profit, and eventually discovers an optimal setting. The random value for material density is preserved through this series of experiments, without which there would be no sense in the model.

10. In a model of this sort, it is important to note that we have used a criterion variable, in this case, gross profit. The optimal ratio between resulting good units versus bad units is not decided simply by maximizing the number of good units. Rather, it will be a function of the respective revenue and cost values. Where the cost of scrap is small compared with the gross profit per good unit, a less cautious policy might be more readily accepted than where the reverse is the case.

Outcomes and Expertise

The observations for the least squares equation will, in an actual application, be taken from production data for the operation of the machine. Due to personnel turnover and other considerations, in an actual application the operator may or may not in fact possess expertise in operation of the machine. Where expertise is present, the only value of the simulation model is in illustrating the range of expected outcomes for the operation of the machine, which may be of considerable value if this model is part of a larger simulation of an entire plant or sequential production process.

Where an expert operator is not available, the simulation model can be of much greater value in its application to the management of a single machine station. Assuming model validity and the ability to run the model quickly, by obtaining a set of multiple outcomes with confidence intervals for a number of experimental recalibrations, we can advise the operator on optimal recalibration after the trial run with the new batch of material. In this case, the simulation model truly substitutes experiment for human expertise.

Limitations of the Modeling Strategy

The limitations of this modeling strategy for support of factory floor machine management are two: time and the cost of simulation expertise. Assuming a hardware/software configuration which is both powerful and cost-effective, the required time for discovering the optimal recalibration may still be excessive. This time expenditure could result mostly from the facts that dozens, if not hundreds of experiments might be necessary to discover the optimal settings, and that thinking time would often be necessary, that is, the analyst must consider the trends of the experiments together with the model results and react accordingly.

Furthermore, it is usually the case that the time spent on modeling must be that of a simulation specialist, whose availability and fees are both constraints on the feasibility of this decision support strategy.

Far worse is the fact that every time there is a change in material density, experimentation must be carried out again. This is not a set of limitations of the value of this particular modeling problem, but rather a representative set of limitations concerning the use of simulation in general for real-time decision support.

In other chapters of this book, simulation strategies put the decision maker in the loop through a very simple and effective modeling approach. However, this approach will be cost-effective only in the sort of problem where it is demonstrated. In other words, an inventory policy problem does not involve complex time relations and collision of events of the sort found in the machine control problem discussed here, such as, machine jams, bad units, and hundreds of time sequences simulated during each run of the many required to generate the confidence interval for just one experiment. Therefore, the strategy used for the inventory problem is clearly not effective for the machine control problem.

Numerous efforts are reported in the literature over the past several years, which develop expensive and complex modeling environments which provide an intelligent user interface and also control experimentation. To the best of our knowledge none of this work provides a consistent, reliable, and cost-effective success to date.

NEURAL NETS AS A SOLUTION TO THE PROBLEM

Simulated neural nets are indeed a special form of simulation in general. On a very simplified and abstracted level, they model some of the features of neural connections in biological organisms' nervous systems, where such connections represent the learning of patterns relevant to knowledge.

Neural nets, which came initially onto the computer scene in the 1960s in the Perceptron mode, soon ran into intractable problems and subsequent eclipse, and emerged again in the 1980s with the development of the feed-forward, back-propagation method. In more recent years, very high-powered algorithms have been added to the neural net process producing important answers to problems in a few iterations of the neural net as contrasted with millions of iterations, as well as numerous trial-and-error strategies.

A simulated neural net (typically referred to as just neural net) represents in program variables a network of nodes linked by paths. Nodes are arranged in rows or layers. Each layer has one or more nodes. There is a minimum of an input layer, at least one hidden or inner layer, and an output layer. An example of a neural net is shown in Figure 8.1.

The classic simple illustration of a neural net is the truth-functional relation of the exclusive disjunction (either/or). Where truth has the value 1 and falsity has the value 0, the inputs and outputs are shown in Table 8.1. As shown in Figure 8.1, each node in each layer is connected to every node in the next layer. Along each path connecting the nodes is a numeric weight, say ranging between negative and positive 2. To teach the neural net the exclusive either/or, the four sets of 1 and 0 values are entered in

Figure 8.1
Simple Neural Net

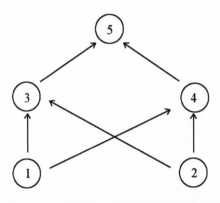

the input nodes. The weight values on the paths are initially generated randomly. Each 1 or 0 is multiplied by the weight on the path, and the products are summed at the receiving node, after which the sum of products is converted by an exponential function to an output value between 0 and 1. The process is continued to the output layer. This is the feed-forward part of the process.

When the output value is incorrect, equations are used to adjust the weights along the paths. This is the back-propagation part of the process. The process is repeated for numerous presentations until one set of weights is found for the network of paths which results in something numerically very close to the correct answer for all four cases of the exclusive either/or. At this point the trained net will always give the correct answer when asked about any of the four cases. What distinguishes this methodology from others is that the process has arrived at a set of saved weights, rather than an equation as a solution.

A very active field of experimentation continues in the use of neural nets to solve problems which have been resistant to solution by other methods, a trait shared with the field of simulation in general. Training of a net is not always successful for a particular problem. Considerations of "gradients of change" in net values, represented through several constants, are managed by an experimenter with more or less of a requirement of human trial and error, depending on the type of solution procedure used. Neural nets are often successful in solving problems despite incomplete

Table 8.1
Truth-Functional Relationship of the Exclusive Disjunction

A	B	A or B
1	1	0
1	0	1
0	1	1
0	0	0

and sometimes even inconsistent data. It is sometimes argued that they perform as well as they do because they capture some of the very powerful capacity of the process whereby the animal brain learns, that is, through pattern recognition as opposed to rule-based processes.

All of this suggests that a neural net application, if it can be achieved, might well be an ideal way to provide cost-effective decision support, quick and virtually automatic, for a simulation model of the extrusion machine and its recalibration. Certainly the relation between the percentage adjustment of machine settings and observed values of good and bad units, speed and pressure, would appear to be a question of recurring patterns rather than of rules, where an expert system might be more appropriate. If the strategy is successful, a trained neural net could select the recalibration values with no additional trial-and-error searching with the simulation model whatsoever. A real-time answer could be provided.

At this point it appears reasonable to inquire as to whether a trained neural net could be captured in the simulation language code of the model. If so, then a model guided by artificial intelligence can be run with no problems of linking to other software or data bases. This indeed does turn out to be the case.

A Successful Simulation/Neural Net Experiment

The methodology involving a trained neural net embedded in GPSS code has been applied to the machine problem discussed in this chapter by Madey and Weinroth in 1991. The model was written in GPSS\PC and the neural net was trained "off-line" in the netware product MacBrain 2.0. Lloyd and Weinroth subsequently developed a GPSS/H™ model in a mainframe environment which, making use of a FORTRAN call, trains the neural net "on-line" within the simulation code. These results were presented at the 1991 Pittsburgh Modeling Conference.

In the Madey and Weinroth experiment, the simulation model generated initial machine settings for speed and pressure randomly, along with random values for the material density. The objective was to provide a robust set of examples for the use of training. Optimal solutions were determined for the recalibration problem, through laborious trial-and-error experimentation with the model for each of twenty cases. Input and output values for speed, pressure, good units and bad, were converted to index values between 0 and 1 as suitable values for the neural net. One case of the twenty was discarded as a statistical outlier, thirteen were used to train the net, and six were saved to test the net against cases it had not seen.

Table 8.2 shows examples of the values submitted to the net for training. Table 8.3 shows the degree of accuracy of the trained net in (1) representing the proper calibrations for the thirteen examples on which it trained and (2) representing the proper recalibrations for the six examples it had not seen.

All in all the results were very good. This can be contrasted with the possible but not promising strategy of analyzing the data by regression, given that almost none of the requisite conditions such as normality of the

Table 8.2
Sample Simulation Output: Model Utilized
to Train a Neural Net

Case	1	2	3	4	5
Good units	812.0	1,062.0	961.0	1,107.0	1,246.0
Bad units	123.0	55.0	55.0	184.0	64.0
Pressure (pounds/inch^2)	10.0	10.5	10.7	10.7	10.4
Speed (minutes/unit)	1.5	1.2	1.4	1.1	1.0
Profit ($)	3,200.0	8,240.0	7,410.0	3,710.0	9,900.0
% Change to pressure	0.0	-4.3	-6.1	-6.8	-3.4
% Change to speed	2.0	-55.3	-59.3	41.5	-51.9
New profit ($)	3,660.0	11,160.0	9,590.0	3,940.0	12,470.0

Table 8.3
Performance of Neural Net in Achieving Target Values

	Average Error	Maximum Error
Machine Speed		
Known cases	6.43%	16.70%
Unknown cases	11.05%	17.73%
Pressure		
Known cases	0.65%	1.29%
Unknown cases	3.32%	13.33%

data are available without extensive rework and in any case no guarantee of success.

One further experiment was conducted, with exciting implications. Since the trained neural net was able to be represented in simulation code, it could constitute part of the executable model. In this way a new model generated a set of new problem examples, ran the trial process to get initial values for good and bad units, ran the results through the embedded trained net to generate recalibrations, and simulated a second run with the same material density, in parallel, one with the recalibrations and one without. Average simulated profit was improved by about 14 percent.

One final technical note, which we will not try to explain. Careful effort revealed something which does not surprise neural net practitioners. A neural net trained on averages for the thirteen scenarios in the training set gave very poor results compared with a neural net trained on one arbitrary simulation run for each of the thirteen scenarios. This appears to contradict a basic premise of simulation methodology. It does in fact point to one of the ways in which neural nets are unlike anything else used in analysis and computer processing, that is, they can, paradoxically, be overtrained, much like people.

Appendix 8.1
Simulation Code

```
100   * neuro4.gps   7/22/89 machine shop w/embedded neural net
110   XPDIS FUNCTION  RN2,C24
0, 0/.1, .104/.2, .222/.3, .355/.4, .509/.5, .69/.6, .915/.7, 1.2/.75, 1.38
.8, 1.6/.84, 1.83/.88, 2.12/.9, 2.3/.92, 2.52/.94, 2.81/.95, 2.99/.96, 3.2
.97, 3.5/.98, 3.9/.99, 4.6/.995, 5.3/.998, 6.2/.999, 7/.9998, 8
120   PROB1 FUNCTION  RN1,C2
0,1/1,1001
130   DFECT1 FVARIABLE 1131.859-.792#X$SPEED
140 DFECT2 FVARIABLE .952#((X$LBS^2)/1000)-X$BETA3#X$LBS/1000 150
DEFECT FVARIABLE V$DFECT1+V$DFECT2
160   DOWN FVARIABLE  (X$SPEED#25)#FN$XPDIS
170   REPAIR FUNCTION  RN2,C2
0,100/1,201
180   PROFIT FVARIABLE 10#X$UNITS-40#X$BAD
190   BETA FUNCTION  RN2,C2
0,1850/1,1948
200   RATE FUNCTION  RN2,C2
0,50/1,151
210   PRESS FUNCTION  RN2,C2
0,900/1,1101
220   IDENT VARIABLE  (P1-1)#5+P2
230   VALUES EQU    1
240   VALUES MATRIX  ,3,5
250   START1 FUNCTION  P1,D4
1, 1062/2, 55/3, 1045/4, 123
260   START2 FUNCTION  P1,E4
1,X$UNITS/2,X$BAD/3,X$LBS/4,X$SPEED
270   WEIGHT1 FUNCTION  V$IDENT,D20
1, 1/2, -2/3, 3/4, -4/5, 5/6, -10/7, 10/8, -10/9, 10/10, -10/11, 5/12, -4/13,3
14, -2/15, 1/16, -10/17, 10/18, -10/19, 10/20, -10
280   VALUE2 FVARIABLE FN$WEIGHT1#P3
290   SIG2 FUNCTION  MX1(2,P1),C2
-5, -1/5, 1
300 ORIGIN2 FVARIABLE  MX1(2,P1)#FN$SIG2#10000
310   VALUE3 FVARIABLE FN$WEIGHT2#P3/1000000
320   WEIGHT2 FUNCTION  V$IDENT2,D10
```

```
1, 1/2, -1.5/3, .25/4, -.5/5, .75/6, -1.25/7, 1/8, -1/9, .2/10, -.2
330  IDENT2 VARIABLE  (P1-1)#2+P2
340  NEWBAD VARIABLE  N$BAD-X$BAD1
350  LBS2 FVARIABLE  ((MX1(3,1)+1000)/1000)#X$LBS
360  SPEED2 FVARIABLE ((MX1(3,2)+1000)/1000)#X$SPEED
500  * neuro1.gps
510  * unit segment
520   GENERATE  X$SPEED          ;FEED UNITS TO SYSTEM
530   GATE FV  MACHINE,EXIT      ;AVOID ARTIFICIAL QUEUE
540   ASSIGN  1,FN$PROB1         ;TO TEST FOR DEFECT (10)
550   SEIZE  MACHINE             ;SEIZE MACHINE
560   ADVANCE  X$SPEED           ;DETERMINISTIC
570   RELEASE  MACHINE           ;RELEASE MACHINE
580   TEST G  P1,X$TEST1,BAD     ;VS.EXPECTED PROB.
590   SAVEVALUE UNITS+,1         ;ANOTHER GOOD UNIT
600  EXIT TERMINATE
610  * breakdown segment
620   GENERATE  ,,,1             ;SEED XACT
630   SAVEVALUE  SPEED,FN$RATE   ;RANDOMIZE SPEED
640   SAVEVALUE  BETA3,FN$BETA   ;RANDOMIZE COEFFICIENT
650   SAVEVALUE  LBS,FN$PRESS    ;RANDOMIZE PRESSURE
660   SAVEVALUE  TEST1,V$DEFECT  ;SAVES PROCESSOR TIME
670  NEXTIME ADVANCE  V$DOWN     ;TO NEXT BREAKDOWN
680   MARK  1                    ;STATS ON DOWN TIME
690   FUNAVAIL  MACHINE          ;MACHINE JAMS
700   ADVANCE  FN$REPAIR         ;REPAIR TIME
710   SAVEVALUE  DTIME+,MP1      ;KEEP STATS
720   FAVAIL  MACHINE            ;REPAIR DONE
730   TRANSFER  ,NEXTIME         ;NEXT BREAKDOWN
732  * bad unit segment
734  BAD  TERMINATE
740  * timer segment
750   GENERATE  144000           ;8 HOURS
755   SAVEVALUE  BAD,N$BAD       ;RECORD FOR PROFIT
760   SAVEVALUE  PROFIT1,V$PROFIT ;STORE FOR RESULT FILE
800  * neuro3.gps 7/22/89 for trained net embedded in model
820   SPLIT  3,ROW1,1            ;4 CELLS IN ROW 1
830  ROW1 ASSIGN  3,FN$START2    ;P3 = CURRENT VALUE
840   SPLIT  4,ROW2,2            ;p2 = TARGET CELL
```

```
850  ROW2 MSAVEVALUE 1+,2,P2,V$VALUE2      ;CUMULATE VALUES
860    ASSEMBLE 20
870    ASSIGN  1,0                         ;CLEAR FOR SPLIT
880    ASSIGN  2,0                         ;CLEAR FOR SPLIT
890    SPLIT  4,ORIG2,1                     ;P1 = ORIGIN CELL
900  ORIG2 ASSIGN  3,V$ORIGIN2              ;NEW OUTPUT VALUE
910    SPLIT  1,ROW3,2                       ;P2 = TARGET CELL
920  ROW3 MSAVEVALUE 1+,3,P2,V$VALUE3       ;FINAL VALUES
930    ASSEMBLE 10
940    SAVEVALUE LBS,V$LBS2                  ;RESET FROM NET
950    SAVEVALUE SPEED,V$SPEED2              ;RESET FROM NET
960    SAVEVALUE TEST1,V$DEFECT              ;RECALCULATE PROB.
970    SAVEVALUE UNITS,0                     ;CLEAR FOR PROFIT2
980    SAVEVALUE BAD1,N$BAD                  ;FOR LATER CLEAR
990    ADVANCE 144000                        ;SECOND SHIFT
1000   SAVEVALUE BAD,V$NEWBAD                ;FOR RUN 2
1010   SAVEVALUE PROFIT2,V$PROFIT
1020   TERMINATE 1
```

Like other simulation languages, GPSS\PC lends itself quite effectively to this representation. The output values in the layers of nodes are represented in cells in the rows of a matrix. The arrived at changing weights are represented in a Function. The traversal of the paths between the nodes by the input values is achieved by a priming transaction which splits the required number of times based on the required number of paths, and represents the impulses along the several paths by parameter values of the parent and offspring transactions. The ASSEMBLE block is in turn useful for producing one output from each node after the summing of products and exponential function is executed.

9

Modeling Facility Location as Related to Emergency Retrieval Systems

The study of health services, and more specifically, emergency services is an important area related to public safety. Within this discipline, the planning of capacity is critical in meeting the demand of consumers requiring health care. Whereas the tactical aspects of capacity/staffing were once manageable without formal analysis, the evolution and growth of major metropolitan areas has increased the complexity involved in the determination of optimal policies, namely, those leading to high quality service. This chapter explores the issue of capacity management as it applies to emergency retrieval systems.

Simply stated, when a crisis occurs leading to increased risk in an individual's health, it becomes critical to provide the means by which the injured party may be transported to the nearest emergency medical facility. Unfortunately, it is often the case that the response time for this request is inexplicably delayed. In these cases, a systematic appraisal and review of the underlying processes involved in responding to these calls may be warranted. While on the surface the basic ambulance service process may seem simple—a call arrives, an ambulance is dispatched, the requested caller is picked up and transported to the nearest emergency medical facility—the underlying tactical decisions which must be made are not so transparent. These issues are investigated, via simulation, in this chapter.

When calls are received, a dispatcher must first decide whether an ambulance should be dispatched immediately. For example, when two calls are received and only one ambulance is available, one call must remain on queue while the other call is serviced. Other dispatch decisions involve determining the location from where the ambulance should be sent (if multiple locations are available), as well as routing the ambulance so as to avoid areas of congestion, based on the time of day. While ambulances have historically been based only at emergency facilities, increased levels of congestion within city limits and increased calls from suburbs have virtually mandated that ambulances also be located at satellite locations. The desired net benefit of this decision is lower response time, and ideally, fewer lives lost.

This chapter considers a prototypical example involving ambulance service, in which an emergency facility is considering siting a satellite dispatch center whose location has been targeted. To begin, and set the stage for the simulation process, the problem is discussed in general terms.

THE EMERGENCY RETRIEVAL

The city of Whitecap, New Hampshire, is concerned with the quality of service provided in responding to emergency calls (911 calls) at the city's only hospital, Whitecap Memorial, which houses the city's only emergency care unit. The hospital is located slightly northwest of the center of the metropolitan area. When the facility was constructed in 1930, this location was determined to be suitable, falling near the epicenter of the city. Consequently, this location was able to cater to the needs of the city's populace with great ease.

As the city's industrial base grew, many of Whitecap's residents began to move out from the downtown area into the suburbs. This shift involved the movement of many residents to the southwest suburbs of the city. Considering that Whitecap is bordered to the northwest by Lake Whinitango, and the Osgood River to the north (beyond which lies a major seaport area) relatively few calls are received from north of the facility. However, the recent development of new industrial parks in the southeast area of the city has precipitated a large influx of 911 calls to Whitecap Memorial, as it remains the closest emergency treatment facility available. This, in addition to the demographic redistribution of existing workers and/or residents, has increased the volume of emergency calls which the hospital must respond to. While the metropolitan area which Whitecap

Memorial serves is only two miles square, the large concentration of industrial zones together with the growing base of residential populace has led to an unanticipated large volume of 911 calls which the hospital must respond to. It is estimated that as many as 34,000 people either work or live within this highly concentrated area, with emergency calls totaling approximately 0.4 percent of this population per work day. More specifically, recent estimates indicate that 911 calls to the hospital occur at a mean rate of seventeen calls per hour during peak load hours (9 A.M.–5 P.M.) Monday through Friday. The hospital is able to meet the lower demand of off-peak calls in a highly efficient manner, with satisfactory response time.

Whitecap Memorial currently houses ten ambulances at the hospital, with no alternate satellite dispatch location. Historically, dead on arrival (DOA) rates for emergency calls have averaged approximately 6.8 percent, when the patient is mortally wounded. However, over the past two years this figure has increased to approximately 7.0 percent. While this increase may not appear significant, taken over fifty-two weeks, this amounts to approximately seventy-one additional lives lost. The management of Whitecap Memorial is primarily concerned with this increase, and believes this trend can be reversed through careful planning and an analysis of their ambulance service procedures.

Discussions with ambulance service administrative personnel indicate that the emergency care department feels (1) inundated with calls during peak load and (2) that increased round-trip response time over the past two years has led to a shortage of available ambulances when calls arrive. It is felt that a significant part of this increased response time is attributable to the newly developed industrial parks. A task force has already been charged with making recommendations as to how this increased congestion may be alleviated. Initially, it was suggested that additional ambulances be obtained, but the task force has noted that additional ambulances may not alleviate the increased DOA rate, which is more a function of distance traveled rather than insufficient ambulances. Alternatively, it was proposed that a redistribution of existing ambulances and the development of a satellite dispatch center should be considered.

Cost considerations support this proposal. New ambulances cost approximately $50,000 apiece, while costs involved in renting, maintaining, and operating a satellite facility would run in the neighborhood of $5,000 per month. Hospital personnel have approved these recommendations, and a potential satellite dispatch site has been located and is available. This site is located in the southeastern sector of the city, a desirable location due to it's proximity to the industrial park area. Hospital management believes that the utilization of this satellite dispatch center may help decrease the inflated DOA rate which Whitecap Memorial currently faces.

In order to further study this proposal, a simulation team is gathered to perform a feasibility study and report on results.

The Simulation Model

In performing the simulation for this study, the simulation team (together with Whitecap Memorial's management team) must ascertain parameters and define the problem's objective. It is decided that the metropolitan area will be segmented into sixteen identically shaped sectors, forming a four-by-four grid. Arrival rates for calls will be differentiated by area. It is assumed that the mean arrival rate for each sector is invariant with time between the peak-load hours of 9 A.M. to 5 P.M. In actuality, it is more likely that arrival rates do vary during the course of the day, but this degree of precision will be omitted for the present time, and may be seen later as a "bump" to the system. For purposes of a feasibility study many details are often omitted, as the purpose of the study is to give management a feel for how appropriate the methodology is in resolving the issue at hand. 911 calls arriving during off-peak hours will be excluded, as the DOA rates over these hours are significantly lower, and Whitecap Memorial is very pleased with their level of service during these hours. Information is obtained from hospital records regarding arrival rates, and is displayed in Table 9.1. The entries in the table indicate the sector number, followed by the mean hourly arrival rate for 911 calls. The notation H indicates the hospital sector, while S indicates the sector containing the potential satellite location.

As noted, the hospital is slightly northwest of center, while the available satellite location is in a southeast sector near the industrial zone. Mean

Table 9.1
Sectors and Hourly 911 Arrival Rates

I, 0.25	II, 0.25	III, 0.50	IV, 1.25
V, 0.25	VI, 0.50 (H)	VII, 0.50	VIII, 0.75
IX, 0.50	X, 0.50	XI, 1.00 (S)	XII, 2.50
XIII, 0.75	XIV, 1.50	XV, 2.75	XVI, 3.25

arrival rates for 911 calls are also consistent with the general demographics of the city, that is, heavy volume to the southeast, with moderate volume in the southwest suburbs. Unfortunately, it is infeasible to relocate the hospital, and no plans are under consideration for the construction of either a new hospital or a new emergency care facility. The location of the available satellite facility is desirable and Whitecap memorial hopes that this will decrease DOA rates by yielding quicker response times to 911 calls generated from these southeast sectors.

Prior to beginning, an evaluatory measure must be agreed upon. This measure will be used to determine the effectiveness of various policies which will be tested. Two suggestions include minimizing the (1) mean response time and (2) DOA rate. While intuition might suggest that the optimal policy will satisfy both criterion, that is not the case, as will be demonstrated later. In consideration of the fact that hospital management is specifically concerned with the increase in DOA rates over the past two years, criteria (2) will be utilized. As noted, while criteria (1) will yield a lower mean response time than criteria (2), it is quite possible that it will actually yield higher DOA rates. This would be the case if criteria (1) were to yield a very low response time for the majority of calls, with a fairly high response time for the remainder of the incoming 911 calls, many of which may be highly critical in terms of severity. Criteria (2), on the other hand, may yield higher response times on average, by increasing response times for those calls which are not critical in exchange for decreasing response times for those 911 calls which are more critical. The end result of policy (2) may be an overall increase in mean response time, but a decrease in response time for the subset of calls considered most critical, which in turn may decrease the DOA rate.

The effectiveness of the policy incorporating the satellite will be determined by comparing the current DOA rate to that which may be expected through the utilization of the satellite, which raises two additional questions: (1) What is the appropriate level of utilization for the satellite. In particular, how many of the ten existing ambulances should be housed at the satellite? and (2) What dispatch rule should be employed? For example, incoming calls may be answered on a first-come-first-serve basis, or a prioritized dispatch rule.

A third issue involving the placement of the satellite may also be pursued, but is unnecessary as only one site is being considered, and the location for this site is predetermined.

Having defined the measure of effectiveness to be used in the objective, details regarding the generation of arrivals and the simulation steps required in responding to calls are now considered. It is agreed that 911 calls arrive randomly to the emergency facility. Statistically, this implies that each call arrives independently. Each of these arrivals has three characteristics: location, time, and severity. Hospital data indicates that arrivals are uniformly distributed within each sector, or equally likely to occur at any spot. In order to determine the specific origin of a call, each sector (which is .25 miles^2, or .5 miles per side) is divided into 625 subsectors, each .02 miles wide and .02 miles long. When a call is generated from a sector, the specific origin of the call is the center of one of these 625 subsectors. To generate the arrival times for calls, it is noted that the independence assumption for incoming 911 calls (which would hold as long as the calling population is reasonably large) implies that the number of arrivals occurring over nonoverlapping time periods must follow what is known as a Poisson process. This further implies that the time between calls, or interarrival time, must be exponentially distributed. Hence, once call x is generated, the time for call $x + 1$ is determined by (1) generating an exponential interarrival time, and (2) adding this inter-arrival time to the arrival time of call x. For example, if call #1 arrives at time 5.0, and the generated exponential interarrival time equals .50, then call #2 would arrive at time 5.5. Proceeding in this manner, an arrival stream for each sector may be generated for each sector contained within the metropolitan area surrounding Whitecap Memorial.

As some calls are clearly more critical than others, 911 calls are to be classified into three severity (or critical) classes I, II, or III, with severity class I reserved for those calls that are most critical (e.g., heart attack). After determining what types of injuries or illnesses are to be classified in each severity class, emergency room data indicates that the incidence rate for each class in terms of percentage is roughly the same. Hence, once a point of origin and time are generated for a 911 call, the call is classified according to severity, with severity classes being equiprobable.

Attention is now turned to the dispatch function for the ambulances. In order to respond to a call, the following information must be provided:

1. outbound travel time for the ambulance between the dispatch point and the origin of the call, where this time represents the amount of

time the ambulance requires, if it proceeds unimpeded with no congestion from its dispatch point to the origin of the call,

2. outbound delay time to account for deviations from the outbound travel time due to traffic congestion and related factors,

3. pickup time for the patient, which involves time for on-site emergency treatment and loading time,

4. inbound travel time,

5. inbound delay time,

6. drop-off time to account for unloading and transporting the patient to the emergency room where treatment can begin.

The outbound travel time is determined by assuming that the mean speed of an ambulance on an emergency dispatch is s MPH. Since the metropolitan area surrounding Whitecap Memorial is predominately composed of city blocks, travel is assumed to be rectilinear (i.e., vertical and horizontal directions only). Assuming that the locations of the hospital and a call and given by Cartesian coordinates (x_0,y_0) and (x_1,y_1), respectively, then it may be shown that the inbound and outbound travel time, T_1 and T_0, for an ambulance responding to this call equals:

$$\left\{ \frac{(|x_1 - x_0| + |y_1 - y_0|)}{s} \right\} \cdot (.60) = T_1 = T_0 = T$$

For simulation purposes, it is assumed $s = 35$. Sensitivity or postoptimality analysis can be considered after the model is run in order to see how changes in this parameter impact solutions. Next, variations in travel time must be accounted for. The travel time, T, represents the minimum time required if the ambulance proceeds unimpeded to the call's origin and back to the emergency center. Any congestion effects must now be added to this time. This added time will be called delay time. Close inspection of travel logs from the emergency center indicates that the resulting delay time is approximately normally distributed with a mean of 1.75 minutes and a standard deviation of .35 minutes. Both outbound and inbound delay times (given by D_0, D_1, respectively) are then generated for each dispatch. Delay times might be differentiated by time and route, however, this consideration will be left as an extension to the basic model developed here. On the other hand, it is also reasonable to suggest that if proper right-of-way procedures are maintained, delay times may be very similar regardless of the time and location.

A pickup time must also be generated for each call. This includes the time required to provide support functions to the passenger on-site, load the passenger onto a stretcher, and transport the patient to the ambulance. Initially it is assumed that either a normal or a uniform distribution might apply, but eventually the decision is made to use the Weibell distribution. The normal distribution is ruled out because it allows any value to occur (including negatives), and hospital management argues that regardless of the severity of the call, the minimum pickup time for any 911 call is no less than three minutes. The uniform distribution is also unlikely, as pickup times are not likely to be equally probable, but mound shaped in nature. As the Weibell distribution is both mound shaped and possesses a minimum feasible value, it is chosen to represent the pick-up distribution function. By utilizing 207 pieces of historical data, a software program titled UNIFIT determines that the appropriate mean and standard deviation for the Weibell distribution are 6.3 and 3.2 minutes, respectively, for the pickup time, P.

The final characteristic to be generated regarding dispatch is the drop-off time (D) at the hospital, which involves unloading the passenger and placing him in the appropriate emergency room where medical service can continue. Since, on occasion, unloading time can be very rapid (less than one minute in severe circumstances), the normal distribution is considered, with a mean of 3 minutes and a standard deviation of .75 minutes. While it can be argued that pickup and drop-off times might vary with severity class, these considerations can be examined more closely at a later time, if desired.

In addition to the total travel time for the ambulance, time also exists between the placement of the call and the dispatch of the ambulance. This time would be positive under the circumstances when (1) an ambulance were unavailable at the time of the call or (2) an available ambulance were not dispatched immediately after the call was received. The second instance is likely to occur if a low priority call arrives when only one or two ambulances are available, in which case the dispatcher may hold the ambulance temporarily until additional ambulances are available. This would allow the emergency center to respond to a high priority call which arrives in the interim. This wait time for each call is not determined through the use of a probability distribution. Rather, it depends specifically on the dispatch rule incorporated into the model. Designating this time W, the total response time for a call, or the total time (*TT*) elapsing between the receipt of the 911 call and the placement of the patient in the emergency room, is given by the following:

$$TT = T_0 + D_0 + P + D_1 + D + W$$

The simulation must keep track of *TT* for each incoming 911 call. In monitoring the system's performance, DOA rates must also be maintained. In order to track DOA rates, each incoming call must be assigned a critical time. Critical time indicates the maximum allowable response time after which it is assumed that the patient expires. If the response time exceeds the call's critical time, it is assumed that the patient arrives DOA. This assumption could be relaxed by assuming that the critical time is the *expected* maximum response time, where the likelihood of arriving DOA beyond the critical time is probabilistic. This is again left as an extension to the basic model. A check through hospital records indicates that the following critical-time distributions apply to the different severity classes: severity class I, uniformly distributed between 12 and 28 minutes; severity class II, uniformly distributed between 18 and 42 minutes; severity class III, uniformly distributed between 24 and 56 minutes. Note the overlap between classes, accounting for the ambiguous nature involved in classifying calls. It is assumed that the severity class is correctly assigned to each call, although a more realistic assumption would entail occasional misclassifications, with the resulting true critical time not equaling the critical time generated for the assigned class.

One final time must be established for ambulance cleanup after each 911 call. When a patient is dropped off, the dispatched ambulance must be cleaned and resupplied at the location from which it was dispatched. This time varies depending upon factors such as supplies used and quantities of blood and other fluids which may have been spilled. It is determined that this time varies between 5 and 15 minutes, uniformly distributed.

At this point the simulation team announces that they are ready to proceed with the simulation runs. By comparing the actual response time per call with the critical time, a running percentage of DOA calls can be maintained from which the optimality of a suggested policy can be examined. The policy which yields the minimum percent of DOA calls will be considered, for purposes of the feasibility study, to be optimal.

In order to proceed with the simulation, a dispatch rule must be chosen. To begin, the simple first-come-first-serve rule will be incorporated. While this rule is commonly used in practice, it has been shown to have severe limitations in terms of optimality. Other dispatch rules, such as SPT (shortest processing time) and EDD (earliest due date) have been shown to yield significantly superior results in terms of efficiency. For example, if a number of jobs await processing on a queue, processing the jobs in increasing order of processing time (SPT rule) minimizes the total mean time that the total group of jobs spend in the system, waiting and processing times combined. Similar beneficial results apply to EDD, as well as other scheduling and processing rules.

While the idea of using separate queues for the satellite and hospital was considered, it is decided that this would only decrease the efficiency of the system. This is based on the queuing theory result that a single queue feeding two servers is more effective than the assignment of two dedicated queues, one per server. Consequently, all 911 calls will be queued on a common queue.

Simulation Results

To begin, the first simulation replicates the ambulatory care facility as it is currently operating, where calls are placed on a common queue and responded to first-come-first-serve. Ten ambulances are available, all stationed at the hospital. The simulation will run for a duration of 480 hours (sixty peak-load periods) simulated time, after which results are compiled. This will allow adequate time to generate fairly reliable results. The simulation team concedes that the model is incomplete due to the exclusion of off-peak hours, but is fairly confident that the generated results will strongly replicate peak-load results which are being witnessed.

The results for 911 call generation are shown in Table 9.2, grouped by sector and severity class. Note the pleasing result that the resulting call pattern is similar to the expected volume of calls (shown in the right hand column) over sixty peak-load periods. Also note that the calls are fairly evenly distributed between severity classes. (Actual arrival times and locations are also generated, but these results are not shown.)

The simulation is now run to completion, with ambulances being dispatched to calls on a first-come-first-serve basis. For identification purposes, and also in order to keep track of utilization, ambulances are

Table 9.2
Call Information

Sector	Calls	Severity I	Severity II	Severity III	Expected
1	114	29	35	50	120
2	125	42	43	40	120
3	230	76	73	81	240
4	524	175	173	177	600
5	140	48	52	40	120
6	257	83	96	78	240
7	281	98	88	95	240
8	224	86	79	59	360
9	255	88	87	80	240
10	241	66	92	83	240
11	479	145	167	167	480
12	1097	394	351	352	1200
13	309	97	119	93	360
14	642	228	203	211	720
15	1201	421	379	401	1320
16	1403	449	519	435	1560
Total	7522	2524	2556	2442	8160

numbered one through ten. If two or more ambulances are available, a
lower numbered ambulance is always dispatched prior to a higher numbered one. This will eventually allow the simulators to check on how often
the tenth ambulance is required, a necessary piece of information if the
question of additional ambulance acquisition is to be considered. Resulting information of DOA rates is displayed in Table 9.3.

Note that the DOA rates are lowest in sectors 5, 6, 7, 8, 9, and 10,
which happen to be the sectors in the immediate vicinity of Whitecap
Memorial. The highest DOA rates are those found in 13, 15, and 16, two
of which are the highly congested southeast industrial park areas, the
other representing a suburban region. Also note that the simulated DOA
percentages match the currently stated figure of approximately 7 percent
as quoted earlier by hospital officials. This close fit indicates that the

Table 9.3
DOA Information, Current Environment

Sector	DOA				% Calls DOA
	Type I	Type II	Type III	Total	
1	4	1	0	5	4.4
2	6	0	0	6	4.8
3	12	1	0	13	5.7
4	31	2	0	33	6.3
5	0	0	0	0	0.0
6	8	2	0	10	3.9
7	9	0	0	9	3.2
8	9	1	0	10	4.5
9	7	2	0	9	3.5
10	3	2	0	5	2.1
11	17	5	1	23	4.8
12	58	11	1	70	6.4
13	25	4	1	30	9.7
14	40	0	1	41	6.4
15	92	12	3	107	8.9
16	124	29	0	153	10.9
Total	445	72	7	524	7.0

results of the simulation are somewhat reliable, allowing the simulation to continue.

In order to ascertain whether the recent increase in the DOA rate is less a function of the number of ambulances available as opposed to the actual distribution and location of the ambulances, the utilization rate (percent of time busy) for each ambulance is now checked. The utilization of ambulance #10, which is only used when all other ambulances are dispatched, equals .33. This implies down time of 67 percent for this ambulance. While this number is not overwhelmingly high, it is high enough to suggest with reasonable confidence that the DOA rate is more sensitive to response time than the number of vehicles. If the down time for ambulance

#10 were only 10 percent, this would suggest the opposite, namely, DOA increases are a direct result of insufficient vehicular capacity. Given the results thus far, the recommendation that a satellite dispatch location be considered becomes increasingly attractive as a viable alternative.

The simulation now proceeds by incorporating the satellite facility, and increasing the number of ambulances at the facility incrementally from zero to ten. One 480-hour simulation is performed for each distribution of ambulances. The dispatch policy remains first-come-first-serve. The corresponding DOA rates for this simulation are illustrated in Figure 9.1.

Figure 9.1 illustrates that the DOA percentage is minimized when eight of the ten ambulances are placed at the satellite. The resulting minimum DOA percentage is 6.5, a significant decrease from the 7.0 percent figure which currently exists. Observe how the smooth curve drawn through the points illustrates convexity, a result which may have been intuitively arrived at. The utilization of nonlinear regression analysis can be employed to help determine the location of the minimum point in cases where the scattergram does not illustrate the U-shaped convexity such as that present in Figure 9.1. For example, a quadratic regression model would determine the best fitting quadratic curve to the points shown, where the

Figure 9.1
DOA Rates, First-Come-First-Serve

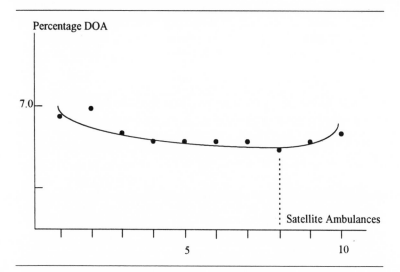

curve would assume a contour similar to the one superimposed in the figure.

Consider next the wait times, W. It is interesting to note, as shown in Table 9.4, that the average wait time increases as the number of ambulances at the satellite increases

Within Table 9.4, "Percent Calls with Wait" indicates the percent of calls for which a dispatch was not immediately made. The corresponding wait times represent the average amount of time between the receipt of the call and the dispatch of the ambulances, averaged over the number of 911 calls with positive wait time. Despite the fact that, in general, wait time appears to increase as the number of satellite ambulances increases, it was noted earlier that the DOA percentage does not increase as a function of the number of ambulances at the satellite. In fact, as shown in Figure 9.1, the DOA rate is convex and decreases initially as more satellite ambulances are utilized. This confirms the earlier hypothesis that wait times and DOA rates are not necessarily positively correlated. This is clearly a nonintuitive result. One would naturally believe that the policy which minimizes (1) the percent of calls which must wait for an ambulance and (2) the average wait time for a dispatch would be that policy which would minimize the DOA rate. Fortunately, tools such as simulation allow us to

Table 9.4
Wait Time, First-Come-First-Serve

Satellite Ambulances	Percent Calls with Wait	Mean Wait (minutes)
1	16.5	4.56
2	16.9	4.68
3	17.9	4.73
4	18.3	4.77
5	18.6	4.75
6	19.4	4.87
7	20.2	4.99
8	20.8	5.02
9	21.9	5.24
10	22.5	5.29

determine when preconceived and well-accepted intuitive conclusions may be erroneous.

In order to improve upon the current policy of using a first-come-first-serve dispatch rule with eight satellite ambulances, we now consider an alternate dispatch rule of the following form: no severity class, i, calls may be responded to if a severity class, j, call is waiting, where $j < t$. In other words, calls are prioritized by severity class. This rule reflects the intuitive suspicion that some severity class III calls are being responded to while severity I calls build in the queue, resulting in increased severity class I DOA rates. Many of the severity class III patients serviced might still arrive at the emergency room within their critical time even if their calls were responded to after servicing any queued severity class I and II calls.

The hypothesis is supported through simulation. Utilizing the same arrival stream, and incrementing the number of satellite ambulances from zero to ten, eleven 480-hour simulations are run utilizing the critical class priority dispatch rule. The corresponding DOA rates are shown in Table 9.5.

It is interesting that the results indicate a local minimum DOA rate when three ambulances are located at the satellite. However, both the simulation team and hospital management agree that the general relationship between the DOA rate and the number of satellite ambulances suggests that the appropriate number of ambulances which should be housed at the satellite equals eight. This is based on the fact that excluding this one result for three satellite ambulances, DOA rates are

Table 9.5
DOA Rates, Critical Class Priority Dispatch

Satellite Ambulances	Percent DOA	Satellite Ambulances	Percent DOA
0	6.6	6	6.2
1	6.4	7	6.2
2	6.4	8	5.9
3	6.1	9	6.2
4	6.4	10	6.2
5	6.3		

again convex with an apparent minimum at eight satellite ambulances. While it would be possible to confirm this suspicion by performing additional simulations, the group makes note of the local minimum result and decides to forego this additional work for the moment.

Since it has been shown that priority dispatch appears beneficial, perhaps prioritizing by critical time may lead to further improvements. While it is true that the average critical time for severity class I patients is lower than that for severity classes II and III patients, individual cases vary. Critical class is often used to classify a call based on the type of care, expertise, and transport materials needed to successfully transport the patient to the emergency facility, rather than the critical time required for the patient to be transported from the call's point of origin to the facility. Consequently, it may be the case that a severity class II call will have a lower critical time than a particular severity class I call, as noted by the overlapping critical times utilized. In that case it may make more sense to prioritize calls by critical time, rather than critical class.

The corresponding DOA rates for the simulation using a critical time dispatch rule are shown in Table 9.6. The number and length of the simulations are identical to those performed for first-come-first-serve and critical class priority dispatch. Once again the initial arrival stream is utilized.

Comparing Tables 9.5 and 9.6, one sees that the DOA rates are smaller for every case in Table 9.6. Apparently, prioritizing by critical time leads to improvements in the system's efficiency. Again, a local minimum (with regard to DOA rate) appears at the solution with three

Table 9.6
DOA Rates, Critical Time Priority Dispatch

Satellite Ambulances	Percent DOA	Satellite Ambulances	Percent DOA
0	6.6	6	6.1
1	6.3	7	5.9
2	6.3	8	5.8
3	6.0	9	5.8
4	6.2	10	5.7
5	6.1		

satellite ambulances, with the global minimum occurring when all ambulances are housed at the satellite. While this result may appear optimal from a numerical standpoint, institutional constraints ordinarily forbid reallocating all ambulances to a remote location, simply because there are instances when ambulance service is required at the main facility, excluding 911 calls. While the three-ambulance satellite solution was disregarded earlier, further simulation analysis appears to be warranted in light of the fact that it now yields a local optimum for both priority dispatch rules.

While it was noted that results for the critical time priority dispatch rule suggest that all ambulances relocate at the satellite, hospital management decides that it is satisfactory to place eight ambulances at the satellite, with a resulting DOA rate of 5.8 percent. The additional 0.1 percent benefit achieved by moving the remaining two ambulances to the satellite does not outweigh the qualitative benefits involved in housing those two ambulances at the hospital. This type of analysis is embedded within the principle of satisficing, as opposed to optimizing. Satisficing ordinarily occurs in situations where qualitative elements, which are sometimes immeasurable quantitatively, are involved, or conflicting constraint requirements eliminate all feasible solutions. Tradeoffs are often considered involving both sacrifices and gains with regard to various conflicting problem attributes. In these cases, one seeks solutions which provide reasonable improvements, and policies which make all parties better off to the extent that each party is satisfied with the resulting solution.

While improvements have been made in the DOA rate, it is interesting to note that (1) the percentage of callers with positive wait time and the average time spent waiting for those calls without immediate dispatch show no benefit (as discussed earlier) and (2) the utilization of the ambulances has actually increased! The individual ambulance utilization for first-come-first-serve (FCFS), no satellite scenario, and the critical time priority dispatch (CTPD) scenario with eight satellite ambulances are shown in Table 9.7. Again, while intuition might suggest that lower DOA rates might imply lower levels of utilization, the opposite is found to be true.

At this point, the simulation team concludes the feasibility study, feeling confident that the simulation has proven useful in illustrating the feasibility and optimality of (1) the satellite location and (2) the critical time priority dispatch rule.

Table 9.7
Ambulance Utilization

FCFS, No Satellite		CTPD, Eight Satellites	
Ambulances	*Utilization*	*Ambulances*	*Utilization*
1	.88	1	.89
2	.86	2	.88
3	.84	3	.84
4	.79	4	.81
5	.74	5	.77
6	.67	6	.72
7	.61	7	.66
8	.53	8	.57
9	.43	9	.50
10	.33	10	.39

FINAL COMMENTS

The simulations presented in this chapter highlight a typical approach for conducting a feasibility study for a service provider. Essentially, the purpose of the simulation is (1) to provide benchmark solutions through which alternatives may be evaluated, albeit loosely, and (2) to illustrate the potential benefits of using a particular methodology (in this instance, simulation). A feasibility study also allows policy makers to determine whether the particular method employed allows enough flexibility to merit further use.

In this study, many factors which might be included in a full-scale study have been omitted, but the usefulness of simulation as an optimization tool has been illustrated. From the study, it was shown that benefits in ambulance service may be achieved through the redistribution of existing resources rather than additional capital expenditures in the procurement of more vehicles. While additional vehicles would also impact solutions, the low utilization rate for lower numbered ambulances, together with the fact that the DOA rate was highest for those sectors distant from the hospital suggests that a redistributing, rather than increasing ambulances might prove more beneficial.

The simulation also illustrated the impact of dispatch rules on DOA rates. Both critical-class and critical-time dispatching were shown to lower the DOA rate, with superior gains attained by utilizing the latter. The overall decreased DOA rate from 7.0 to 5.8 percent would save approximately 424 additional lives:

$$\frac{17\ calls}{hour} \cdot \frac{8\ hours}{day} \cdot \frac{360\ weekdays}{year} \cdot .012 = 424$$

Hospital management would clearly support the notion that the value of 424 additional lives saved is immense. However, prior to concluding that this is indeed the effect of implementing the policies suggested earlier, a full study would need to be conducted taking many other factors into account, such as,

- time-differentiated arrival rates and delay times,
- more specific and realistic probability distributions,
- off-peak hours,
- additional dispatch rules,
- optimal routing, other than simple rectilinear movement,
- investigation of local optimum points, such as the three-ambulance satellite solution,
- cleaning of satellite ambulances at the hospital and vice versa,
- hospital ambulances being dispatched from the satellite if calls are waiting, and vice versa,
- ambulance down time for maintenance,
- different ambulance speeds,
- critical class differentiated pickup and drop-off times,
- probabilistic death rate when critical time is missed, among others.

Incorporating these elements into the problem would increase the reliability and precision of solutions, and assist policy makers further in their determination of a satisfactory ambulance service management policy.

The overall importance of simulation in the area of health care is borne out when one notes that despite the existence of sophisticated mathematical models, the numerous stochastic elements, such as, random arrival times, delay times, and pickup times, together with complicated routing and distribution facets, present in the problem limit their applicability. For these situations, simulation seems appropriate. While simulationists must make concessions regarding the unavailability of guarantees that solutions generated are necessarily optimal, the tradeoff involves a reasonably good solution to the problem at hand (using simulation) versus an optimal solution to a model which replicates the given problem only to a limited extent (using a mathematical model).

Throughout this book this has been the case. While we do not contend that simulation is in fact superior to quantitative methods, we hope that the material presented here has helped the reader recognize that simulation is a viable, important quantitative tool that can be utilized in conjunction with well-known quantitative methods to strengthen the analysis of systems which are complex in nature. The scope and potential of simulation are vast, and its appropriate use can assist policy makers in many areas by guiding them toward optimal solutions, and solutions which increase the welfare of all involved.

Appendix 9.1
Simulation Code

```
SIMULATE
  REALLOCATE COM,200000
TYPE FUNCTION  RN5,D3
0.3333,1/0.6667,2/1.0,3
PTYPE FUNCTION  PH9,E3
1,FN(CRIT1)/2,FN(CRIT2)/3,FN(CRIT3)
CRIT3 FUNCTION  RN5,C9
0.0,24/0.125,28/0.25,32/0.375,36/0.5,40/0.625,44/0.75,48/0.875,52
1.0,56
CRIT1 FUNCTION  RN5,C9
0.0,18/0.125,21.5/0.25,24/0.375,27.5/0.5,30/0.625,33.5/0.75,36
0.875,39.5/1.0,42
CRIT2 FUNCTION  RN5,C9
0.0,12/0.125,14/0.25,16/0.375,18/0.5,20/0.625,22/0.75,24
0.875,26/1.0,28
CLEAN FUNCTION  RN5,C6
0.0,5/0.2,7/0.4,9/0.6,11/0.8,13/1.0,15
GROW FUNCTION  PH1,D16
1,1/2,1/3,1/4,1/5,2/6,2/7,2/8,2/9,3/10,3/11,3/12,3/13,4/14,4/15,4/16,4
GCOL FUNCTION  PH1,D16
1,1/2,2/3,3/4,4/5,1/6,2/7,3/8,4/9,1/10,2/11,3/12,4/13,1/14,2/15,3/16,4
LOCUS FVARIABLE  (FRN6*625)+1
DROW FVARIABLE  (PH2/25)+1
DCOL FVARIABLE  PH2@25
MGROW FVARIABLE  PH3+((PH5-1)*25)
MGCOL FVARIABLE  PH4+((PH6-1)*25)
TIME FVARIABLE  ((((V(VDIFF)*0.02)+(V(HDIFF)*0.02))*60)/35)+PL8
PICK FVARIABLE  3.00538+3.24828*EXP(LOG(RVEXPO(4,1.))/.98373)
VDIFF VARIABLE  ABS(PH7-37)
HDIFF VARIABLE  ABS(PH8-38)
TRIP VARIABLE  (PL1+PL2+PL3+PL4)
DEAD BVARIABLE  PL5'L'V(TRIP)
PDOA FVARIABLE  (MH1(PH1,5)/MH1(PH1,1))*1000
DISPT BVARIABLE  BV(DISP1)'E'1+BV(DISP2)'E'1
DISP1 BVARIABLE  PH10'E'2+PH10'E'4+PH10'E'6+PH10'E'8
DISP2 BVARIABLE  PH10'E'10
```

```
1   MATRIX   H,16,9
OTIME TABLE   PL1,2,1,10              SET UP TABLE PARAMETERS
PICUP TABLE   PL2,3,2,14              SET UP TABLE PARAMETERS
ITIME TABLE   PL3,2,1,10              SET UP TABLE PARAMETERS
DPOFF TABLE   PL4,1,.5,10             SET UP TABLE PARAMETERS
CTIME TABLE   PL5,15,5,12             SET UP TABLE PARAMETERS
DELAY TABLE   PL8,.5,.5,10            SET UP TABLE PARAMETERS
CLEAN TABLE   PL6,5,1.5,10            SET UP TABLE PARAMETERS
OTIM1 TABLE   PL1,2,1,10              SET UP TABLE PARAMETERS
PICP1 TABLE   PL2,3,2,14              SET UP TABLE PARAMETERS
ITIM1 TABLE   PL3,2,1,10              SET UP TABLE PARAMETERS
DPOF1 TABLE   PL4,1,.5,10             SET UP TABLE PARAMETERS
HOMEB TABLE   PL1,2,1,10              SET UP TABLE PARAMETERS
*************************************************************************
     GENERATE  RVEXPO(1,60),,,,,10PH,8PL ARRIVAL REQUESTS
     ASSIGN  1,1,H                    ASSIGN POSITION ON THE 4X4 GRID
     TRANSFER  ,RED1                  SEND TO THE MAIN FLOW
     GENERATE  RVEXPO(1,60),,,,,10PH,8PL ARRIVAL REQUESTS
     ASSIGN  1,2,H                    ASSIGN POSITION ON THE 4X4 GRID
     TRANSFER  ,RED1                  SEND TO THE MAIN FLOW
     GENERATE  RVEXPO(1,30),,,,,10PH,8PL ARRIVAL REQUESTS
     ASSIGN  1,3,H                    ASSIGN POSITION ON THE 4X4 GRID
     TRANSFER  ,RED1                  SEND TO THE MAIN FLOW
     GENERATE  RVEXPO(1,30),,,,,10PH,8PL ARRIVAL REQUESTS
     ASSIGN  1,4,H                    ASSIGN POSITION ON THE 4X4 GRID
     TRANSFER  ,RED1                  SEND TO THE MAIN FLOW
     GENERATE  RVEXPO(1,60),,,,,10PH,8PL ARRIVAL REQUESTS
     ASSIGN  1,5,H                    ASSIGN POSITION ON THE 4X4 GRID
     TRANSFER  ,RED1                  SEND TO THE MAIN FLOW
     GENERATE  RVEXPO(1,60),,,,,10PH,8PL ARRIVAL REQUESTS
     ASSIGN  1,6,H                    ASSIGN POSITION ON THE 4X4 GRID
     TRANSFER  ,RED1                  SEND TO THE MAIN FLOW
     GENERATE  RVEXPO(1,30),,,,,10PH,8PL ARRIVAL REQUESTS
     ASSIGN  1,7,H                    ASSIGN POSITION ON THE 4X4 GRID
     TRANSFER  ,RED1                  SEND TO THE MAIN FLOW
     GENERATE  RVEXPO(1,30),,,,,10PH,8PL ARRIVAL REQUESTS
     ASSIGN  1,8,H                    ASSIGN POSITION ON THE 4X4 GRID
     TRANSFER  ,RED1                  SEND TO THE MAIN FLOW
     GENERATE  RVEXPO(1,120),,,,,10PH,8PL    ARRIVAL REQUESTS
```

```
        ASSIGN   1,9,H                         ASSIGN POSITION ON THE 4X4 GRID
        TRANSFER ,RED1                         SEND TO THE MAIN FLOW
        GENERATE  RVEXPO(1,120),,,,,10PH,8PL     ARRIVAL REQUESTS
        ASSIGN   1,10,H                        ASSIGN POSITION ON THE 4X4 GRID
        TRANSFER ,RED1                         SEND TO THE MAIN FLOW
        GENERATE  RVEXPO(1,120),,,,,10PH,8PL     ARRIVAL REQUESTS
        ASSIGN   1,11,H                        ASSIGN POSITION ON THE 4X4 GRID
        TRANSFER ,RED1                         SEND TO THE MAIN FLOW
        GENERATE  RVEXPO(1,120),,,,,10PH,8PL     ARRIVAL REQUESTS
        ASSIGN   1,12,H                        ASSIGN POSITION ON THE 4X4 GRID
        TRANSFER ,RED1                         SEND TO THE MAIN FLOW
        GENERATE  RVEXPO(1,60),,,,,10PH,8PL      ARRIVAL REQUESTS
        ASSIGN   1,13,H                        ASSIGN POSITION ON THE 4X4 GRID
        TRANSFER ,RED1                         SEND TO THE MAIN FLOW
        GENERATE  RVEXPO(1,60),,,,,10PH,8PL      ARRIVAL REQUESTS
        ASSIGN   1,14,H                        ASSIGN POSITION ON THE 4X4 GRID
        TRANSFER ,RED1                         SEND TO THE MAIN FLOW
        GENERATE  RVEXPO(1,120),,,,,10PH,8PL     ARRIVAL REQUESTS
        ASSIGN   1,15,H                        ASSIGN POSITION ON THE 4X4 GRID
        TRANSFER ,RED1                         SEND TO THE MAIN FLOW
        GENERATE  RVEXPO(1,120),,,,,10PH,8PL     ARRIVAL REQUESTS
        ASSIGN   1,16,H                        ASSIGN POSITION ON THE 4X4 GRID
        TRANSFER ,RED1                         SEND TO THE MAIN FLOW
RED1    ASSIGN   2,V(LOCUS),H                  FIND A GRID LOCATION (1-625)
        ASSIGN   3,V(DROW),H                   FIND ROW IN 25X25 GRID
        ASSIGN   4,V(DCOL),H                   FIND COLUMN IN 25X25 GRID
        ASSIGN   5,FN(GROW),H                  FIND ROW LOCATION IN 4X4 GRID
        ASSIGN   6,FN(GCOL),H                  FIND COLUMN LOCATION 4X4 GRID
        ASSIGN   7,V(MGROW),H                  FIND ROW IN 100X100 GRID
        ASSIGN   8,V(MGCOL),H                  FIND COLUMN IN 100X100 GRID
        ASSIGN   9,FN(TYPE),H                  PICK UP PATIENT TYPE
        ASSIGN   8,RVNORM(2,1.75,.35),PL       PICK UP DELAY TIME
        TABULATE DELAY                         PUT THE TIME IN A TABLE
        MSAVEVALUE 1+,PH1,1,1,H                ADD TO COUNT FROM GRID SECTOR
        MSAVEVALUE 1+,PH1,(PH9+1),1,H          ADDS TO COUNT OF PATIENT TYPE
        QUEUE    AMBUL                         GET IN LINE FOR AN AMBULANCE
        TRANSFER ALL,RED2,RED11,3              GET A FREE AMBULANCE
RED2    SEIZE    1                             AN AMBULANCE IS AVAILABLE
        ASSIGN   10,1,H                        STORE THE AMBULANCE NUMBER
```

```
    TRANSFER  ,RED12          SEND TO THE TRAVEL ROUTINE
RED3 SEIZE   2                AN AMBULANCE IS AVAILABLE
    ASSIGN   10,2,H           STORE THE AMBULANCE NUMBER
    TRANSFER  ,RED16          SEND TO THE TRAVEL ROUTINE
RED4 SEIZE   3                AN AMBULANCE IS AVAILABLE
    ASSIGN   10,3,H           STORE THE AMBULANCE NUMBER
    TRANSFER  ,RED12          SEND TO THE TRAVEL ROUTINE
RED5 SEIZE   4                AN AMBULANCE IS AVAILABLE
    ASSIGN   10,4,H           STORE THE AMBULANCE NUMBER
    TRANSFER  ,RED16          SEND TO THE TRAVEL ROUTINE
RED6 SEIZE   5                AN AMBULANCE IS AVAILABLE
    ASSIGN   10,5,H           STORE THE AMBULANCE NUMBER
    TRANSFER  ,RED12          SEND TO THE TRAVEL ROUTINE
RED7 SEIZE   6                AN AMBULANCE IS AVAILABLE
    ASSIGN   10,6,H           STORE THE AMBULANCE NUMBER
    TRANSFER  ,RED16          SEND TO THE TRAVEL ROUTINE
RED8 SEIZE   7                AN AMBULANCE IS AVAILABLE
    ASSIGN   10,7,H           STORE THE AMBULANCE NUMBER
    TRANSFER  ,RED12          SEND TO THE TRAVEL ROUTINE
RED9 SEIZE   8                AN AMBULANCE IS AVAILABLE
    ASSIGN   10,8,H           STORE THE AMBULANCE NUMBER
    TRANSFER  ,RED16          SEND TO THE TRAVEL ROUTINE
RED10 SEIZE  9                AN AMBULANCE IS AVAILABLE
    ASSIGN   10,9,H           STORE THE AMBULANCE NUMBER
    TRANSFER  ,RED12          SEND TO THE TRAVEL ROUTINE
RED11 SEIZE  10               AN AMBULANCE IS AVAILABLE
    ASSIGN   10,10,H          STORE THE AMBULANCE NUMBER
    TRANSFER  ,RED16          SEND TO THE TRAVEL ROUTINE
RED12 DEPART  AMBUL          GET OUT OF THE WAITING LINE
    ASSIGN   1,V(TIME),PL     FIND OUTBOUND TRAVEL TIME
    TABULATE  OTIME           PUT THE TIME IN A TABLE
    ASSIGN   2,V(PICK),PL     FIND PICK-UP TIME
    TABULATE  PICUP           PUT THE TIME IN A TABLE
    ASSIGN   8,RVNORM(2,1.75,.35),PL   PICK UP DELAY TIME
    TABULATE  DELAY           PUT THE TIME IN A TABLE
    ASSIGN   3,V(TIME),PL     FIND INBOUND TRAVEL TIME
    TABULATE  ITIME           PUT THE TIME IN A TABLE
    ASSIGN   4,RVNORM(2,3,.7),PL   FIND DROP OFF TIME
    TABULATE  DPOFF           PUT THE TIME IN A TABLE
```

```
ASSIGN   5,FN(PTYPE),PL           PICK UP CRITICAL TIME
TABULATE CTIME                    PUT THE TIME IN A TABLE
ASSIGN   6,FN(CLEAN),PL           PICK UP CLEAN-UP TIME
TABULATE CLEAN                    PUT THE TIME IN A TABLE
MSAVEVALUE 1+,PH1,5,BV(DEAD),H    COUNT THE DEAD ARRIVALS
MSAVEVALUE 1,PH1,6,V(PDOA),H      PROVIDE PERCENT OF D.O.A.S
ADVANCE  PL1                      TRAVEL TO LOCATION
ADVANCE  PL2                      PICK-UP TIME
ADVANCE  PL3                      TRAVEL FROM LOCATION
ADVANCE  PL4                      DROP-OFF TIME
ADVANCE  PL6                      CLEAN-UP AMBULANCE FOR NEXT CALL
RELEASE  PH10                     FREE UP THE AMBULANCE
TERMINATE
TIME1 FVARIABLE  ((((V(VDIF1)*0.02)+(V(HDIF1)*0.02))*60)/35)+PL8
VDIF1 VARIABLE  ABS(PH7-63)
HDIF1 VARIABLE  ABS(PH8-62)
TIME2 FVARIABLE  ((((V(VDIF2)*0.02)+(V(HDIF2)*0.02))*60)/35)+PL8
VDIF2 VARIABLE  ABS(PH7-37)
HDIF2 VARIABLE  ABS(PH8-38)
HOME  FVARIABLE  ((((V(VDIF3)*0.02)+(V(HDIF3)*0.02))*60)/35)+PL8
VDIF3 VARIABLE  ABS(63-37)
HDIF3 VARIABLE  ABS(62-38)
RED16 DEPART  AMBUL               GET OUT OF THE WAITING LINE
   ASSIGN   1,V(TIME1),PL         FIND OUTBOUND TRAVEL TIME
   TABULATE OTIM1                 PUT THE TIME IN A TABLE
   ASSIGN   2,V(PICK),PL          FIND PICK-UP TIME
   TABULATE PICP1                 PUT THE TIME IN A TABLE
   ASSIGN   8,RVNORM(2,1.75,.35),PL  PICK UP DELAY TIME
   TABULATE DELAY                 PUT THE TIME IN A TABLE
   ASSIGN   3,V(TIME2),PL         FIND INBOUND TRAVEL TIME
   TABULATE ITIM1                 PUT THE TIME IN A TABLE
   ASSIGN   4,RVNORM(2,3,.7),PL   FIND DROP OFF TIME
   TABULATE DPOF1                 PUT THE TIME IN A TABLE
   ASSIGN   5,FN(PTYPE),PL        PICK UP CRITICAL TIME
   TABULATE CTIME                 PUT THE TIME IN A TABLE
   ASSIGN   8,RVNORM(2,1.75,.35),PL  PICK UP DELAY TIME
   TABULATE DELAY                 PUT THE TIME IN A TABLE
   ASSIGN   7,V(HOME),PL          PICK UP TO HOME BASE TIME
   TABULATE HOMEB                 PUT THE TIME IN A TABLE
```

```
ASSIGN   6,FN(CLEAN),PL          PICK UP CLEAN-UP TIME
TABULATE  CLEAN                  PUT THE TIME IN A TABLE
MSAVEVALUE  1+,PH1,5,BV(DEAD),H  COUNT THE DEAD ARRIVALS
MSAVEVALUE  1,PH1,6,V(PDOA),H    PROVIDE PERCENT OF D.O.A.S
ADVANCE   PL1                    TRAVEL TO LOCATION
ADVANCE   PL2                    PICK-UP TIME
ADVANCE   PL3                    TRAVEL FROM LOCATION
ADVANCE   PL4                    DROP-OFF TIME
ADVANCE   PL7                    TRAVEL TO HOME BASE
ADVANCE   PL6                    CLEAN-UP AMBULANCE FOR NEXT CALL
RELEASE   PH10                   FREE UP THE AMBULANCE
TERMINATE
GENERATE  ,,1440,1               SEND IN THE TIMER
TERMINATE  1                     SHUT OFF THE SIMULATION
START   1
END
```

Selected
Bibliography

Allata, J. T., I. D. Jacobson, and M. A. Townsend. 1993. Evaluation of new technologies in a show manufacturing plant using simulation. *Simulation 61*, no. 5: 303–313.

Banks, J., and J. S. Carson II. 1984. *Discrete-event system simulation*. Englewood Cliffs, NJ: Prentice-Hall.

Bendall, A., D. Solomon, and J. M. Carter. 1995. Evaluating project completion times when activity times are erlang distributed. *Journal of the Operational Research Society 46*, no. 7: 867–882.

Bobillier, P. A., B. C. Kahan, and A. R. Probst. 1976. *Simulation with GPSS and GPSS V.* Englewood Cliffs, NJ: Prentice-Hall.

Canabarro, Eduardo. 1995. Where do one-factor interest rate models fail? *Journal of Fixed Incomes 5*, no. 2: 31–52.

Chakrovorty, Satya S., and J. Brian Atwater. 1995. Do JIT lines perform better than traditionally balanced lines? *International Journal of Operations and Production Management 15*, no. 7: 77–88.

Clymer, John R. 1995. System design and evaluation using discrete-event simulation with AI. *European Journal of Operational Research 84*, no. 1: 213–225.

Coats, Pamela. 1990. Combining an expert system with simulation to enhance planning for bank networks. *Simulation 54*, no. 6: 253–264.

Cochran, Jeffrey K., Gerald T. Mackulak, and Paul A. Savory. 1995. Simulation project characteristics in industrial settings. *Interfaces 25*, no. 4: 104–113.

Cochran, Mark J., James W. Richardson, and Clair Nixon. 1990. Economic and financial simulation for small business: A discussion of the small business economic, risk, and tax simulator. *Simulation 54*, no. 4: 177–188.

Collins, Michael J. 1995. Benchmarking with simulation: How it can help your production operations. *Production 107*, no. 7: 50–51.

Computer simulation predicts employee response to contemplated plan redesigns. 1995. *Employee Benefit Plan Review 49*, no. 9: 24–26.

Dyner, Isaac, Ricardo Smith, and Gloria E. Pena. 1995. Systems dynamics modeling for residential energy efficiency analysis and management. *Journal of the Operational Research Society 46*, no. 10: 1163–1173.

Freeman, J. M. 1995. Estimating quality costs. *Journal of the Operational Research Society 46*, no. 6: 675–686.

Goyal, S. K., Kapil Mehta, Rambabu Kodali, and S. G. Desmukh. 1995. Simulation for analysis of scheduling rules for a flexible manufacturing system. *Integrated Manufacturing Systems 6*, no. 5: 21–26.

Graybeal, W. J., and U. W. Pooch. 1980. *Simulation principles and methods.* Cambridge, MA: Winthrop.

Gregory, Annie. 1995. Simulation cuts the risk and costs of change. *Works Management 48*, no. 1: 14–17.

Halpern, Marc. 1995. Simulation payoffs. *Computer Aided Engineering 14*, no. 8: 56.

Hoover, Stewart V., and Ronald F. Perry. 1989. *Simulation: A problem solving approach.* Reading, MA: Addison-Wesley.

Law, A. M., and W. D. Kelton. 1982. *Simulation modeling and analysis.* New York: McGraw-Hill.

Law, A. M., and M. G. McComas. 1991. Secrets of successful simulation studies. In *Conference proceedings of the 1991 winter simulation conference*, edited by B. Nelson, W. Kelton, and G. Clark, 21–27. Phoenix, Arizona.

Lawrence, Stephen R. 1995. Estimating flowtimes and setting due dates in complex production systems. *Transactions 27*, no. 5: 657–668

Lenz, John, and Ray Neitzel. 1995. Cost modeling: An effective means to compare alternatives. *Industrial Engineering 27*, no. 1: 18–19.

Lai, K. K., Kokin Lam, and W. K. Chan. 1995. Shipping container logistics and allocation. *Journal of Operational Research Society 46*, no. 6: 687–697.

Lovas, Gunnar G. 1995. On performance measures for evacuation systems. *European Journal of Operational Research 85*, no. 2: 352–367.

Matta, Khalil F., and Diptendu Sinha. 1995. Policy and cost approximations of two-echelon distribution systems with a procurement cost at the higher echelon. *IIE Transactions 27*, no. 5: 638–645.

Mukherjee, Arup K. 1991. A simulation model for management of operations in the pharmacy of a hospital. *Simulation 56*, no. 2: 91–103.

Nersesian, R. L. 1990. *Computer simulation in financial risk management.* New York: Quorum Books.

Nersesian, R. L. 1990. *Corporate planning, human behavior, and computer simulation.* New York: Quorum Books.

Owen, Jean V. 1995. Simulation: Art and science. *Manufacturing Engineering 114*, no. 2: 61–63.

Polajnar, Andrej, Borut Buchmeister, and Marjan Leber. 1995. Analysis of different transport solutions in the flexible manufacturing cell using computer simulation. *International Journal of Operations and Production Management 15*, no. 6: 51–58.

Pooch, U. W., and J. A. Wall. 1993. *Discrete event simulation: A practical approach.* Boca Raton, FL: CRC Press.

Prakash, Avneesh, and Mingyuan Chen. 1995. A simulation study of flexible manufacturing systems. *Computers and Industrial Engineering 28*, no. 1: 191–199.

Prakash, Subramanian, and Robert E. Shannon. 1993. Development of a goal-directed simulation environment for discrete part manufacturing systems. *Simulation 61*, no. 2: 102–115.

Rao, Kavuri, K. N. Krishnaswamy, and B. G. Raghavendra. 1995. Structured systems technology for evaluation of random interruptions in continuous type manufacturing systems. *IIE Transactions 27*, no. 4: 435–443.

Schreiber, T. J. 1974. *Simulation Using GPSS.* New York: John Wiley and Sons.

Schreiber, T. J. 1991. *An Introduction to Simulation Using GPSS/H.* New York: John Wiley and Sons.

Selladurai, V., P. Aravindan, P., S. G. Ponnambalam, and A. Gunasekaran. 1995. Dynamic simulation of job shop scheduling for optimal performance. *International Journal of Operations and Production Management 15*, no. 7: 106–120.

Sengupta, Sumantra, and Rick Combes. 1995. Optimizing and simulation Kraft General Foods' manufacturing environment. *IIE Transactions 27*, no. 8: 30–35.

Shannon, R. E. 1975. *Systems simulation: The art and science.* Englewood Cliffs, NJ: Prentice-Hall.

Solomon, S. L. 1983. *Simulation of waiting-line systems.* Englewood Cliffs, NJ: Prentice-Hall.

Spiegler, Israel, and Jerome Herniter. 1993. Forecasting retail sales and dealer inventories: A simulation and decision support system. *Simulation 61*, no. 4: 268–274.

Steigum, Erling, Jr., and Oystein Thogersen. 1995. Petroleum wealth, debt policy, and intergenerational warfare: The case of Norway. *Journal of Policy Modeling 17*, no. 4: 427–442.

Taha, H. A. 1988. *Simulation modeling and SIMNET.* Englewood Cliffs, NJ: Prentice-Hall.

Tannock, James D. T. 1995. Choice of inspection strategy using quality simulation. *International Journal of Quality and Reliability Management 12*, no. 5: 75–84.

Thesen, A., and L. E. Travis. 1992. *Simulation for decision making.* St. Paul, MN: West.

Warren, James R., Robert L. Crosslin, and Paul James MacArthur. 1995. Simulation modeling for BPR: Steps to effective decision support. *Information Systems Management 12*, no. 4: 32–42.

Watson, H. J., and J. H. Blackstone, Jr. 1989. *Computer Simulation.* New York: John Wiley and Sons.

Index

ABOUT THE AUTHORS

KEITH KLAFEHN is Professor of Management and Health Care Systems at the University of Akron, and president of SIMUTECH, Inc., a simulation and animation company he founded in 1993. He has published widely in various professional and academic journals and has consulted to industry and health care organizations for more than 20 years, specializing in simulation in the analysis of processes and systems.

JAY WEINROTH is Associate Professor and Chair of the Department of Administrative Sciences, Kent State University. He specializes in systems simulation, information technology, and systems development, and focuses his research on linking simulation with Artificial Intelligence and Expert Systems technology. With many publications in the scientific and technical journals serving his field, he has co-edited two Proceedings in Simulation for Business Management for the Society for Computer Simulation and has made presentations at simulation conferences here and in Europe.

JESS BORONICO is Professor of Quantitative Analysis and Operations Research at Monmouth University. He has published internationally in scholarly journals and conducts research in the area of mathematical programming and applied optimization. His consulting experience has been with firms in both the private and public sectors, including the United States Postal Service.

ISBN 0-89930-732-9

HARDCOVER BAR CODE